ASSESSING ENGLISH LANGUAGE PROFICIENCY IN U.S. K–12 SCHOOLS

Assessing English Language Proficiency in U.S. K–12 Schools offers comprehensive background information about the generation of standards-based, English language proficiency (ELP) assessments used in U.S. K–12 school settings. The chapters in this book address a variety of key issues involved in the development and use of those assessments: defining an ELP construct driven by new academic content and ELP standards, using technology for K–12 ELP assessments, addressing the needs of various English learner (EL) students taking the assessments, connecting assessment with teaching and learning, and substantiating validity claims. Each chapter also contains suggestions for future research that will contribute to the next generation of K–12 ELP assessments and improve policies and practices in the use of the assessments. This book is intended to be a useful resource for researchers, graduate students, test developers, practitioners, and policymakers who are interested in learning more about large-scale, standards-based ELP assessments for K–12 EL students.

Mikyung Kim Wolf is Senior Research Scientist at the Center for English Language Learning and Assessment Research at Educational Testing Service.

Innovations in Language Learning and Assessment at ETS

Series Editors: John M. Norris, Sara Cushing, Steven John Ross, and Xiaoming Xi

The goal of the *Innovations in Language Learning and Assessment at ETS* series is to publish books that document the development and validation of language assessments and that explore broader innovations related to language teaching and learning. Compiled by leading researchers, then reviewed by the series editorial board, volumes in the series provide cutting-edge research and development related to language learning and assessment in a format that is easily accessible to language teachers and applied linguists as well as testing professionals and measurement specialists.

Volume 1: *Second Language Educational Experiences for Adult Learners*
John M. Norris, John McE. Davis, and Veronika Timpe-Laughlin

Volume 2: *English Language Proficiency Assessments for Young Learners*
Edited by Mikyung Kim Wolf and Yuko Goto Butler

Volume 3: *Automated Speaking Assessment:*
Using Language Technologies to Score Spontaneous Speech
Edited by Klaus Zechner and Keelan Evanini

Volume 4: *Assessing English Language Proficiency in U.S. K–12 Schools*
Edited by Mikyung Kim Wolf

ASSESSING ENGLISH LANGUAGE PROFICIENCY IN U.S. K–12 SCHOOLS

Edited by Mikyung Kim Wolf

Routledge
Taylor & Francis Group

NEW YORK AND LONDON

First published 2020
by Routledge
52 Vanderbilt Avenue, New York, NY 10017

and by Routledge
2 Park Square, Milton Park, Abingdon, Oxon, OX14 4RN

Routledge is an imprint of the Taylor & Francis Group, an informa business

© 2020 Taylor & Francis

The right of Mikyung Kim Wolf to be identified as the author of the
editorial material, and of the authors for their individual chapters, has
been asserted in accordance with sections 77 and 78 of the Copyright,
Designs and Patents Act 1988.

Library of Congress Cataloging-in-Publication Data
A catalog record for this title has been requested

ISBN: 978-1-138-58939-1 (hbk)
ISBN: 978-1-138-58940-7 (pbk)
ISBN: 978-0-429-49168-9 (ebk)

Typeset in Bembo
by Integra Software Services Pvt. Ltd.

CONTENTS

SECTION III
Some Future Considerations in K–12 ELP Assessment

SERIES EDITORS' FOREWORD

We are pleased to welcome volume 4 in the series, a collection edited by Mikyung Kim Wolf, Senior Research Scientist at ETS. The focus of this volume is on *Assessing English Language Proficiency in U.S. K–12 Schools*, and it is intended to highlight recent research and development work undertaken in response to the specific assessment needs of learners of English as a second language in primary and secondary school settings in the United States. Wolf, along with Yuko Goto Butler, edited volume 2 in this series with a focus on general issues in assessing young language learners and the development of ETS young learner assessments that are used internationally. By contrast, this new volume reflects a heightened awareness of the academic and social English language demands experienced by a growing population of English language learners in the context of K–12 schooling in the United States. Several chapters of this volume highlight the cutting-edge practices that ETS has spearheaded in developing useful, fair, and valid English language proficiency (ELP) assessments in response to the needs of U.S. teachers, schools, and diverse educational policies.

Assessing English Language Proficiency in U.S. K–12 Schools begins by providing a critical update on the current status quo of ELP assessments for K–12 English learners in response to new learning standards, accountability requirements, and changing population characteristics in the U.S. K–12 environment. Of particular interest here are the ways in which evolving federal and state policies have interacted with educational practices to result in new trajectories as well as challenges for defining the construct of ELP in large-scale, standardized assessments. The book then goes on to explore a variety of research, development, and validation issues that have been addressed in recent work completed by ETS researchers and scholarly collaborators as they have produced large-scale ELP assessments for use in the United States. This work has focused on developing ELP assessments that accurately identify English learners, track their progress, and help determine when they are likely to be able to succeed in mainstream English-medium classrooms. Chapters emphasize diverse theoretical and practical issues, including construct definition, validity claims, task design, learners' test-taking processes, accessibility issues, score reporting, and collaboration with stakeholders such as policymakers, educators, teachers, and others, to determine best practices in test-score-based interpretations. The book concludes with a forward-looking section on the emerging uses of technology in ELP assessments—including the very intriguing yet challenging use of automated scoring of learners' spoken and written English production—and important considerations in attempting to connect large-scale assessments with teachers' and learners' classroom practices. The final chapter of the book then calls for a system-wide validation effort with special attention to consequences for accountability testing.

This volume is uniquely authoritative, drawing both on ETS expertise and leading K–12 education scholars to clearly define major issues in the contemporary landscape of large-scale ELP assessment. Collectively, the chapters paint a complex picture of the many factors that shape assessment design and that must be addressed by test providers if they seek to maintain professional standards and deliver trustworthy tests. The book also delivers the key message that the consequences of such assessments for K–12 English learners are potentially dramatic—even life-changing—hence the critical importance of investigating, understanding, and improving on the design and use of these powerful tests.

Series editors

John M. Norris, Sara T. Cushing, Steven J. Ross, Xiaoming Xi

ACKNOWLEDGMENTS

This volume is the culmination of the collaboration and supportive efforts of many dedicated individuals. First and foremost, I would like to thank the authors of the chapters for sharing their work and perspectives in this volume. To make a coherent volume, the authors were asked to write about specific topics and were involved in multiple rounds of review and revision. The effort required numerous emails, phone calls, and in-person meetings with authors to discuss their chapters from outlines to implications over the course of the project. I was privileged to collaborate with these authors to bring the language testing and K–12 education fields together. I am also grateful for their dedication to shedding light on best practices in serving English learner (EL) students and their educators.

All chapters in this volume drew upon authors' research or experience working with students and educators. I would like to acknowledge those students and educators who have participated in research projects. Their participation and input are invaluable in guiding researchers and test developers as they pursue the path forward.

I also wish to thank several individuals for their helpful feedback and guidance. The series editors, John Norris, Sara Cushing, Steve Ross, and Xiaoming Xi, provided detailed and insightful feedback for early drafts of all chapters. John, in particular, was readily available to offer guidance and suggestions throughout the production of this volume. I deeply appreciate all series editors' support to bring this volume to the field. I am also thankful to the publisher and editorial team, including Helena Parkinson, Ze'ev Sudry, and Sunantha Ramamoorthy for their guidance and flexibility throughout the production process.

I would also like to convey my sincere appreciation to ETS peer reviewers, associate editor, Don Powers, and editorial manager, Kim Fryer of the ETS technical review system for their generous help with reviewing chapters contributed by ETS authors. I am particularly indebted to Don for his thorough review and valuable suggestions to further strengthen the chapters.

Finally, special thanks go to my family for their understanding and encouragement while I worked on this volume. It is my hope that this volume is useful to the field and worthy of the dedication of all of the contributors.

Mikyung Kim Wolf

CONTRIBUTORS

Traci Albee, Education Research and Evaluation Administrator, English Language Proficiency and Spanish Assessments (ELPSA) Office, California Department of Education

David P. Anderson, Assessment Designer, Research & Development, Educational Testing Service

Alison L. Bailey, Professor, Graduate School of Education and Information Studies, University of California, Los Angeles (UCLA)

Heidi Liu Banerjee, Research Project Manager, Teachers College, Columbia University

Patricia Baron, Strategic Advisor, Student & Teacher Assessment, Educational Testing Service

Micheline B. Chalhoub-Deville, Professor, Educational Research Methodology Department, School of Education, University of North Carolina at Greensboro

Mark Chapman, Director of Test Development, WIDA, University of Wisconsin-Madison

Keelan Evanini, Research Director, Research & Development, Educational Testing Service

Timothy Farnsworth, Associate Professor, School of Education, Hunter College, City University of New York

Yoko Futagi, Capability Implementation Manager, Research & Development, Educational Testing Service

Georgia Earnest García, Professor Emerita, College of Education, University of Illinois, Urbana-Champaign

Danielle Guzman-Orth, Research Scientist, Research & Development, Educational Testing Service

Maurice Cogan Hauck, Senior Strategic Advisor, Research & Development, Educational Testing Service

Min Huang, Research Associate, Innovation Studies, WestEd

Ahyoung Alicia Kim, Researcher, WIDA, University of Wisconsin-Madison

Robert Linquanti, Project Director & Senior Researcher, WestEd

Alexis A. Lopez, Research Scientist, Research & Development, Educational Testing Service

Emilie Pooler, Client Management Director, National Assessment of Educational Progress (NAEP), Educational Testing Service

Edynn Sato, CEO & Chief Research Scientist, Sato Education Consulting LLC

Lorraine Sova, Assessment Specialist, Research & Development, Educational Testing Service

Cathryn Still, Executive Director, the English Language Proficiency Assessment for 21st Century (ELPA21), National Center for Research on Evaluation, Standards, and Student Testing (CRESST), UCLA

Karen D. Thompson, Associate Professor, College of Education, Oregon State University

Joyce Wang, Lead Psychometrician, Accessible Teaching, Learning, and Assessment Systems (ATLAS), Achievement and Assessment Institute, University of Kansas

Phoebe Winter, Independent Consultant

Mikyung Kim Wolf, Managing Senior Research Scientist, Research & Development, Educational Testing Service

Hanwook Yoo, Managing Senior Psychometrician, Research & Development, Educational Testing Service

Eric Zilbert, Educational Research and Evaluation Administrator, Psychometrics, Evaluation and Data Office, California Department of Education

ILLUSTRATIONS

Figures

Tables

ACRONYMS

2PLM	Two-parameter Logistic Model
AAAL	American Association for Applied Linguistics
ABV	Argument-Based Validity
ACCESS	Assessing Comprehension and Communication in English State-to- State for English Language Learners
AERA	American Educational Research Association
AI	Artificial Intelligence
AMAO	Annual Measurable Achievement Objective
APA	American Psychological Association
ASL	American Sign Language
ASR	Automatic Speech Recognition
AUA	Assessment Use Argument
AZELLA	Arizona English Language Learner Assessment
CAL	Center for Applied Linguistics
CALPADS	California Longitudinal Pupil Achievement Data System
CCR standards	College- and Career-Ready standards
CCSS	Common Core State Standards
CCSSO	Council of Chief State and School Officers
CDE	California Department of Education
CELDT	California English Language Development Test
DOE	Department of Education
DIF	Differential Item Functioning
EAG	Enhanced Assessment Grant
EAP	Expected a posteriori
EBAE	English Braille, American Edition
EEOA	Equal Educational Opportunity Act

EFL	English as a foreign language
EL	English Learner
ELA	English Language Arts
ELD	English Language Development
ELL	English Language Learner
ELP	English Language Proficiency
ELPA21	English Language Proficiency Assessments for the 21st Century
ELPAC	English Language Proficiency Assessments for California
ELSCDs	English Learners with the Most Significant Cognitive Disabilities
ELSWDs	English Learners with Disabilities
EO	English-Only
ESEA	Elementary and Secondary Education Act
ESSA	Every Student Succeeds Act
ETS	Educational Testing Service
GPCM	Generalized Partial Credit Model
IA	Interpretive Argument
IDEA	Individuals with Disabilities Education Act
IEP	Individualized Education Program
IFEP	Initially Fluent English Proficient
ILTA	International Language Testing Association
IRT	Item Response Theory
IA/IUA	Interpretation and Use Argument
L1	First Language
L2	Second Language
LEA	Local Educational Agency
LIEP	Language Instruction Education Program
MC	Multiple-choice
MIRT	Multidimensional Item Response Theory
ML	Maximum Likelihood
NAEP	National Assessment of Educational Progress
NCLB	No Child Left Behind
NCME	National Council on Measurement in Education
NGSS	Next-Generation Science Standards
NLP	Natural Language Processing
NYSESLAT	New York State English as a Second Language Achievement Test
ODE	Oregon Department of Education
OELA	Office of English Language Acquisition
PARCC	Partnership for Assessment of Readiness for College and Careers
PL	Performance Levels
PLD	Performance Level Descriptor

R&D	Research and Development
RFEP	Reclassified Fluent English Proficient
RFPs	Request for Proposals
SEA	State Education Agency
SIA	Social Impact Assessment
Smarter Balanced	Smarter Balanced Assessment Consortium
TCC	Test Characteristic Curve
TE	Technology-enhanced
TELL	Test of English Language Learning
TELPAS	Texas English Language Proficiency Assessment System
TOA	Theory of Action
VA	Validation Argument
VS	Vertical Scaling
WCAG	Web Content Accessibility Guidelines
WER	Word Error Rate

Introduction

1

INTRODUCTION

Assessing K–12 English Learners' English Language Proficiency

Mikyung Kim Wolf

Nowadays, it is not uncommon to encounter linguistically diverse students in any K–12 public school in the United States. Coming from homes where languages other than English are predominantly spoken, these students include both foreign-born and U.S.-born children from immigrant families. While some states (e.g., California, Florida, and Texas) have long had a sizable linguistically diverse student population, other states (e.g., Georgia, Nevada, and North Carolina) have experienced a dramatic growth of these students over the past decades. It is clear that significant changes are taking place in the demographic profile of the United States, and the linguistically diverse students who are part of these changes have unique potential to make a positive contribution to increasingly diverse communities and a globalized workforce (National Academies of Sciences, Engineering, and Medicine [NASEM], 2017).

Educating these students appropriately has been a pressing challenge in the United States, as many of these students require language support to participate meaningfully in a school setting. Schools, in fact, have a legal obligation to identify English learner (EL) students in need of language support, as determined by "a valid and reliable English language proficiency (ELP) assessment" (U.S. Department of Justice & U.S. Department of Education, 2015). Once students are officially classified as ELs, they are entitled to receive appropriate language assistance for instruction and assessments (e.g., bilingual and ESL programs and language-related accommodations).

Note that the term, "English learner (EL)" is used in this volume mainly because of its prevalence in many federal and state documents. In some literature, other terms—including language minority students, second language learners, and emergent dual/multilingual students—are often used to avoid any negative connotations that the label "EL" might carry. However, as used in federal documents, including the reauthorized *Elementary and Secondary Education Act*, the term "EL" reinforces the legal rights of this subgroup of students. Irrespective of the terminology used to refer to these students, it is important to note the current prevailing asset-based view of EL students, which recognizes their linguistic and cultural diversity as a valuable resource for U.S. schools and society (e.g., Hakuta, 2011; NASEM, 2017; Valdés, Kibler, & Walqui, 2014).

Keen attention has been paid to EL students in recent years, due not only to the rapid growth of this population but also to the persistent and substantial achievement gap they experience relative to their non-EL peers. For example, in the 2019 National Assessment of Education Progress (NAEP) Grade 8 reading assessment, 72% of EL students scored below the "Basic" level, as compared to 24% of non-EL students (the NAEP proficiency levels include "Basic," "Proficient," and "Advanced."). Even though EL students are by definition those identified as needing English language support to perform academic tasks, the proportion of them scoring below the Basic level is disconcerting. The results of the 2019 NAEP Grade 8 mathematics assessment raise similar concerns in that 72% of EL students scored below "Basic," as compared to 28% of non-EL students (U.S. Department of Education, n.d.; results available at www.nationsreportcard.gov/).

Research suggests that a number of factors account for this achievement gap, including the challenge of learning academic content and academic English simultaneously, having unequal opportunities to learn in school, low socioeconomic status, and lack of teacher training in educating EL students (Abedi & Herman, 2010; Callahan & Shifrer, 2016; Estrada, 2014; Samson & Lesaux, 2015; Umansky, 2016). Helping EL students improve their ELP is of utmost importance in efforts to close the achievement gap and foster EL students' academic and vocational success.

The 2002 reauthorization of the *Elementary and Secondary Educational Act*, also known as *No Child Left Behind*, highlighted the importance of EL students' ELP development. This education law requires that, once students are identified as ELs, a school must assess their ELP annually to monitor their progress toward proficiency. The act holds schools, local educational agencies (LEAs), and state educational agencies (SEAs) accountable for ensuring EL students' appropriate ELP attainment.

This mandate has led to the creation of large-scale, standards-based ELP assessments across the United States, with high-stakes uses at both the student and school levels (Boals et al., 2015). At the individual student level, ELP assessments are used to make decisions about the types of instructional services and accommodations an EL student will receive. The results are also used to determine whether a student can exit EL services and be relieved of the required annual ELP assessment. At the school level, ELP assessment results are used for accountability purposes, including program evaluation and funding allocation. They also influence schools' decisions about resource allotment and curriculum planning for their EL students. Considering the significant uses of

ELP assessments and their impact on various stakeholders, the quality of state-wide large-scale ELP assessments is crucial. The development of appropriate ELP assessments must be guided by a rigorous process that is informed by empirical investigations and supported by robust theoretical bases.

This edited volume is intended to inform the fields of language testing and K–12 education about key considerations in the development and use of large-scale, standards-based ELP assessments for EL students. As mentioned above, the No Child Left Behind Act spawned the first generation of large-scale, standards-based K–12 ELP assessments across states. Since the act was passed in 2002, the field has made considerable strides in conceptualizing the kinds of academic language proficiency to be assessed in ELP assessments (Bailey, 2007; DiCerbo, Anstrom, Baker, & Rivera, 2014; Schleppegrell, 2012; Snow & Uccelli, 2009), and in systematically measuring students' language skills in listening, reading, speaking, and writing from kindergarten through high school. Abedi (2007) documents this major undertaking and the characteristics of the first-generation standards-based ELP assessments in the United States. In a way, the present volume provides a collective account of the second (or current) generation of standards-based ELP assessments, which has resulted from the substantial reform of academic content standards and the subsequent changes in ELP standards across many states.

This volume contains a collection of conceptual and empirical articles describing the historical landscape of K–12 ELP assessments including various endeavors in the development of the current generation of ELP assessments. Readers will, I hope, gain a better understanding of the contexts of large-scale K–12 ELP assessments and the variety of empirical research and advancements that underlie them. The chapters in this volume are designed to stimulate discussion and future research that will contribute to the next generation of ELP assessments and improve policy-making and practices that are facilitated by such assessments. Thus, the intended audience of this volume is wide, encompassing researchers, graduate students, test developers, educators, and policymakers. Although the volume focuses on U.S. K–12 education, information presented in this volume should be useful and applicable in other contexts and countries dealing with ELP assessment for students learning English as an additional language. Note that this volume is concerned with statewide, summative ELP assessments that are used largely for accountability purposes. While equally important, other types of ELP assessments and native language assessments for diagnostic and formative purposes, for example, are beyond the scope of this volume.

In this introductory chapter, I provide a brief overview of EL students, the role of large-scale standards-based ELP assessments, and policies that have engendered such ELP assessments. I also highlight major issues to consider in the development and use of K–12 ELP assessments and describe how these issues are covered across chapters.

English Learners in U.S. K–12 Schools

According to data from the school year 2015–2016, students officially identified as ELs numbered approximately 4.9 million nationwide, comprising 10% of the total U.S. K–12 public school enrollment (U.S. Department of Education, Office of English Language Acquisition [OELA], 2018b). Identifying EL students typically begins with a home language survey when students first enroll in school. Those who indicate in their survey responses that they speak a language other than English at home are administered an ELP assessment. The ELP assessment results, in conjunction with other inputs from teachers and parents/guardians, determine whether a student is officially designated an EL (Linquanti & Cook, 2013; Wolf et al., 2008).

Understanding the heterogeneity of EL students' demographic and education backgrounds is essential for the development and use of ELP assessments. While Spanish is most often the language reported as spoken at home by EL students (approximately 75%), more than 400 different languages and dialects are reported by EL students (U.S. Department of Education, OELA, 2018a). The number of home languages alone speaks to the tremendous diversity of EL students' linguistic and cultural backgrounds. EL students' ELP profiles in listening, reading, speaking, and writing vary widely among and within students. Students' ELP levels are also varied from beginning to intermediate-high ELP levels, irrespective of any given grade levels. Some EL students are more proficient in receptive skills (e.g., listening, reading) than in productive skills (e.g., speaking, writing), and some have better developed oral proficiency than written language skills.

EL students' formal education background is an important aspect related to their language skills. Some EL students enter U.S. schools with only limited formal schooling (e.g., refugee students). Moreover, some of these students have limited literacy skills even in their native language. In contrast, some EL students with formal schooling experience (particularly older immigrant students) have proficient literacy skills in their native language as well as content knowledge and skills. Considering the effect of the onset age of second language (L2) acquisition as well as the effect of first language (L1) transfer on L2 development (Gass & Selinker, 2001), diverse paths of students' ELP development are highly conceivable.

Many EL students were born in the United States (Batalova & Zong, 2016), and they have developed their oral proficiency and social/interpersonal language skills in immersive language environments. On the other hand, recently arrived EL students, who have little familiarity with American culture, will likely need to develop both academic language and social/interpersonal language skills. The diversity of EL students' backgrounds reinforces the need for the careful choice of what is to be measured by ELP assessments (e.g., social and academic language skills, sociolinguistic competence).

It is also worth noting that most EL students are in the primary grades. This is because EL identification usually takes place when students first enroll in a U.S. public school, often in kindergarten. As it takes time to develop sufficient English proficiency to exit EL status, there is a higher proportion of EL students in the primary grades than in the upper grades. Given that learners from kindergarten to Grade 2 have relatively little familiarity with standardized testing, an evidence-based design of appropriate assessments is critical (Bailey, Heritage, & Butler, 2014; Wolf & Butler, 2017).

Research also points to the socioeconomically disadvantaged characteristics of the EL population, which impact students' opportunities to learn and their academic performance (Menken, 2010; Samson & Lesaux, 2015). Demographic data indicate that EL students disproportionally reside in high-poverty areas and attend schools with limited resources. Examining the Early Childhood Longitudinal Study-Kindergarten (ECLS-K) dataset, Samson and Lesaux (2015) found that linguistic minority students constitute a disproportionately high percentage of those in the low socioeconomic status quintiles (more than 70%, compared to 37% of their counterparts). As current large-scale ELP testing is increasingly technology-based, EL students' degree of familiarity with technology (which may be less for socioeconomically disadvantaged students) should be an important consideration in the development and use of ELP assessments.

Roles of Standards-Based K–12 ELP Assessments

As described earlier, large-scale standards-based ELP assessments were created to meet federal mandates. These mandates stress the important role of assessments in enforcing students' civil rights as well as accountability in EL education. That is, ELP assessments are a critical means of identifying EL students and monitoring their ELP progress. ELP assessments also play a fundamental role in teaching and learning, since the results yield important information about EL students' linguistic needs, which helps schools provide appropriate support and interpret their academic performance accurately.

ELP assessments play a pivotal role in standards-based education reform efforts. Current U.S. K–12 education reforms center on new academic content standards that are intended to help all students prepare for college and careers. These standards, generally referred to as college- and career-ready (CCR) standards, feature increased academic rigor, technology literacy, and academic language demands. The CCR standards currently adopted by most states include the Common Core State Standards-English Language Arts and Mathematics (National Governors Association Center for Best Practices, Council of Chief State School Officers, 2010) and the Next-Generation Science Standards (NGSS Lead States, 2013). New ELP standards were also developed to reflect the academic language skills needed to meet the high language demands embedded in the CCR standards (Wolf, Guzman-Orth, & Hauck, 2016).

The alignment of academic content and ELP standards is stipulated explicitly in the 2015 reauthorization of the Elementary and Secondary Educational Act, known as the *Every Student Succeeds Act*: "Each State plan shall demonstrate that the State has adopted English language proficiency standards that ... (iii) are aligned with the challenging State academic standards" (ESSA, Section 1111 (b) (2)(F)). WIDA and ELPA21, two multistate consortia focused on ELP, modified their existing ELP standards and developed new ELP standards, respectively. The state of California, which has the nation's largest EL population, also developed new 2012 English language development standards to replace the 2004 standards. Consequently, almost all states have been implementing new ELP assessments based on the new standards. The new assessment items and tasks are designed to provide teachers with concrete examples of the knowledge and skills required by the new standards, the descriptions of which are sometimes overly general or ambiguous (Llosa, 2011).

Key Research Areas for Supporting Best Practices of ELP Assessment

To fully realize the intended benefits of ELP assessments for students and other stakeholders (e.g., SEAs, LEAs, schools, educators), a few key areas of assessment development and use need to be taken into account. In this section, I describe four key areas and the ways in which the chapters in this volume address them.

Defining an ELP Construct

In principle, the construct of an assessment (i.e., what will be measured) depends on the specific intended uses of the assessment (Bachman & Palmer, 1996). As described earlier, large-scale K–12 ELP assessments serve multiple purposes (i.e., accountability, classification, progress-monitoring, instructional support, and standards-based education). The complex interplay of policy and practical requirements has made it challenging to define an ELP construct for current K–12 ELP assessments. The ELP construct of these assessments should not only reflect the language skills manifested in current standards but also be grounded in a defensible framework or model of English language ability and academic language proficiency.

The challenge of defining an ELP construct is illustrated in the literature, which suggests that academic language proficiency is an evolving concept that can be operationalized differently in ELP assessments depending on its theoretical model (Frantz, Bailey, Starr, & Perea, 2014; Wolf & Faulkner-Bond, 2016). Since Cummins' (1981) seminal work to differentiate academic language proficiency from basic interpersonal communicative skills, a number of language researchers have endeavored to establish a framework for the academic language proficiency of K–12 EL students. The distinction of academic and social language has also been revisited with the acknowledgment of the dynamic nature of language-use situations (Snow & Uccelli, 2009; van Lier & Walqui, 2012).

One approach to defining academic language focuses on academic language functions and the specific linguistic forms used to perform such functions. This approach adopts systemic functional linguistics theory (Halliday, 1994). Some researchers have used this approach to examine academic tasks and their linguistic characteristics in order to define school language or academic language (Bailey, 2007; Christie, 2012; Schleppegrell, 2004). Uccelli and her colleagues (2015) recently expanded on this concept and articulated a core set of academic language skills. These frameworks or models can be useful in unpacking the language skills manifested in standards and in defining an ELP construct.

In this volume, chapters 2 through 4 consider the ELP construct issue for current K–12 ELP assessments. In chapter 2, Sato and Thompson provide a historical account of ELP assessments and evolving constructs of ELP that are driven by policy and standards. They also offer a general overview of the characteristics of these large-scale standards-based K–12 ELP assessments implicated by current policy and practices. In chapter 3, Bailey and Wolf delve into CCR academic content standards to illustrate the types of academic language EL students need in order to access core content learning. They also discuss theories of second language acquisition that help to define an ELP construct. In chapter 4, complementing the previous two chapters, Kim, Chapman, and Banerjee review the characteristics of current K–12 ELP assessment items and provide readers with a concrete representation of the ELP construct measured in these assessments. These chapters pose fundamental questions about what and how to measure ELP for K–12 EL students.

Sustaining Validation Research

Needless to say, inferences and decisions made from ELP assessments should be supported by empirical validity evidence. As ELP assessments undergo changes in both construct and item types, along with a changing test-taking population, continual validation efforts must be made to accumulate and update empirical evidence. Validation research should be conducted not only to develop sound assessments but also to monitor their appropriate use. A validity framework is of crucial importance in the collection of comprehensive evidence throughout assessment development and use. For instance, using a framework such as a unitary construct validity model (Messick, 1989), an interpretation/use argument framework (Kane, 2001), an assessment use argument framework (Bachman & Palmer, 2010), or an evidence-centered design (Mislevy, Steinberg, & Almond, 2003) offers a systematic approach to gathering validity evidence to evaluate the adequacy of assessment uses.

In chapters 5 and 13, respectively, Farnsworth and Chalhoub-Deville delineate various validity models and approaches. In chapter 5, Farnsworth also reviews publicly available validation research and evidence conducted by test developers and researchers. He further identifies where validity evidence is lacking and calls for specific validation research. In chapter 13, Chalhoub-Deville argues for a system-wide validation framework with an emphasis on the consequences of accountability assessments that will lead to improved education policy and reform. These two chapters set out current and future-looking validation frameworks and research agendas for K–12 ELP assessments.

This volume includes a select set of studies conducted during the ELP assessment development processes. These empirical studies have yielded evidence-based, practical recommendations for improving assessment design. In so doing, they help to substantiate validity claims for given assessments. Chapters 6 through 10 present an array of key development considerations for K–12 ELP assessments.

Hauck and Pooler, in chapter 6, discuss teachers' roles in ELP assessment development and the ways in which teacher involvement strengthens the validity of score interpretations. They pinpoint key development stages where teachers' input and involvement are critical, including item development, standard-setting, piloting, and field-testing stages.

In chapter 7, Wolf, Guzman-Orth, Still, and Winter report on a cognitive laboratory study that investigated EL students' response processes while engaging in newly developed item types. The study showcases how researchers and test developers can collaborate to finalize item design and administration methods during development of the assessment. It also demonstrates critical validity evidence based on test-takers' response processes to ensure that items measure the intended construct.

In chapter 8, Yoo, Wang, Anderson, and Zilbert address technical and practical considerations for reporting scores on K–12 ELP assessments. In the context of developing a score report for one state's new ELP assessment, this chapter includes dimensionality and vertical scaling analyses based on large-scale field test data. The dimensional analysis supplies evidence to confirm the internal test structure of the intended ELP construct and of the possible subscores or composite scores for a score report. The vertical scaling analysis provides validity evidence to support monitoring of students' ELP progress, a chief use of ELP assessments.

Similarly, chapter 9 addresses validity evidence for another critical use of ELP assessments; that is, to establish different ELP levels and to determine EL exit decisions (i.e., determining proficiency). Baron, Linquanti, and Huang demonstrate a variety of techniques to establish and validate proficiency levels using one U.S. state's data.

Finally, in chapter 10, Guzman-Orth, Sova, and Albee point out accessibility issues in the context of the development and administration of ELP assessments for EL students with disabilities. These issues are critical but have previously overlooked validity and fairness concerns. This chapter lays out important accessibility principles for ELP assessment development, along with an empirical study conducted during the recent ELP assessment development in one state.

All of these chapters suggest the significance of validation work in the development of sound assessments and their appropriate use. Notably, these studies exemplify the areas of validity research needed during assessment development. Due to space limitations, other major validation research areas (e.g., alignment, relationships between ELP assessments and other measures, and consequences) are not fully discussed in this volume. The important roles and purposes of K–12 ELP assessment intensify the need for expanded and continued validation work.

Using Technology in ELP Assessments

Another key research area for K–12 ELP assessments is concerned with technology. The use of technology is increasing in U.S. K–12 education settings and, as noted earlier, academic standards explicitly delineate certain expectations about technology literacy (e.g., integrating information from multimedia and diverse sources including the internet, sharing work using technology). To keep abreast of current trends and to prepare students to meet new standards, the use of technology in ELP assessments is inevitable. Indeed, more than 40 states are currently implementing computer-based K–12 ELP assessments. Major advantages of using technology in assessments are well documented in the literature (Bennett, 2018; Fulcher, 2003; Ockey, 2009), including the efficiency of test administration and the effective manifestation of the intended construct by increasing the authenticity and the interactiveness of assessment items. On the other hand, some characteristics of K–12 EL students (e.g., diverse formal schooling experience, young learners, socioeconomic disadvantages) pose concerns for the appropriate use of technology in ELP assessments.

This volume contains chapters that address both challenges and opportunities in improving the ways technology is used in K–12 ELP assessment. Kim et al. in chapter 4 delineate innovative features that have already been implemented in ELP assessment task designs. They also discuss areas needing empirical investigation. Wolf et al. in chapter 7 and Guzman-Orth et al. in chapter 10 also explore technology issues, including EL students' interaction with computer-based ELP assessments and enhancing accessibility using technology for EL students with disabilities.

While these chapters address technology features used in existing K–12 ELP assessments, in chapter 11, Evanini, Futagi, and Hauck discuss the emerging demand for automated scoring for current computer-based K–12 ELP assessments. Considering the burden imposed on teachers when scoring spoken and written responses, the high costs of human scoring in large-scale assessments, and the long time needed to score and report scores, automated scoring holds compelling promise for K–12 ELP assessment. Evanini et al. consider both technical aspects and practical constraints in applying automated scoring for K–12 ELP assessments.

As use of computer-based K–12 ELP assessments is a recent development, empirical research on EL students' technology use in assessment and instructional settings is relatively limited. In recognition of the increased digital learning occurring in classrooms, the U.S. Department of Education (2018, 2019) recently issued guidance documents for educators about the use of technology for EL students. However, the effectiveness of such guidance and the advantages of using technology in ELP assessments warrants further empirical research.

Connecting ELP Assessment and Instruction

The final key area of research for the effective use of ELP assessments pertains to the interface between assessment and instruction to achieve the ultimate goal of assessment, improving EL students' learning outcomes. The ELP assessments discussed in this volume are large-scale summative assessments designed for accountability. During the No Child Left Behind era, these assessments were subject to the widespread criticism that they offered little information to improve instruction (Herman, 2004). To address this criticism, states and test developers are now more proactive in developing a theory of action to articulate the vital role that assessments can play in improving teaching and learning (e.g., ELPA21, 2014). They have also made conscious efforts to improve the design and implementation of current accountability assessments including K–12 ELP assessments to inform instruction. For instance, they have made available sample ELP assessment items with detailed item specifications along with targeted ELP standards.

In chapter 12, Lopez and García focus on the issue of connecting large-scale K–12 ELP assessments to instruction. Based on a focus group study with teachers, they provide important insights on teachers' perspectives and on the challenges of using the results of K–12 ELP assessments for instruction. The challenges discussed suggest areas of further research. Hauck and Pooler, in chapter 6, also discuss the need for professional support to increase teachers' assessment literacy so as to integrate assessment and instruction more effectively to improve student learning.

Concluding Remarks

Driven by education policies, large-scale standards-based K–12 ELP assessments in the United States have a significant impact on EL students' academic paths. To ensure that these assessments are used to promote the intended effects, including equitable education for EL students, high-quality assessments and empirical bases are needed to support their appropriate use. The present volume contains a collection of selected articles that describe the complicated contexts and the various stakeholders involved in K–12 ELP assessments. Policies and high-stakes use of K–12 ELP assessments create both challenges and opportunities to advance the education and language-testing fields. Current ELP standards and assessments have undergone major paradigm shifts that reflect the academic and disciplinary language proficiency that EL students need in order to access content learning. Nevertheless, more empirical evidence is needed to support current ELP standards and to facilitate both their refinement and their advancement. The chapters in this volume illustrate current undertakings and encourage further work to improve K–12 ELP assessment practices. Language assessments can play a major role in the development of language policies (Menken, 2017; Shohamy, 2007). While U.S. standards-based K–12 ELP assessments are shaped by current policy, they can also help formulate future policies. Shohamy (2007) emphasizes that valid language policies can be developed by using language assessments that incorporate research-based empirical evidence. I hope that the conceptual and empirical research presented in this volume provides a useful foundation as well as direction for future research to improve practices and policies on K–12 ELP assessment.

References

Abedi, J. (2007). *English language proficiency assessment in the nation: Current status and future practice.* Davis, CA: University of California.

Abedi, J., & Herman, J. (2010). Assessing English language learners' opportunity to learn mathematics: Issues and limitations. *Teachers College Record, 112*(3), 723–746.

Bachman, L. F., & Palmer, A. S. (1996). *Language testing in practice.* Oxford: Oxford University Press.

Bachman, L. F., & Palmer, A. S. (2010). *Language assessment in practice.* Oxford: Oxford University Press.

Bailey, A. L. (2007). *The language demands of school: Putting academic English to the test.* New Haven, CT: Yale University Press.

Bailey, A. L., Heritage, M., & Butler, F. A. (2014). Developmental considerations and curricular contexts in the assessment of young language learners. In A. J. Kunnan (Ed.), *The companion to language assessment* (pp. 423–439). New York, NY: John Wiley & Sons, Inc.

Batalova, J., & Zong, J. (2016, November 11). *Language diversity and English proficiency in the United States.* Washington, DC: Migration Policy Institute. Retrieved from www.migrationpolicy.org/article/language-diversity-and-english-proficiency-united-states

Bennett, R. (2018). Educational assessment: What to watch in a rapidly changing world. *Educational Measurement: Issues and Practice, 37*(4), 7–15.

Boals, T., Kenyon, D. M., Blair, A., Cranley, M. E., Wilmes, C., & Wright, L. J. (2015). Transformation in K–12 English language proficiency assessment changing contexts, changing constructs. *Review of Research in Education, 39*(1), 122–164.

Callahan, R. M., & Shifrer, D. (2016). Equitable access for secondary English learner students: Course taking as evidence of EL program effectiveness. *Educational Administration Quarterly, 52*(3), 463–496.

Christie, F. (2012). *Language education throughout the school year: A functional perspective.* West Sussex, UK: John Wiley & Sons Ltd.

Cummins, J. (1981). The role of primary language development in promoting educational success for language minority students. In California State Department of Education (Ed.), *Schooling and language minority students: A theoretical framework* (pp. 3–49). Los Angeles, CA: National Dissemination and Assessment Center.

DiCerbo, P., Anstrom, K., Baker, L., & Rivera, C. (2014). A review of the literature on teaching academic English to English language learners. *Review of Educational Research, 84*(3), 446–482.

English Language Proficiency Assessment for the 21st Century. (2014). *Theory of action.* Los Angeles, CA: National Center for Research on Evaluations, Standards, and Student Testing (CRESST).

Estrada, P. (2014). English learner curricular streams in four middle schools: Triage in the trenches. *The Urban Review, 46*(4), 535–573.

Frantz, R. S., Bailey, A. L., Starr, L., & Perea, L. (2014). Measuring academic language proficiency in school-age English language proficiency assessments under new college and career readiness standards in the United States. *Language Assessment Quarterly, 11* (4), 432–457.

Fulcher, G. (2003). Interface design in computer-based language testing. *Language Testing, 20*(4), 384–408.

Gass, S., & Selinker, L. (2001). *Second language acquisition: An introductory course* (2nd ed.). Hillsdale, NJ: Lawrence Erlbaum Associates, Inc.

Hakuta, K. (2011). Educating language minority students and affirming their equal rights: Research and practical perspectives. *Educational Researcher, 40*(4), 163–174.

Halliday, M. A. K. (1994). *An introduction to functional grammar* (2nd ed.). New York, NY: Routledge.

Herman, J. L. (2004). The effects of testing in instruction. In S. Fuhrman & R. Elmore (Eds.), *Redesigning accountability systems for education* (pp. 141–165). New York, NY: Teachers College Press.

Kane, M. (2001). Current concerns in validity theory. *Journal of Educational Measurement, 38*(4), 319–342.

Linquanti, R., & Cook, G. (2013). *Toward a common definition of English learner.* Washington, DC: Council of Chief State School Officers.

Llosa, L. (2011). Standards-based classroom assessments of English proficiency: A review of issues, current developments, and future directions for research. *Language Testing, 28*(3), 367–382.

Menken, K. (2017). High-stakes tests as de facto language education policies In E. Shohamy, I. Or, & S. May (Eds.), *Language testing and assessment, encyclopedia of language,* (pp. 385–396). New York, NY: Springer.

Menken, K. (2010) NCLB and English language learners: Challenges and consequences. *Theory Into Practice, 49*(2), 121–128.

Messick, S. (1989). Validity. In R. L. Linn (Ed.), *Educational measurement* (3rd ed., pp. 13–103). New York, NY: Macmillan.

Mislevy, R. J., Steinberg, L. S., & Almond, R. G. (2003). On the structure of educational assessments. *Measurement: Interdisciplinary Research and Perspectives,* 1(1), 3–62.

National Academies of Sciences, Engineering, and Medicine. (2017). *Promoting the educational success of children and youth learning English: Promising futures.* Washington, DC: The National Academies Press.

National Governors Association Center for Best Practices, Council of Chief State School Officers. (2010). *Common Core State Standards.* Washington, DC: Author.

NGSS Lead States. (2013). *Next generation science standards: For states, by states.* Washington, DC: The National Academies Press.

Ockey, G. J. (2009). Developments and challenges in the use of computer-based testing for assessing second language ability. *The Modern Language Journal, 93*(s1), 836–847.

Samson, J. F., & Lesaux, N. (2015). Disadvantaged language minority students and their teachers: A national picture. *Teachers College Record, 117*(2), 1–26.

Schleppegrell, M. J. (2004). *The language of schooling: A functional linguistics perspective.* Mahwah, NJ: Lawrence Erlbaum.

Schleppegrell, M. J. (2012). Academic language teaching and learning: Introduction to the special issue. *Elementary School Journal, 112*(3), 409–418.

Shohamy, E. (2007). Language tests as language policy tools. *Assessment in Education, 14* (1), 117–130.

Snow, C. E., & Uccelli, P. (2009). The challenge of academic language. In D. R. Olson & N. Torrance (Eds.), *The Cambridge handbook of literacy* (pp. 112–133). Cambridge: Cambridge University Press.

U.S. Department of Education. (2018). *National study of English learners and digital learning resources, educator toolkit: Using educational technology—21st century supports for English learners.* Washington, DC. Retrieved from www2.ed.gov/about/offices/list/opepd/ ppss/reports.html

U.S. Department of Education. (2019). *Supporting English learners through technology: What districts and teachers say about digital learning resources for English learners.* Washington, DC. Retrieved from www2.ed.gov/about/offices/list/opepd/ppss/reports.html

U.S. Department of Education, Office of English Language Acquisition. (2018a, August). Fast facts: Languages spoken by English learners (ELs). Retrieved from https://ncela. ed.gov/files/fast_facts/FastFacts-Languages-Spoken-by-ELs-2018.pdf

U.S. Department of Education, Office of English Language Acquisition. (2018b, April). Fast facts: Profiles of English learners (ELs). Retrieved from https://ncela.ed.gov/ files/fast_facts/Profiles_of_ELs_4.12.18_MM_Final_Edit.pdf

U.S. Department of Justice & U.S. Department of Education. (2015). *Dear colleague letter: English learner students and limited English proficient parents.* Retrieved from www2.ed. gov/about/offices/list/ocr/letters/colleague-el-201501.pdf

Uccelli, P., Barr, C. D., Dobbs, C. L., Phillips Galloway, E., Meneses, A., & Sánchez, E. (2015). Core academic language skills (CALS): An expanded operational construct and a novel instrument to chart school—Relevant language proficiency in pre-adolescent and adolescent learners. *Applied Psycholinguistics, 36*(5), 1077–1109.

Umansky, I. (2016). Leveled and exclusionary tracking: English learners' access to academic content in middle school. *American Educational Research Journal, 53*(6), 1792–1833.

Valdés, G., Kibler, A., & Walqui, A. (2014). *Changes in the expertise of ESL professionals: Knowledge and action in an era of new standards.* Alexandria, VA: TESOL International Association.

van Lier, L., & Walqui, A. (2012). *Language and the Common Core State Standards.* Retrieved from http://ell.stanford.edu/papers/language

Wolf, M. K., & Butler, Y. G. (2017). An overview of English language proficiency assessments for young learners. In M. K. Wolf & Y. G. Butler (Eds.), *English language proficiency assessments for young learners* (pp. 3–21). New York, NY: Routledge.

Wolf, M. K., & Faulkner-Bond, M. (2016). Validating English language proficiency assessment uses for English learners: Academic language proficiency and content assessment performance. *Educational Measurement: Issues and Practice, 35*(2), 6–18.

Wolf, M. K., Guzman-Orth, D., & Hauck, M. C. (2016). *Next-generation summative English language proficiency assessments for English learners: Priorities for policy and research.* (ETS Research Report No. RR-16-08). Princeton, NJ: Educational Testing Service.

Wolf, M. K., Kao, J., Herman, J. L., Bachman, L. F., Bailey, A., Bachman, P. L. ... Chang, S. M. (2008). *Issues in assessing English language learners: English language proficiency measures and accommodation uses—Literature review* (CRESST Technical Report 731). Los Angeles, CA: University of California, National Center for Research on Evaluation, Standards, and Student Testing (CRESST).

Contexts and Fundamental Considerations in the Development of K–12 ELP Assessments

2

STANDARDS-BASED K–12 ENGLISH LANGUAGE PROFICIENCY ASSESSMENTS IN THE UNITED STATES

Current Policies and Practices

Edynn Sato and Karen D. Thompson

There is a long history of English language proficiency (ELP) assessment in U.S. schools. The purposes of these assessments include identifying and classifying English learners (ELs), determining appropriate instructional programs and services for these students, monitoring their progress toward proficiency, and evaluating how they are learning relative to their English-proficient peers (National Research Council [NRC], 2011). Until the reauthorization of the Elementary and Secondary Education Act (ESEA) in 2001, commonly referred to as the No Child Left Behind (NCLB) Act, ELP assessments typically focused on discrete phonological and basic interpersonal communication skills and tended not to have clear scholastic purposes (Abedi, 2007; Bauman, Boals, Cranley, Gottlieb, & Kenyon, 2007; Francis & Rivera, 2007; Lara et al., 2007). A consequence of such foci was that many EL students could score well on these assessments without having mastered the English language skills essential for learning academic content in classes instructed in English (Lara et al., 2007).

Current ELP assessments of students in kindergarten through Grade 12, largely shaped by NCLB and continuing under the Every Student Succeeds Act (ESSA, 2015), measure state-adopted ELP standards that include expectations related to learning the academic language necessary for success in school and for college and career preparedness (e.g., Common Core State Standards and other next-generation standards). These assessments are also standardized, and their use includes accountability for ensuring that students are learning and mastering the English language knowledge and skills needed to progress through their education and achieve success in school, higher education, and their careers (Hauck, Wolf, & Mislevy, 2016).

The purpose of this chapter is to provide an overview of the history and characteristics of K–12, large-scale, standards-based ELP assessments in the United States. The chapter begins with a brief review of significant court cases and legislation that have influenced ELP assessment in the United States. We then describe the characteristics of current K–12, large-scale, standards-based ELP assessments. Specifically, we explore the content of current ELP assessments, the entities that create the assessments, and the ways in which the assessments are administered. We hope this chapter provides key contextual information, improves understanding on how K–12 ELP assessments have evolved in the United States, and identifies areas in which further research and improvement in K–12 ELP assessment are needed.

Significant Court Cases and Legislation Relevant to ELP Assessment

ELP assessment policy and practice have been shaped by several key court cases and by legislation. These legal developments reflect a shift toward standards-based accountability in education, as well as academic, more rigorous, clearly and purposefully linked ELP expectations.

Lau v. Nichols

The landmark Supreme Court case *Lau v. Nichols* (1974) serves as the key foundation underlying EL policy and practice, including ELP assessment. In *Lau*, the Court held that school districts must provide specialized services for English learners. The case was brought against the San Francisco Unified School District (SFUSD) by parents of nearly 1,800 Chinese-origin students who were not proficient in English. One of these students was failing school because he could not understand the lessons in his classes, which were instructed in English only. This student was given no special assistance or supplemental courses in the English language, and the district maintained that its policies were not discriminatory because it offered the same instruction to all students. Lower courts ruled in favor of the SFUSD. However, in 1974, the U.S. Supreme Court overturned these decisions and found for the plaintiffs. In a much-quoted ruling, the Court held, "[T]here is no equality of treatment merely by providing students with the same facilities, textbooks, teachers, and curriculum; for students who do not understand English are effectively foreclosed from any meaningful education."

As a result of the Court's decision, individual school districts were responsible for taking affirmative measures toward providing equal educational opportunities for all students. However, there were no specifications regarding the nature of such measures.[1] Therefore, the U.S. Department of Education's Office of Civil

Rights created the Lau Remedies, which applied to all school districts and established standards for compliance. The Lau Remedies specified appropriate approaches, methods, and procedures for (1) identifying and evaluating national-origin-minority students' English-language skills, (2) determining appropriate instructional treatments, (3) deciding when EL students were ready for mainstream classes, and (4) determining the professional standards required of teachers of language-minority children. Generally, under the Lau Remedies, schools were required to provide EL students special English-as-a-second-language instruction in addition to academic subject-matter instruction in a manner that was comprehensible to the student, until the student achieved a level of English proficiency needed to effectively learn from English-only instruction (Lyons, 1995).

The core of *Lau v. Nichols* was codified into federal law though the Equal Educational Opportunities Act (EEOA) of 1974. This law prohibits discrimination in schools based on race, nationality, color, or sex and applies to faculty, staff, and students. Additionally, it requires that education agencies take action to overcome barriers to equal participation by all students, including ELs. Thus, although Lau, its associated remedies, and the EEOA did not explicitly mandate ELP assessments or define their characteristics, these assessments were developed to evaluate students' English-language skills and to determine their readiness for mainstream classes.

Castañeda v. Pickard

In a second key court case shaping EL policy and practice, *Castañeda v. Pickard* (1981) established a three-prong test for determining whether the EL services implemented by districts were appropriate. In this case, the Raymondville Independent School District in Texas was charged with failing to address the needs of its EL students, as required by the EEOA. In finding for the plaintiffs, the Fifth Circuit stipulated that educational programs for ELs must be (1) based on sound theory supported by qualified experts, (2) implemented with sufficient resources and personnel, and (3) evaluated regularly to determine their effectiveness in enabling students to overcome language barriers. This three-prong test, the *Castañeda Standard*, did not explicitly mention ELP assessments. However, this case also implies that such assessments were necessary to monitor if EL students were learning English.

No Child Left Behind Act of 2001

The reauthorization of the ESEA in 2001, known as the No Child Left Behind Act (NCLB), represented a major shift in ELP assessment policy. For the first time, this legislation required that states receiving federal funds for ELs administer ELP assessments and report the results of these assessments. Specifically, the law stipulated that each state implement "a valid and reliable assessment of English proficiency" that provided information about students' "speaking, listening, reading, and writing skills in English" (NCLB, 2002). Moreover, the law required that states establish Annual Measurable Achievement Objectives (AMAOs) to report on ELs' progress, with two of the three AMAOs tied directly to ELP assessment results. NCLB stipulated that each year states report the percentage of ELs who were (1) making progress in attaining English proficiency (AMAO 1), (2) attaining English proficiency (AMAO 2), and (3) meeting academic content standards (AMAO 3). Just as NCLB established an accountability system linked to content assessments in reading and math, with the creation of AMAOs, the law established an accountability system linked to ELP assessment results. If districts repeatedly failed to meet AMAO targets established by states, NCLB outlined a variety of consequences that states could implement, including requiring the district to modify its instructional program for ELs, withholding Title III (Language Instruction for Limited English Proficient and Immigrant Students) funding, and replacing personnel.

In order for states to meet NCLB's requirement of implementing a valid and reliable ELP assessment, states also had to establish ELP standards. Guidance from the U.S. Department of Education (2003) stated that the purpose of ELP standards was to "define progressive levels of competence in the use of English in the four domains of speaking, listening, reading, and writing," including a label for each proficiency level, a narrative description outlining the key characteristics of the level, and "an assessment score that determines the attainment of the level" (p. 8). The guidance further clarified that ELP standards should be linked[2] to state's content standards but that states could not use their language arts standards as their ELP standards.

NCLB established a very tight implementation timeline. After passage of the law in 2001, states had until the 2002–2003 school year to adopt both ELP standards and an ELP assessment linked to the standards. By the same year, states also had to establish AMAO targets for the proportion of ELs who should make progress toward and attain English proficiency each year. As the U.S. Department of Education's evaluation of Title III found, these provisions proved very challenging for states to meet (Boyle, Taylor, Hurlburt, & Soga, 2010). Prior to NCLB, the majority of ELP assessments used by local education agencies were designed for placement purposes, not for measuring growth (Boyle et al., 2010). Thus, not only did states need to implement new statewide ELP assessments, they also had little if any empirical data about ELP growth trajectories to use when establishing their AMAO targets (Zehr, 2003).

Common Core State Standards

Soon after most states adopted ELP standards that were aligned with their state academic content standards, efforts mounted to develop new college- and career-ready content standards shared across states. This effort, launched by the National Governors' Association and the Council of Chief State School Officers, ultimately led to the development of the Common Core State Standards (CCSS) in English Language Arts and Mathematics. Several U.S. Department of Education policies incentivized states to adopt these new, more rigorous standards. CCSS adoption was a requirement for states to be eligible for the federal Race to the Top grant program (Baird, 2015).[3] Similarly, in order to be eligible for waivers from some of NCLB's provisions, states had to have adopted the CCSS. By 2013, 45 states had adopted these new academic content standards, though some states later replaced them with their own locally developed college and career-ready standards (Common Core State Standards Initiative, 2015).

Because federal guidance stipulated that states' ELP standards had to be linked to their academic content standards, adoption of the CCSS ultimately triggered shifts in states' ELP standards as well as the associated ELP assessments (see Bailey & Wolf, 2020, in this volume for more details on the shifts in ELP standards). California and a consortium of states called the English Language Proficiency Assessment for the 21st Century consortium (ELPA21), for example, developed their respective ELP standards to be linked to new academic content standards (i.e., CCSS). These new academic and ELP standards spawned a new generation of ELP assessments.

Every Student Succeeds Act

The reauthorization of the ESEA in 2015, this time called the Every Student Succeeds Act (ESSA), marked important changes to ELP assessment and accountability policies, coupled with the advent of new standards. ESSA maintains the provision that states annually assess all EL students using an ELP assessment. ESSA also maintains the provision that states have ELP standards that are aligned to their academic content standards. However, accountability measures for ELs have changed substantially under ESSA. The new legislation eliminates AMAOs as defined under Title III in NCLB. Instead, as one of many indicators in their overall accountability systems for all students, states now have relatively wide latitude to establish their own indicators measuring "progress in achieving English language proficiency, as defined by the State [ELP assessment] … , within a State-determined timeline for all English learners" (ESSA, 2015). ESSA moves this accountability for English language proficiency from Title III to Title I, thus increasing its significance (U.S. Department of Education, 2016).

Under this new legislation, states are required to develop and submit plans that describe how their educational systems will comply with ESSA. Guidance for the development of ESSA plans requires that states describe various features of their EL progress indicators, including how they established their timeframes for achieving English proficiency. Importantly, under ESSA, states may establish different timeframes for ELs to attain English proficiency depending not only on students' initial ELP levels but also on "students' time in language instruction educational programs, grade level, age, native language proficiency level, or limited or interrupted formal education" (U.S. Department of Education, 2017, p. 7). In addition to the latitude they have in defining the EL progress indicators themselves, states have wide latitude in determining the weight given to EL progress indicators when determining which schools are in need of support and improvement (ESSA, 2015).

Another significant change under ESSA is that states must now establish "uniform entry and exit procedures" for ELs. In other words, states must use uniform procedures to determine who qualifies as an EL at school entry and when students are ready to exit EL services. Many states have used ELP assessment results as the sole or primary criterion for making exit decisions (Linquanti, Cook, Bailey, & MacDonald, 2016). However, in the past, some states and districts have incorporated a wide variety of other criteria into these decisions in some locations, including content assessment results, grades, teacher recommendations, and parent input. In addition, research has shown substantial variation in the criteria considered part of exiting decisions both across and within states (Linquanti et al., 2016; Wolf et al., 2008). Because ESSA stipulates that states must use "uniform procedures" but does not specify uniform criteria, the allowability of past practices, such as the use of teacher recommendations, remains somewhat ambiguous.

Characteristics of Current ELP Assessments

The court cases and legislation described in the previous section profoundly influenced policy and practice regarding the assessment of ELP. In this section, we attempt to characterize current large-scale, standards-based K–12 ELP assessments (e.g., ELPA21 and WIDA consortia assessments) in terms of their content, the entities that create them, and the ways in which they are administered, with reference to relevant policies and practices. In doing so, we describe some key challenges with current ELP assessments, identifying areas in which further research and improvement are needed.

Assessment Content

NCLB in particular marked the beginning of a shift to standards-based accountability in education that reflected more rigorous content expectations, as well as explicit ELP expectations linked to these content expectations (Hauck et al., 2016; National Clearinghouse for English Language Acquisition, 2014). States were required to implement valid and reliable ELP assessments linked to ELP standards that articulated progressive levels of English proficiency in the four domains of speaking, listening, reading, and writing (No Child Left Behind Act of 2001, 2002).

Language Domains

Prior to NCLB, ELP assessments, with some exceptions (e.g., Language Assessment Scales), typically focused on the oral domains of language (i.e., listening and speaking), measured discrete phonological knowledge and basic interpersonal communication skills and tended not to have clear scholastic purposes (Abedi, 2007; Francis & Rivera, 2007; Lara et al., 2007). Title III of NCLB required states to establish ELP standards that were derived from the four domains of speaking, listening, reading, and writing and that aligned with expectations of rigorous academic content and achievement standards. Similarly, Title I of ESSA requires states to establish ELP standards derived from the four domains that are aligned with rigorous academic standards. Additionally, similar to NCLB, ESSA requires that ELP standards address different ELP levels. Thus, consistent with ESSA requirements, current ELP assessments measure students' proficiency in speaking, listening, reading, and writing and the English language knowledge and skills critical for students to achieve academically.

Researchers generally agree that the four language domains are interrelated. Although currently there is no consensus on the exact nature of the relationship among the modalities and related pedagogical implications (e.g., Francis, Rivera, Lesaux, Kieffer, & Rivera, 2006; Goldenberg, 2011), oral language skills typically facilitate the development of reading and writing skills and serve as a foundation for aspects of reading comprehension (e.g., Catts, Fey, Tomblin, & Zhang, 2002; Dutro & Helman, 2009; Lesaux & Geva, 2006; Roskos, Tabors, & Lenhart, 2009; Shanahan & Lonigan, n.d.; Storch & Whitehurst, 2002). Research suggests that for EL students, aspects of oral language in English (e.g., phonological and phonemic awareness, syntactic and structural knowledge, and metalinguistic awareness) influence literacy development and oral language and literacy may be acquired simultaneously (e.g., August & Shanahan, 2008; Clay, 2004; Elley & Mangubhai, 1983; Helman, 2009; Wagner & Torgesen, 1987). Additionally, EL students' development of listening comprehension and vocabulary can positively impact their development of reading comprehension (Verhoeven & Van Leeuwe, 2008).

The implications of such interrelationships are reflected in current ELP standards, which describe integrated language skills that correspond to the development of complex academic language demands of college and career readiness standards. However, current K–12 ELP assessments do not reflect the newer emphasis on the integration of the skills across domains. That is, while current ELP standards represent the four domains as integrated, current K–12 ELP assessments continue to measure and report traditional, distinct conceptualizations of each of the four domains, likely because federal law has been interpreted to require that these assessments provide separate scores in each domain. This mismatch poses both technical and practical challenges in terms of, for example, reporting and interpretation of student assessment outcomes (Wolf, Guzman-Orth, & Hauck, 2016).

Standardized Content

The standards-based assessment and accountability of NCLB brought about greater consistency across K–12 ELP assessments in terms of the English language knowledge and skills that they measured (Abedi, 2007). As mentioned previously, one of the shifts that came about with NCLB was a focus on language necessary for students to succeed in academic content areas, given the language demands of the more rigorous academic standards (Butler, Lord, Steven, Borrego, & Bailey, 2004; Wolf et al., 2016; Zwiers, O'Hara, & Pritchard, 2013). Reflective of this shift, ELP standards and assessments more explicitly addressed academic English language skills. NCLB required states to develop ELP standards that corresponded to the language students needed to achieve academically, administer assessments that measured students' progress toward these standards, establish targets for performance on these assessments, and prepare interventions for schools and districts that did not meet performance targets (Hamilton et al., 2007). Although ELP assessments are not tests of academic content, they were purposefully designed and intended to assess the English language knowledge and skills students needed to access and learn core academic content (NRC, 2011).

In addition to the greater consistency of English language knowledge and skills measured across ELP assessments (e.g., in terms of linkage to state content standards), NCLB also brought about greater consistency in the technical quality of these assessments (Abedi, 2007). The uses of assessment outcomes for accountability purposes are possible in part because of the technical qualities of an assessment (e.g., validity, reliability, freedom from bias) (Sireci & Faulkner-Bond, 2015). In order to ensure state assessments met requirements at a level of technical rigor that supported the high-stakes decisions and consequences associated with their outcomes, the U.S. Department of Education established a peer review process that evaluated state assessments against specified criteria (e.g., U.S. Department of Education, 2015). States prepared and submitted documentation that addressed the Peer Review criteria, and their submission was evaluated by Peer Reviewers who were national experts in the fields of standards and assessments. The Peer Review expectations and criteria for technical quality for state content assessments recently were extended to state ELP assessments, and the technical quality of these assessments was evaluated by national experts in standards, assessments, second language acquisition, and language testing (U.S. Department of Education, 2018).

Content That Reflects Language Development/Growth within and across Grades

States are required to develop ELP standards and administer assessments that measure students' progress toward these standards. Current ELP assessments are designed to measure growth in ways that reflect the increasing complexity of language vis-à-vis ELP expectations at various grade levels. For example, the two most widely used current ELP assessments have test forms for a variety of grade bands (i.e., kindergarten, Grade 1, and grade bands 2–3, 4–5, 6–8, and 9–12). For each grade level or grade band, tests are designed to differentiate across proficiency levels (e.g., Beginning, Early Intermediate, Advanced). Narrative descriptions that characterize stages of English language knowledge and skills development are articulated for each level of proficiency (e.g., language proficiency levels, proficiency level descriptors). Prior to NCLB, assessments typically clustered more grade levels together (e.g., early elementary, late elementary, middle school, high school) and were not purposefully designed to reflect and allow for the measurement of students' English development in much granularity (National Research Council, 2011).

Assessment Consortia and Independent States

In addition to shifts in the content of ELP assessments, there have been important shifts in the entities developing ELP assessments. After NCLB passed in 2001, states had a very short timeframe in which to develop ELP standards and an aligned ELP assessment. In some cases, the limited capacity of state education agencies, particularly those in smaller states, led these states to seek out collaborations that would support them in fulfilling this policy requirement (National Research Council, 2011).

Consortia

Currently, there are two large consortia for English language proficiency assessments: WIDA, which has 35 member states, and ELPA21, which has seven member states, as of 2019. In addition to using a common ELP assessment, member states in each consortium have shared ELP standards. Both ELP assessment consortia grew out of Enhanced Assessment Grants (EAGs) from the U.S. Department of Education (Mitchell, 2015; WIDA, n.d.). After first receiving federal funding in 2002, WIDA completed development of ELP standards in 2004, and the associated assessment, known as ACCESS for ELLs became operational in the 2005–2006 school year (WIDA, n.d.). Following the creation of the Common Core standards, in 2011, WIDA received another federal grant to revise its standards and assessments to align with these new academic standards (Mitchell, 2015). A new version of WIDA's assessment, ACCESS for ELLs 2.0, became operational in 2015–2016, with changes to the cut scores necessary for students to be considered English-proficient implemented in 2016–2017 (Mitchell, 2017; WIDA, n.d.). Meanwhile, ELPA21 launched ten years after WIDA. Its standards were finalized in 2013 and were aligned to the CCSS from the outset. The ELPA21 assessment was field tested in 2014–2015 and became operational the following school year (Mitchell, 2015). Each assessment consortium includes a diverse array of states, including states with small and large EL populations.

A variety of policy factors impacted the development of ELP assessment consortia. As noted above, the federal government awarded an EAG assessment grant to WIDA, enabling this collaboration. In fact, three other ELP assessment consortia received federal funding after the passage of NCLB; however, only WIDA remains active (National Research Council, 2011). The same time pressure came into play ten years later when states had policy incentives to revise their ELP standards (and therefore their ELP assessments) to be aligned to the new, more rigorous content standards (i.e., CCSS). Once again, these policy changes fueled the growth of consortia, with federal funding supporting the consortia's creation/revision of ELP assessments.

Independent States

The remaining eight independent states each has its own distinct ELP assessments. These independent states include three of the four states with the largest EL populations (California, Texas, and New York). A key reason that these eight states have remained independent is that joining one of the assessment consortia would have required modifying or changing state ELP standards or practices more than was acceptable to these states. For example, California was initially considering membership in the ELPA21 consortium. However, the state had recently adopted new ELP standards that it did not want to abandon (Maxwell, 2013).

Variation in Approaches to Challenges in Assessment Administration

In the process of implementing their standards-based ELP assessments, states have encountered challenges related to test administration and have developed a variety of approaches to addressing these challenges. Discussion of states' different approaches to the assessment of very young ELs and to the mode of assessment administration follows.

Assessment of Very Young ELs

Federal law mandates that states administer content-area assessments in reading and mathematics beginning in Grade 3 (ESSA, 2015). In contrast, ELP assessments must be available for students in Grades K–12. Developmental features of young children pose a variety of challenges to valid and reliable standardized assessment. As researchers have noted, young children may have "short attention spans, high levels of activity, high distractibility, low tolerance for frustration, and are likely to fatigue easily" (Nagle, 2007), impacting their assessment performance. In addition, students may have had limited experience with formal testing environments, and this lack of familiarity with the context may also adversely impact their performance (Lopez, Pooler, & Linquanti, 2016; Wolf & Butler, 2017). Further-more, the rapid developmental change typical of young language learners poses challenges to the valid and reliable assessment of their language proficiency (Lopez et al., 2016).

Despite these challenges, standardized ELP assessments for students in the early grades are required in order to identify and exit ELs across the K–12 spectrum. Current ELP assessments include specific design features in an effort to address the needs of young children. For example, in contrast to its ELP assessment for Grades 1–12, WIDA's kindergarten ELP assessment is paper-based, administered one on one, and scored locally (WIDA, 2014). In New York's ELP assessment, students in Grades 3–12 record answers on a separate machine-scorable answer sheet. However, students in Grades K-2 record answers in their testing booklet; then educators transfer their responses to separate answer sheets (New York City Department of Education, 2018).

Computer-Based Assessment

Though not required by federal law, the two major ELP assessment consortia, ELPA21 and WIDA, developed computer-based ELP assessments. Each student (K–12 for ELPA21 and Grades 1–12 for WIDA) taking the computer-based assessment must have access to a computer or tablet, including headphones and a microphone. The launch of these assessments led to concerns about schools' technology resources in some states; however, other states had prior experience with administering state assessments via computer and thus had an easier transition (Mitchell, 2015). In addition, WIDA allowed states to choose whether to offer a paper-based or computer-based assessment (WIDA, n.d.). Some independent states also use a hybrid approach. For example, in Texas, students in Grades K-1 take a paper-and-pencil ELP assessment, and students in Grades 2–12 take the assessment via computer (Texas Education Agency, 2017).

A considerable amount of prior research has investigated whether the mode in which assessments are administered impacts performance. Findings suggest that scores from computer-based assessments are generally equivalent to scores from paper-and-pencil versions (e.g., Kingston, 2008; Wang, Jiao, Young, Brooks, & Olson, 2008). However, several factors seem to impact this relation-ship, including the amount of prior computer experience students have and the content area being assessed (e.g., Kingston, 2008; Russell, Goldberg, & O'Con-nor, 2003). In particular, student performance on writing assessments may be impacted by students' keyboarding skills and the extent of their comfort level and experience with writing via paper and pencil and via computer (Russell et al., 2003; Tate, Warschauer, & Abedi, 2016). In one example of an effort to address the role of prior computer experience, ELPA21 allows students without the necessary computer skills (such as keyboarding/mouse skills) to have a test administrator assist with test navigation (Oregon Department of Education,

2018). Meanwhile, in WIDA states, the writing assessment is typically completed via computer for students in Grades 4–12. However, students may complete responses to writing questions via paper and pencil rather than online if the students do not have the necessary experience or comfort level to enter their response via computer (WIDA, 2015).

One-on-One Assessment

In addition to variation across ELP assessments in mode of administration, the assessments vary in the extent to which they involve one-on-one interactions between students and test administrators. For example, in New York's ELP assessment, all items designed to assess speaking, at all grade levels, are administered to students one on one (New York State Education Department [NYSED], 2018). In contrast, in the ELPA21 assessment, all test items, including speaking, are administered via the online test interface (ELPA21, 2018).

The qualifications for test administrators vary across ELP assessments as well. For example, WIDA requires that test administrators complete specific online training courses for the particular tests they will be administering, trainings range from 1.5–3 hours. After successfully passing quizzes associated with the training courses, individuals become certified to administer the WIDA-created assessments (WIDA, 2014). In contrast, New York requires that test administrators complete training but does not have a formal certification process. However, unlike WIDA, New York requires that test administrators be certified teachers (NYSED, 2018). Thus, while federal legislation has led to increased standardization of ELP assessments, considerable variability remains in how ELP assessments are operationalized and administered across states.

Concluding Remarks

This chapter provided an overview of the history and characteristics of K–12, large-scale, standards-based ELP assessments in the United States. Over the past two decades, the attention paid to ELP assessments has increased, and in keeping with current policies, research, and best practices, there is increasing evidence of their rigor and technical quality. States have established integrated systems of ELP standards, assessments, and objectives that are linked to rigorous academic content and achievement standards in order to ensure that all students, including EL students, meet high academic expectations (National Research Council, 2011). Specifically, ELP assessments now address language needed for success in college and careers rather than discrete phonological or grammatical knowledge. In addition, the technical quality of ELP assessments has improved as well, allowing for more valid interpretations of results.

Nonetheless, there is much work to be done to further improve the nature and quality of ELP assessments. For example, ELP standards now reflect a research-based understanding of the ways in which speaking, listening, reading, and writing are integrated skills; however, current K–12 ELP assessments still measure these skills as discrete entities and there is not a consistent definition of proficiency vis-a-vis performance on these skills. Improvements in ELP assessments are crucial because they have the potential to improve equity and outcomes for EL students. The variability that currently exists in mode and administration, as described previously, for example, should be examined systematically to inform and ensure assessment conditions that best enable students to fully demonstrate what they know and can do. EL students who are inappropriately assessed may be misclassified and consequently provided inappropriate support and instruction that affects their access to academic content and their achievement (Abedi, 2007). As we continue our work to support the learning and success of our EL students, it is critical that we continue research and development of valid, reliable, and fair assessments of students' English proficiency.

Notes

1 The Title VII Bilingual Education Act regulations applied to funded programs only.
2 Some scholars draw a distinction among the terms alignment, correspondence, and linkage. The Council of Chief State School Officers (CCSSO, 2012) noted that "alignment typically refers to a comparison between equivalent 'artifacts', such as standards, assessments, or curricula (e.g., ELP standards to an ELP assessment). Correspondence refers to a comparison between nonequivalent artifacts. For example, the English Language Proficiency Development Standards Framework corresponds to the Common Core State Standards (CCSS) and Next Generation Science Standards (NGSS) because the language practices do not encompass all standards in the CCSS and NGSS (Council of Chief State School Officers, 2012). Some scholars (e.g., Bailey, Butler, & Sato, 2007) used the term 'linkage' to refer to the linking of standards across different content areas on a common dimension." (p. 3).
3 In 2009, the U.S. Department of Education created a competitive grant, Race to the Top, funded by the American Recovery and Reinvestment Act, to encourage and reward innovation and state and local reforms in K–12 education. States were awarded points for satisfying educational policies such as those related to educator effectiveness, adopting common standards, turning around the lowest-performing schools, and building and using data systems. Race to the Top was a critical factor contributing to common standards for K–12 (U.S. Department of Education, n.d.).

References

Abedi, J. (Ed.). (2007). *English language proficiency assessment in the nation: Current status and future practice.* Davis, CA: University of California.

August, D., & Shanahan, T. (Eds.). (2008). Developing reading and writing in second-language learners: Lessons from the report of the National Literacy Panel on Language-minority children and youth. New York, NY: Routledge.

Baird, A. S. (2015). *How have NCLB and RTTT impacted education for DLLs/ELLs?* Washington, DC: New America Foundation. Retrieved from www.newamerica.org/education-policy/edcentral/dllreader9/

Bauman, J., Boals, T., Cranley, E., Gottlieb, M., & Kenyon, D. (2007). Assessing comprehension and communication in English: State to state for English language learners (ACCESS for ELLs®). In J. Abedi (Ed.), *English language proficiency assessment in the nation: Current status and future practice* (pp. 81–91). Davis, CA: University of California.

Boyle, A., Taylor, J., Hurlburt, S., & Soga, K. (2010). *Title III: Behind the numbers.* Washington, DC: U.S. Department of Education.

Butler, F. A., Lord, C., Steven, R., Borrego, M., & Bailey, A. L. (2004). *An approach to operationalizing language for language test development purposes: Evidence from fifth-grade science and math* (CSE report 626). Los Angeles, CA: University of California Center for the Study of Evaluation, National Center for Research on Evaluation, Standards, and Student Testing.

Castañeda, v. Pickard. 648 F.2d 989 (5th Cir. 1981).

Catts, H. W., Fey, M. E., Tomblin, J. B., & Zhang, X. (2002). A longitudinal investigation of reading outcomes in children with language impairments. *Journal of Speech, Language, and Hearing Research, 45,* 1142–1157.

Clay, M. (2004). Talking, reading and writing. *Journal of Reading Recovery, 3*(2), 1–15.

Common Core State Standards Initiative. (2015). *Development process.* Retrieved from www.corestandards.org/about-the-standards/development-process/

Council of Chief State School Officers. (2012). *Framework for English language proficiency development standards corresponding to the Common Core State Standards and the Next Generation Science Standards.* Washington, DC: Author.

Dutro, S., & Helman, L. (2009). Explicit language instruction: A key to constructing meaning. In L. Helman (Ed.), *Literacy development with English learners* (pp. 40–63). New York, NY: The Guilford Press.

Elley, W. B., & Mangubhai, F. (1983). The impact of reading on second language learning. *Reading Research Quarterly, XIX,* 53–67.

ELPA21. (2018). *ELPA21 Test Administration Manual.* Los Angeles, CA: University of California, National Center for Research on Evaluation, Standards, and Student Testing (CRESST).

Every Student Succeeds Act of 2015. (2015). Pub. L. No. 114-95 § 114 Stat. 1177.

Francis, D. J., Rivera, M., Lesaux, N., Kieffer, M., & Rivera, H. (2006). *Practical guidelines for the education of English language learners: Research-based recommendations for instruction and academic interventions.* Portsmouth, NH: RMC Research Corporation, Center on Instruction. Retrieved from www2.ed.gov/about/inits/ed/lep-partnership/interventions.pdf

Francis, D. J., & Rivera, M. O. (2007). Principles underlying English language proficiency tests and academic accountability for ELLs. In J. Abedi (Ed.), *English language proficiency assessment in the nation: Current status and future practice* (pp. 13–31). Davis, CA: University of California.

Goldenberg, C. (2011). Reading instruction for English language learners. In M. L. Kamil, P. D. Pearson, E. Birr Moje, & P. Afferback (Eds.), *Handbook of reading research* (pp. 684–710). New York, NY: Routledge.

Hamilton, L. S., Stecher, B. M., Marsh, J. A., McCombs, J. S., Robyn, A., Russell, J. L., … Barney, H. (2007). *Standards-based accountability under no child left behind: Experiences of teachers and administrators in three states.* Santa Monica, CA: RAND.

Hauck, M. C., Wolf, M. K., & Mislevy, R. (2016). *Creating a next-generation system of K–12 English learner language proficiency assessments* (ETS Research Report No. RR-16-06). Princeton, NJ: Educational Testing Service.

Helman, L. (2009). Factors influencing second language literacy development: A road map for teachers. In L. Helman (Ed.), *Literacy development with English learners* (pp. 1–17). New York, NY: The Guilford Press.

Kingston, N. M. (2008). Comparability of computer-and paper-administered multiple-choice tests for K–12 populations: A synthesis. *Applied Measurement in Education, 22*(1), 22–37.

Lara, J., Ferrara, S., Calliope, M., Sewell, D., Winter, P., Kopriva, R., … Joldersma, K. (2007). The English language development assessment (ELDA). In J. Abedi (Ed.), *English language proficiency assessment in the nation: Current status and future practice* (pp. 47–60). Davis, CA: University of California.

Lau v. Nichols. (1974). 414 U.S. 563.

Lesaux, N., & Geva, E. (2006). Synthesis: Development of literacy in language-minority students. In D. August & T. Shanahan (Eds.), *Developing literacy in second language learners: Report of the national literacy panel on language-minority children and youth* (pp. 53–74). Mahwah, NJ: Lawrence Erlbaum Associates.

Linquanti, R., Cook, H. G., Bailey, A. L., & MacDonald, R. (2016). *Moving toward a more common definition of English learner: Collected guidance for states and multi-state assessment consortia.* Washington, DC: Council of Chief State School Officers.

Lopez, A. A., Pooler, E., & Linquanti, R. (2016). *Key issues and opportunities in the initial identification and classification of English learners.* (ETS Research Report No. RR-16-09). Princeton, NJ: Educational Testing Service.

Lyons, J. (1995). The past and future directions of federal bilingual education policy. In O. García & C. Baker (Eds.), *Policy and practice in bilingual education: Extending the foundations* (pp. 1–15). Clevedon, UK: Multilingual Matters.

Maxwell, L. (2013, February 13). California drops out of ELL assessment consortium. *Education Week.* Retrieved from http://blogs.edweek.org/edweek/learning-the-language/2013/02/california_drops_out_of_ell_as.html

Mitchell, C. (2015, September 23). As ELL tests move online, educators hope for better gauge of skills. *Education Week, 35*(5), 1, 11. Retrieved from www.edweek.org/ew/articles/2015/09/23/as-ell-tests-move-online-educators-hope.html

Mitchell, C. (2017, July 19). Thousands of English-learners fall short on test of language skills. *Education Week, 36*(37), 1, 16–17. Retrieved from www.edweek.org/ew/articles/2017/07/19/thousands-of-english-learners-fall-short-on-test.html

Nagle, R. J. (2007). Issues in preschool assessment. In B. A. Braken & R. Nagle (Eds.), *Psychoeducational assessment of preschool children* (4th ed., pp. 39–48). Mahwah, NY: Lawrence Erlbaum Associates.

National Clearinghouse for English Language Acquisition. (2014). *Standards-based instruction compendium of resources.* Silver Spring, MD: Author.

National Research Council. (2011). *Allocating federal funds for state programs for English language learners.* Washington, DC: National Academies Press.

New York City Department of Education. (2018, April 5). *Assessment Memorandum #16 2017–18.* Retrieved from http://schools.nyc.gov/NR/rdonlyres/6325DBEF-75AD-427F-882F-B0A06E9A17F8/0/MemoNYSESLAT20180405.pdf

New York State Education Department. (2018). *New York State English as a second language achievement test: School administrator's manual, K–12, 2018–19.* Retrieved from www.p12.nysed.gov/assessment/sam/nyseslat/nyseslat-sam-18.pdf

No Child Left Behind Act of 2001. (2002). Pub. L. 107-110, 20 U.S.C. § 6319.

Oregon Department of Education. (2018). *Preliminary 2018–2019 Oregon accessibility manual.* Retrieved from www.oregon.gov/ode/educator-resources/assessment/Documents/accessibility_manual.pdf

Roskos, K. A., Tabors, P. O., & Lenhart, L. A. (2009). *Oral language and early literacy in preschool* (2nd ed.). Newark, DE: International Reading Association.

Russell, M., Goldberg, A., & O'Connor, K. (2003). Computer-based testing and validity: A look back into the future. *Assessment in Education: Principles, Policy & Practice, 10*(3), 279–293.

Shanahan, T., & Lonigan, C. (n.d.). The role of early oral language in literacy development. *Language Magazine.* Retrieved from www.languagemagazine.com/5100-2/

Sireci, S. G., & Faulkner-Bond, M. (2015). Promoting validity in the assessment of English learners. *Review of Research in Education, 39*(1), 215–252.

Storch, S. A., & Whitehurst, G. J. (2002). Oral language and code related precursors to reading: Evidence from a longitudinal structural model. *Developmental Psychology, 38,* 934–947.

Tate, T. P., Warschauer, M., & Abedi, J. (2016). The effects of prior computer use on computer-based writing: The 2011 NAEP writing assessment. *Computers & Education, 101,* 115–131.

Texas Education Agency. (2017). *Educator guide: Texas English language proficiency assessment system.* Retrieved from https://tea.texas.gov/student.assessment/ell/telpas/

U.S. Department of Education. (2003). Final non-regulatory guidance on the title III state formula grant program—Standards, assessments and accountability. Retrieved from www2.ed.gov/programs/nfdp/NRG1.2.25.03.doc

U.S. Department of Education. (2015). Peer review of state assessment systems non-regulatory guidance for states for meeting requirements of the Elementary and Secondary Education Act of 1965, as amended. Retrieved from www2.ed.gov/policy/elsec/guid/assessguid15.pdf

U.S. Department of Education. (2016, September). Non-regulatory guidance: English learners and title III of the Elementary and Secondary Education Act (ESEA), as amended by the Every Student Succeeds Act (ESSA). Retrieved from www2.ed.gov/policy/elsec/leg/essa/essatitleiiiguidenglishlearners92016.pdf

U.S. Department of Education. (2017, January). *Every Student Succeeds Act consolidated state plan guidance.* Retrieved from www2.ed.gov/admins/lead/account/stateplan17/essastateplanguidance.pdf

U.S. Department of Education. (2018). A state's guide to the U.S. Department of Education's assessment peer review process. Retrieved from www2.ed.gov/admins/lead/account/saa.html

U.S. Department of Education. (n.d.). Race to the top fund. Retrieved from www2.ed.gov/programs/racetothetop/index.html

Verhoeven, L., & Van Leeuwe, J. (2008). Prediction of the development of reading comprehension: A longitudinal study. *Applied Cognitive Psychology, 22,* 407–423.

Wagner, R. K., & Torgesen, J. K. (1987, March). The nature of phonological processing and its causal role in the acquisition of reading skills. *Psychological Bulletin, 101*(2), 192–212.

Wang, S., Jiao, H., Young, M. J., Brooks, T., & Olson, J. (2008). Comparability of computer-based and paper-and-pencil testing in K–12 reading assessments: A meta-analysis of testing mode effects. *Educational and Psychological Measurement, 68*(1), 5–24.

WIDA. (2014). *Kindergarten ACCESS for ELLs.* Madison, WI: Author. Retrieved from www.wida.us/assessment/kinder-ACCESS.aspx

WIDA. (2015). ACCESS for ELLs 2.0: Frequently asked questions on accommodations, accessibility tools, and test administration procedures. Retrieved from www.wida.us/assessment/FAQs_ACCESS2%200_Accommodations.pdf

WIDA. (n.d.). *Mission and the WIDA story*. Madison, WI: Author. Retrieved from www.wida.us/aboutus/mission.aspx

Wolf, M. K., & Butler, Y. G. (2017). An overview of English language proficiency assessments for young learners. In M. K. Wolf & Y. G. Butler (Eds.), *English language proficiency assessments for young learners* (pp. 3–21). New York, NY: Routledge.

Wolf, M. K., Guzman-Orth, D., & Hauck, M. C. (2016). *Next-generation summative English language proficiency assessments for English learners: Priorities for policy and research* (ETS Research Report No. RR-16-08). Princeton, NJ: Educational Testing Service.

Wolf, M. K., Kao, J., Griffin, N., Herman, J. L., Bachman, P., Chang, S. M., & Farnsworth, T. (2008). *Issues in assessing English language learners: English language proficiency measures and accommodation uses—Practice review* (CRESST Technical Report 732). Los Angeles, CA: University of California, National Center for Research on Evaluation, Standards, and Student Testing (CRESST).

Zehr, M. A. (2003). English proficiency can take a while in state ESEA plans. *Education Week, 23*(12), 1. Retrieved from www.edweek.org/ew/articles/2003/11/19/12nclb.h23.html

Zwiers, J., O'Hara, S., & Pritchard, R. (2013). Eight essential shifts for teaching the Common Core to academic English learners. Retrieved from https://freeman.wjusd.org/documents/Learning%20Resources/Learning%20Resources%20Locker/8%20Shifts%20for%20Teaching%20CC%20to%20AELs%20-%20PDF.pdf

3

THE CONSTRUCT OF ENGLISH LANGUAGE PROFICIENCY IN CONSIDERATION OF COLLEGE AND CAREER READINESS STANDARDS

Alison L. Bailey and Mikyung Kim Wolf

College- and Career-readiness (CCR) content standards such as the Common Core State Standards (CCSS) and the Next-Generation Science Standards (NGSS) have been implemented across most U.S. states since their dissemination in 2010 for the Common Core in English language arts and mathematics and in 2013 for science. Summative assessments (e.g., the Partnership for Assessment of Readiness for College and Careers [PARCC] and Smarter Balanced Assessment Consortium [Smarter Balanced]) developed in alignment with CCR content standards were first administered in spring 2015. Most states have adopted the CCSS for English language arts and mathematics standards (National Governors Association Center for Best Practices and the Council of Chief State School officers, [CCSSO], 2010) or have developed their own CCR content standards that largely mirror those of the Common Core. Science standards (e.g., NGSS Lead States, 2013) are more recent, and aligning state assessments are newly released or still in development. For example, Washington State began the first phase of assessments aligned to NGSS for 5th, 8th, and 11th grades in 2018, and California had its first operational assessment aligned with the NGSS for 5th and 8th grades, and once during the high school grades in 2019.

These academic content standards in English language arts, mathematics, and science have already exerted a strong influence on a new generation of English language proficiency (ELP) standards[1] and consequently on the assessment of English language skills and knowledge of students who are learning English as an additional language in school. In this chapter, we describe the ELP construct in U.S. K–12 contexts as it has evolved in response to policies, practices (particularly standards), language development theories, and research. We then propose ways in which to identify language knowledge and skills in current CCR content and

ELP standards with concrete examples. By doing so, we aim to offer insights into defining the ELP construct for summative and formative ELP assessment, both of which are critical in supporting EL students' English language development to meet the expectations of current CCR content standards.

Given that much has changed in less than a decade, there is a great need for more research to assist in defining a construct of K–12 ELP that can lead to recommendations for improving ELP assessments. Many important questions abound regarding the connections between CCR content standards and ELP standards (Haas, Grapin, & Lee, 2018; Lee, 2018) and the assessments aligned to both sets of standards (National Academies of Sciences, Engineering, and Medicine, [NASEM], 2017, 2018). For example, what language skills and knowledge are represented in the CCR content standards and ELP standards, respectively? Do ELP standards capture the broad range of language uses in the academic content areas? Will close alignment between the ELP standards and large-scale summative ELP assessment result in measures of student perform-ance that can inform instruction in both English language development (ELD) and academic content areas? What role can formative assessment tied to both the ELP standards and CCR content standards play to complement large-scale assessment with dyadic language usages and classroom interactions?

To address these questions, we first briefly review theories of language acquisition and the implications these theories have for operationalizing the ELP construct for ELP assessments. Further, we review how the construct can be derived from current CCR content standards and ELP-specific standards and how the intended purposes and settings of ELP assessments, either summative or formative, make a difference in defining the ELP construct.

Such an endeavor is important because it can reveal essential language know-ledge and skills that EL students may need to acquire in order to meaningfully participate and succeed in academic learning and assessment. A better understand-ing of the ELP construct might lead to more efficacious ELP assessments—that is, assessments that are more accurate in their estimation of students' ELP progress and *linguistic* readiness for CCR content assessments. Moreover, ideas and approaches suggested in the chapter on the ELP construct could be a useful basis for developing appropriate interventions and instructional materials aligned with the language constructs measured by ELP assessments. Strong construct definitions of ELP can also provide a foundation for effective professional supports for the implementation of the CCR content and ELP standards with EL students.

The Federal Policy Context of ELP Standards and Assessments

We first provide a brief overview of relevant policies that have led to the current ELP standards and assessments for EL students (for more detailed information about these policies, see Sato & Thompson, 2020, in this volume). Federal education law, the *No Child Left Behind Act* (NCLB, 2001), first drew unprecedented attention to students acquiring English as an additional language in U.S. schools by requiring that they be included in annual state assessments and that their scores be reported separately for accountability purposes. In line with NCLB, the latest reauthorization of the *Elementary and Secondary Education Act* (1965), the *Every Student Succeeds Act* (ESSA), continues to emphasize the importance of holding states accountable for the academic achievement and ELP development of EL students as a separate subgroup (ESSA, 2015, Sec. 1111(b)(2)(G)).

The NCLB and ESSA eras have seen major shifts in ELP assessment from measuring social language and discrete language skills to an emphasis on measuring the language proficiency that students need in order to succeed in academic contexts. As a result of the accountability mandates initially set by NCLB, states must annually assess EL students' attainment of ELP and report the number of students who meet the targeted ELP level. The stakes and consequences involved in these ELP assessments are significant for individual students and schools. Heightened attention has subsequently been paid to the ways in which to meaningfully assess the language proficiency of EL students.

Title III (Language Instruction for Limited English Proficient and Immigrant Students) of NCLB first suggested that ELP standards adopted by each state be "linked"—in an unspecified fashion—to the states' academic content standards and that the states' ELP assessments be aligned to their respective ELP standards. This mandate was interpreted by many states as calling for a link between ELP standards and English language arts (ELA) standards (Bailey, Butler, & Sato, 2007). Yet, as state ELA standards vary in their breadth, depth, and emphasis of content, so too can state ELP standards. Furthermore, by linking ELP and ELA standards (e.g., reading and writing skill expectations in both standards), much of the language specific to other disciplines (e.g., mathematics, science, social studies) may go ignored.

Under ESSA, states have needed to formalize college and career readiness expectations for academic content standards and ELP standards within one accountability system. Specifically, ESSA stipulates that states include an indicator to account for EL students' progress in attaining ELP as part of Title I (Improving the Academic Achievement of the Disadvantaged) accountability requirements (previously under NCLB, the ELP indicator was part of Title III requirements that focus on the education of EL students only in contrast to Title I encompassing all students). It further specifies that a state's ELP assessment should be aligned with the state's ELP standards (Sec. 1111(b)(2)(G)) and that ELP standards should be aligned with academic content standards (Sec. 1111(b)(2)(F)). This change highlights a tighter connection between the range of content areas and ELP performance to better understand and support EL students' achievements and needs (Hakuta, 2017) with far-reaching implications for the definition of the ELP construct. (For review of implications of the federal law for ELP and academic content assessment with EL students, see reports by NASEM, 2017, 2018).

As a result of their increased rigor, CCR content standards demand more challenging and sophisticated language use from students than the content standards prior to 2010 (Bailey & Wolf, 2012; Haas et al., 2018; Lee, 2017, 2018; Wolf, Wang, Huang, & Blood, 2014). The nature of this rigor is also largely language-related with a focus on, for example, close reading of challenging texts in ELA and arguing from evidence in science. These disciplinary language practices have had a huge impact on expectations for and challenges to EL students. To ensure that EL students are equipped with the English proficiency they need to meet rigorous CCR content standards at all grade levels, researchers have attempted to draw the public's attention to the increased language demands embedded in the CCR content standards (e.g., Bailey & Heritage, 2014; Bailey & Wolf, 2012; Bunch, Kibler, & Pimentel, 2012; CCSSO, 2012; Lee, 2018; Lee, Quinn, & Valdés, 2013). Inarguably, increased language demands in CCR content standards impose greater challenges on EL students than on English proficient students; EL students face the dual challenges of learning rigorous academic content while developing their English language and literacy skills. However, CCR content standards are at least making many of the high-level language skills needed for academic success explicit so that educators can articulate them and EL students (and others) can focus on developing them.

In contrast with the situation before ESSA, when varied ELP standards and definitions of the language proficiency construct represented major challenges to developing and validating ELP assessments (e.g., Bailey, 2007; Wolf, Farnsworth, & Herman, 2008), a consensus has emerged that one of the goals of ELP assessments should be to measure students' academic language proficiency in order to gauge the accessibility of content instruction for EL students, in addition to EL identification, reclassification, and progress-monitoring purposes. What to measure and how to measure it are key areas for continued investigation. In what follows, we focus primarily on what aspects of language and literacy should be identified and operationalized as constructs in ELP assessments claiming to be tied to CCR content standards.

Role of Language Development Theory in Exploring the ELP Construct

Theories about what aspects of language develop when we consider language use in a school context can guide our understanding of the different facets of the ELP construct (e.g., Bailey, 2017). Language competence models, in particular, can take account of key facets of "language-in-use"—that is, the discourse of real-world, social interactions (e.g., Wetherell, Taylor, & Yates, 2001). For school-age students, this means discourse used for academic functions such as representing ideas and concepts, taking turns to formulate questions about academic content, conveying content knowledge in their answers, explaining a set of skills related to an academic discipline, and so forth. The "language-in-use" facets of the

ELP construct should therefore ideally address the following: (1) how different contexts influence language choices and use, (2) how language functions or has a communicative purpose, (3) how language knowledge becomes used in more sophisticated or complex ways by students over time, (4) how domains or modalities of language can either stand alone or be integrated when used simultaneously and/or integrated into authentic academic uses, and (5) how individual student differences can lead to different rates of acquisition and language proficiency outcomes (e.g., Bailey, 2007, 2017; Bailey & Heritage, 2014; CCSSO, 2012; Halliday, 1989; Schleppegrell, 2012; Wolf & Butler, 2017). Each of these is discussed briefly below:

Understanding Contexts of Language Use

Theories that distinguish among the different registers of language based on the context of use suggest that the ELP construct needs to take account of the social/interpersonal, school navigational, general-academic, and discipline-specific language uses (Bailey & Heritage, 2014). Moreover, this aspect of the ELP construct will entail specificity of communicative modes (e.g., receptive, collaborative, or expressive language uses), type of audiences such as students or teachers, the participation configurations students encounter in classroom contexts (e.g., one-to-one or one-to-many interactions), and a myriad of types of language tasks and social practices (e.g., engaging in academic discussions, writing a research report).

Understanding Language Functions

Language serves a purpose in the classroom—doing things with language, such as describing, presenting, or comparing (Halliday, 1978, 1989). As conceptualized by the *Framework for English Language Proficiency Development Standards Corresponding to the Common Core State Standards and the Next Generation Science Standards* (The *ELPD Framework*, CCSSO, 2012), language has cross-cutting disciplinary uses such as explanation, argumentation, and recounting information and phenomena.

Understanding Linguistic Complexity

Language becomes more sophisticated over time through exposure and instruction at the lexical, syntactic, and discourse levels. This complexity involves increases to the amount of language (e.g., adding to general and technical academic vocabularies, increasing the number of nominalizations and passive structures, etc.), and also enlarging the repertoires of what students can do with language (e.g., increases in the variety of transition words used in discourse and in the variety of synonyms for different words, etc.) (e.g., Bailey, 2017; Bailey & Heritage, 2014; Wolf, Oh, Wang, & Tsutagawa, 2018).

Integrated Language and Literacy Skills

Language can be parsed into four modalities (listening, speaking, reading, and writing), but in reality these discrete language domains are rarely kept apart and students will need integrated language skills in the classroom as well as during assessment of their academic and language development (e.g., Plakans, 2009). The different language domains are mutually supportive in that a language learner shifts between reading for understanding and displaying that comprehension knowledge orally or in writing, for example. One may also use discussions to generate ideas and formulate sentences for later written language production; conversely, one may write notes for a future oral presentation or discussion.

Additionally, integrated language skills can mean integration of language and literacy learning within the teaching of the academic disciplines. While this can involve ELD instruction within any regular content area, one state, California, has expressly created a framework for ELD integration within ELA instruction (California Department of Education, 2015), a convergence between these two areas that we explore further later.

Understanding Individual Differences and Learners' Characteristics

In the second language (L2) acquisition literature, the impact of individual differences such as age of acquisition, first language background, the nature of the input, gender, (dis)ability status, and socioeconomic background, is well-documented in terms of variations in the rate of acquisition as well as in the accuracy, complexity, and fluency of language (e.g., Brantmeier, Schueller, Wilde, & Kinginger, 2007; Ellis, 2008; Hoff, 2013; Larsen-Freeman & Long, 1991; Wolf & Butler, 2017). For instance, younger EL students whose cognition is still developing may find the task of coherently providing explanations more challenging than older EL students do, irrespective of language proficiency level (Bailey, 2017).

Evolving ELP Standards and Constructs in Relation to Academic Content Standards

In the NCLB era, many states rushed to develop or adopt ELP standards and assessments with little guidance on defining the ELP construct (Boals et al., 2015; Wolf et al., 2014). At the time that NCLB-era ELP standards and assessments were developed, the construct of academic English language, or the language of school, was largely unexplored (DiCerbo, Anstrom, Baker, & Rivera, 2014). As a result, the ELP construct was represented in varied ways; for example, predecessor ELP standards and assessments might conceptualize academic and social language, or discrete and integrated language skills differently (Bailey & Huang, 2011; Wolf et al., 2014). Some review studies have pointed out that states differed in their approaches to developing ELP standards and operationalizing those standards as ELP assessment constructs and test items (Bailey & Huang, 2011; Frantz, Bailey, Starr, & Perea, 2014; National Research Council, 2011; Wolf & Faulkner-Bond, 2016).

The CCSS for ELA explicitly specify the language and literacy skills in grades 6 to12 expected for the academic content areas, including history/social studies and science and technical subjects, as part of the ELA standards. That is, these content standards have attempted to establish common language and literacy skills across the different academic content areas. This situation offers language test developers the benefits of target expectations from which to create measures of ELP needed to acquire content (and demonstrate learning) expressed in the academic standards. Indeed, the *ELPD Framework* (CCSSO, 2012) offers precisely this kind of approach to defining the construct of ELP. The *ELPD Framework* was created in part to provide guidance to states working to develop or adapt ELP standards for alignment with the CCSS. The *ELPD Framework* describes the language competencies that students need to achieve in the CCSS and provides a taxonomy to identify language tasks and language skills in CCR standards. For example, the framework suggests that key language tasks and specific language skills (in productive and receptive functions) be organized under each practice identified from the content standards (e.g., making sense of problems, communicating mathematical reasoning, constructing arguments as key practices in CCSS for Mathematics).

Additionally, since the introduction of the CCSS and NGSS, a number of initiatives have attempted to characterize inherent language demands in the content areas in more detail (e.g., Lee et al., 2013). Bunch, Kibler, and Pimentel (2012), for instance, discuss major language and literacy demands in the CCSS ELA including (1) engaging complex texts (reading standards), (2) using evidence in writing and research (writing standards), (3) working collaboratively and presenting ideas (speaking and listening standards), and (4) developing linguistic resources to do the above-mentioned tasks effectively (language standards). The authors also highlight the strong interdisciplinary focus of the language and literacy requirements in the CCSS.

A complementary line of research has also contributed to our understanding of the language skills in the disciplines. For example, LaRusso et al. (2016) conducted a large-scale, longitudinal study on the effects of academic language on student reading abilities. They found that academic language abilities in the fall of the school year significantly and positively predicted Grade 5 through 7 students' deep reading comprehension in the following spring. Specifically, academic language abilities to connect ideas, track themes, organize texts, and understand metalinguistic skills among others were related to students' abilities to apply what they had read to different contexts and perspectives. Given that this manner of reading underpins learning in other text-dependent disciplines such as science and social studies, it is reasonable to expect that the positive connection holds between student academic language abilities and these disciplines as well. A recent review by Truckenmiller, Park, Daboa, and Wu Newton (2019) also reports on the positive impact of academic language instruction on student performance in ELA, science, and social studies in Grades 4 to 8.

As the literature on academic English proficiency and its interconnection with academic content areas has evolved, the two major ELP consortia (i.e., the WIDA consortium and the English Language Proficiency Assessment for the 21st Century [ELPA21] consortium) have also developed new ELP standards including language skills and knowledge tied to CCR standards. Notably, the two consortia have taken different approaches to revising or developing their respective ELP standards. In revising its 2004 standards in 2007 and 2012, WIDA maintained its original structure of four language domains (reading, writing, listening, and speaking) and added descriptions of how each standard is connected to CCSS ELA and mathematics standards (WIDA, 2004, 2007, 2012). Moreover, the new WIDA ELD Instructional Framework (WIDA, 2018) makes more explicit both the academic contexts of English language learning by "increasing emphasis on interaction and meaning-making within common classroom learning experiences for each subject area" (p. 1) and the integration of the four modalities (listening, speaking, reading, writing) into common language uses in the classroom, namely, *arguing, discussing, explaining*, and *recounting*.

In contrast, ELPA21's ELP standards take the Common Core standards as their basis and reflect the prevailing view of integrated language skills in academic contexts (CCSSO, 2013). Thus, ELPA21's ELP standards are not divided into the traditional four language domains of listening, reading, speaking, and writing. Rather, the standards include descriptions of integrated language skills (i.e., oral proficiency that integrates listening and speaking, literacy skills that incorporate reading and writing, receptive skills that focus on listening and reading comprehension, productive skills that focus on oral and written expression), a conception that appears to focus on authentic interactions and more complex uses of language in order to correspond to the deeper content learning and the more rigorous language demands embodied in CCR standards (Mislevy & Durán, 2014; Wolf, Guzman-Orth, & Hauck, 2016).

Next, we examine example CCR and ELP standards for language demands explicitly mentioned in them, as well as for the implied language knowledge students will need to possess in order to meet the standards. These examples shed light on a way to define the ELP construct, connecting content and ELP standards.

Identifying Language Knowledge and Skills in CCR Standards and ELP Standards

In the following seven examples taken from different CCR content standards and ELP standards, we draw on different aspects of the "language-in-use" model described earlier to illustrate the process we envision for analyzing specific language knowledge and skills. From these examples, we will see how ELP standards attempt to converge on language inherent in CCR content standards.

Examples from CCR Content Standards

The first example is taken from the CCSS Reading Standards for Literacy in History/Social Studies, Grades 11 and 12.

Example 1:

> *4. Determine the meaning of words and phrases as they are used in a text, including analyzing how an author uses and refines the meaning of a key term over the course of a text (e.g., how Madison defines faction in Federalist No. 10).*

The standard (and parallel standards at Grades 6 to 9 and in the CCSS Reading Standards for ELA) explicitly mentions what kinds of tasks students must be able to accomplish with language as they read and, in this instance, attempt to comprehend history texts. Expectations for vocabulary knowledge and analysis skill are also clearly stated. These aspects of the standard relate to understanding linguistic complexity as one of the facets of "language-in-use" and are obvious targets for ELP assessment.

The next example is from CCSS Reading Standards for ELA Informational Text, Grades 11 and 12.

Example 2:

> *7. Integrate and evaluate multiple sources of information presented in different formats and media (e.g., visually, quantitatively) as well as in words in order to address a question or solve a problem.*

Despite being a reading standard, Standard 7 (and parallel standards at earlier grades and for Literacy in History/Social Studies, Science and Technical Subjects) focuses on the production of language (integrate, address, solve) as much as on the comprehension of language in texts. In fact, this standard appears to entail the "language-in-use" facet involving integrated language skills of reading, writing, speaking, and listening. It is also notable that more than one literacy task and skill are implied in one single standard (e.g., integrating, evaluating, addressing a question, solving a problem). These higher-order skills themselves are dependent on many complex subskills.

Explicit language demands are also noteworthy in current CCR content standards for mathematics and science. The following example is from the CCSS for Mathematics, High School: Statistics & Probability: Making Inferences & Justifying Conclusions.

Example 3:

B.3. Make inferences and justify conclusions from sample surveys, experiments, and observational studies: Recognize the purposes of and differences among sample surveys, experiments, and observational studies; explain how randomization relates to each.

This standard overtly mentions the production of explanations but additionally entails language uses that can support making inferences and justifications. This range of different language functions inherent within one CCR standard is worth noting, and student understanding in this area is one of the key facets of the "language-in-use" model. The standard is silent on which specific modalities (speaking or writing) the explanation should adopt, but presumably, either or both modalities are candidates for displaying an understanding of randomization.

The next example is from the NGSS: Earth and Space Sciences (Earth's Place in the Universe) high school (Grades 9–12) standards.

Example 4:

1.6: Apply scientific reasoning and evidence from ancient Earth materials, meteorites, and other planetary surfaces to construct an account of Earth's formation and early history.

This standard requires students to not only describe their Earth science knowledge but also support their descriptive language uses with scientific reasoning, including the use of evidence. Similar in situation to the CCSS Mathematics Standard B.3 in Example 3, the only "language-in- use" facet we can safely assume is student understanding of language functions, and the account students must create is not made specific to either writing or oral reporting. This task, however, has its parallels in ELA standards for building persuasive arguments and in that sense comes close to the "language-in-use" facet of integrating language and literacy skills within the non-ELA disciplines.

Examples from ELP Standards

As described in the previous sections, states and ELP consortia (i.e., ELPA21 and WIDA) have endeavored to reflect the language demands manifested in CCR standards in their latest ELP standards. At the time of writing, ELPA21 and WIDA's standards have been adopted by 43 states, while the remaining states with large EL populations (e.g., Arizona, California, New York, Texas) have their own ELP or ELD standards with differing approaches to reflect CCR language demands in their ELP standards. Thus, some convergence and divergence in ELP standards to derive the ELP construct are evident. Below we use a few example ELP standards to illustrate variability across the standards in how they conceptualize the ELP construct, particularly in relation to the facets of language-in-use outlined earlier. To differing degrees, the standards selected demonstrate our argument that the most current ELP standards have shifted to be more aligned with the CCR content standards than in previous renditions of such standards.

The following standard from the New York New Language Arts Progressions (ESL/New Language) is at the highest ELD level (Commanding) for Grades 9 and 10 in Speaking and Listening: Speaking-Centered Activity.

Example 5:

> 1. *Use knowledge of the topic, text or issue, independently, to pose and respond to questions that connect ideas and propel conversations, when speaking in partnership, small group and/or whole class settings.*

This standard focuses on language production, specifically what students need to do discursively with the knowledge they are gaining in the content areas. The diversity in the interactions of content classrooms is emphasized in the different participation configurations that are mentioned (with partners, in small groups, etc.), but in each case the student needs to be able to ask and answer questions tailored to connecting content area concepts and ideas to which they are being exposed. This standard most strongly entails the "language-in-use" facet involving understanding contexts of language use.

The following example is from the California ELD Standards at the highest ELD level (Bridging) for Grades 11 and 12 in Section 2: Elaboration on Critical Principles for Developing Language and Cognition in Academic Contexts: Part I: Interacting in Meaningful Ways.

Example 6:

> 12. *Selecting language resources*
> a) *Use a variety of grade-appropriate general (e.g., alleviate, salutary) and domain-specific (e.g., soliloquy, microorganism) academic words and phrases, including persuasive language, accurately and appropriately when producing complex written and spoken texts.*

This standard focuses on the language production of students in the written and spoken modalities and clearly states that students need to know the circumstances for choosing the different types of academic vocabulary entailing the "language-in-use" facets involving understanding the context of language use. Moreover, the mention of grade-appropriate usage shows some acknowledgment of the "language-in-use" facet focused on the effects of learner characteristics (in this case age/grade) on language production in both the written and spoken modalities. It converges on some of the same genre skills likely necessary for the CCR content standards that also require students to perform some "persuasive" action with language, as in "evaluate multiple sources of information" in CCSS Reading Standards for ELA (Example 2), "justify conclusions" as in CCSS for Mathematics (Example 3), or "apply evidence" as in NGSS: Earth and Space Sciences (Example 4).

The final example is also taken from the California ELD Standards at the highest ELD level (Bridging) for both Grades 9 and 10 and Grades 11 and 12 in Section 2: Elaboration on Critical Principles for Developing Language and Cognition in Academic Contexts: Part I: Interacting in Meaningful Ways.

Example 7:

> *6. Reading/viewing closely*
> *b) Explain inferences and conclusions drawn from close reading of grade-level texts and viewing of multimedia using a variety of verbs and adverbials (e.g., creates the impression that, consequently).*

This standard focuses on productive language (written or spoken is left unspecified) resulting from reading. It entails a number of "language-in-use" facets, including prominently the integration of the different language modalities and overt language functions, as well as understanding linguistic complexity (achieved through use of a variety of forms), and a consideration of learner characteristics (age-appropriateness) with the mention of grade-level texts. Note how the targets of language learning, including the mention of different media uses, described in this example ELD standard strongly converge with the language uses described in the CCSS Reading Standards for ELA Standard 7 (Example 2). "Explain inferences and conclusions drawn from close reading" also echoes the "persuasive language" that cuts across most of the example standards as discussed above in Example 6.

These examples from the CCSS and NGSS standards and the different ELP standards demonstrate the complexities of assessing ELP in a way that is aligned with CCR standards. For example, even if CCSS ELA, Grades 11 and 12, Standard 4 (Example 1) above explicitly delineates language skill expectations where other standards do not, as in Standard 7 (Example 2), it still presupposes a host of additional supporting language skills and knowledge that are not explicitly acknowledged. For instance, to demonstrate the skills covered in Standard 4 (Example 1), students must be able to use the conventions of providing formal definitions, they must be able to talk or write about word choice and semantic refinement as objects of study, and they must understand and use the language of sequencing in order to keep track of word usage across the text. CCSS ELA, Grades 11 and 12, Standard 7 (Example 2), which rather implicitly embeds a wide range of language skills, requires a thorough identification of all the language skills involved. The specific complexity these examples raise is that the CCSS ELA standards may presuppose higher-order skills without providing any information about constituent lower-order skills that students need to master before they get to the higher-order skills.

Considering that the CCR standards by their nature describe the expected end-goals at each grade level, identifying underlying or relevant language skills is a challenging but critical step to take for teaching and assessing EL students. For EL students, we need to specify the entirety of other implicit language skills that will also be needed to meet the standards. Then, the role of ELP assessments is to measure the extent to which EL students are able to meet the language demands of the standards in order to identify where they are in their language learning and what they need instructionally to move their learning forward.

Characterizing the inherent language demands of the CCR standards should be at the heart of attempts to articulate the construct(s) operationalized by ELP assessments given the current conceptualization of ELP standards to contain language knowledge and skills to support EL students' access to academic content learning. As illustrated from the standards examples, not all standards can be adequately assessed in large-scale, standardized assessment settings, and some standards may be more effectively assessed in classroom-based summative and formative assessment (Bailey & Durán, 2020). As we consider convergence of the ELP and CCR standards, it is worth noting that the CCR standards we reviewed here cover language functions, linguistic complexity, and integrating skills, but not the first or the last facets of the "language-in-use" model (contexts & individual differences), which were more explicitly addressed in the ELP standards we reviewed. It will be important to investigate further precisely what language demands are included in the CCR content standards and how they are reflected in current ELP standards on which ELP assessments should be based.

Implications for Determining the Construct(s) to Be Measured by ELP Assessments

In evaluating the quality of ELP assessments, a systematic correspondence of language demands should be determined between ELP assessments and the kinds of tasks or activities that the CCR standards express. Tasks included in CCR standards can serve as "model instantiations" of the language that students will likely encounter in the classroom during different content tasks. For example, to meet CCSS ELA, Grades 11 and 12, Standard 7 (Example 2) given above, language demands include understanding a given question, comprehending the content of multiple oral and written materials, comparing and contrasting the information in the materials, integrating the information in a similar or different theme, and evaluating the relevance of the information to the question. Depending on the topic of the question and materials, knowledge of domain-specific linguistic features (e.g., technical vocabulary, certain grammatical structures) may also be needed. Some of the language skills may overlap with those in other standards. A systematic effort to address whether there is a common set of language knowledge and skills manifested across CCR content standards is therefore still necessary (Lee, 2018). This will be a major analytical undertaking.

The *ELPD Framework* (CCSSO, 2012) has contributed significantly to making the CCR standards useful to educators for understanding how language is used in the different academic disciplines. However, the *ELPD Framework* does not help teachers understand other aspects of language inherent in the CCR standards that teachers need to infer (e.g., transition words). While the *ELPD Framework* does incorporate some facets of the "language-in-use" model of language development (e.g., understanding language functions), others are not salient (e.g., understanding the development of linguistic complexity over time). However, future efforts can identify a common set of language knowledge and skills that can help formulate a core ELP construct to be measured in ELP assessments. Once identified, perhaps along the lines we have illustrated above, the next step is to organize these skills holistically and systematically. This organization can assist in the creation of an ELP construct that cuts across CCR standards and can also aid in future revisions of current ELP standards. If future ELP assessments are built employing this mechanism, alignment with CCR standards and ELP standards will be inherently incorporated into them.

Future research efforts will also be necessary to determine how formative assessment can play a significant role in gathering evidence of student learning for those aspects of the ELP construct that do not readily lend themselves to summative assessment, whether large scale or classroom-based. For example, process characteristics or variables (e.g., asking contingent questions and providing backchannel encouragement of a partner's contributions during student-to-student interaction), in contrast with trait variables (e.g., general English proficiency), would be more readily assessed in formative assessment. These interactions are important and valid facets of the ELP construct as it is articulated in the CCR standards but are not easy to meaningfully measure with a summative assessment, given that they require assigning a score to interactions that are highly dependent on others (Bailey & Durán, 2020).

The ELP construct can be further specified by proficiency levels within grade or grade span. These should describe the extent to which students are able to listen, speak, read, and write within each standard or, at minimum, key or recurring standards. Specifically, language acquisition theory and empirical evidence of language learning progressions can be used to articulate the four modalities, capturing the subskills or prerequisite skills that delineate proficiency levels (including any skills not articulated in the CCR standards but routinely taught in English language development curricula). These can serve to organize ELP associated with the CCR standards for both instructional and assessment purposes.

Developing ELP assessments that measure and report on the language knowledge, skills, and practices that are inherent in the CCR standards could lead to greater ELP data use by both content and language teachers. Moreover, specific language skills for content areas may also need to be assessed, and the results will need to be available to content area teachers. Further, content area teachers can be encouraged to adopt performance data-driven approaches such as formative assessment as part of their instructional practice (Black, Wilson, & Yao, 2011).

What and how teachers teach is influenced by assessment (i.e., washback effects) (Tsagari & Cheng, 2016). We need to guard against washback that could lead to negative impacts on teaching by carefully defining the ELP construct to be measured. One risk is the possibility of de-emphasizing standards that require inter- and intra-personal uses of language necessary for successful engagement in school but are not readily assessable by large-scale assessment. Another is that sole emphasis on academic language may encourage teachers to ignore entirely the language used during social (i.e., non-scholastic) experiences even though such language skills are necessary for becoming fully functional in English across all aspects of a student's life. We should consider ways in which these diverse interactions can be systematically included in ELP assessment. Most likely classroom formative approaches that involve listening to and discussing with students would be efficacious in this context (Bailey & Durán, 2020).

Concluding Remarks

We conclude by proposing four guiding principles for the operationalization of the ELP construct so that future ELP assessment might be more effective.

- Guiding principle 1: The ELP construct should be articulated with a view to language as a social practice and action to enhance meaningful language learning for students (van Lier & Walqui, 2012).
- Guiding principle 2: The ELP construct should be elaborated in ways that can help teachers and students to understand general and specific language demands associated with various school tasks across content areas.
- Guiding principle 3: Content and language should be acknowledged as largely intertwined to help understand the link between ELP and content standards.
- Guiding principle 4: Explicit articulation of different levels of proficiency in ELP should play an important role in establishing developmental progressions to guide teaching and student learning.

By investigating the language demands embedded in academic content standards and ELP standards, their linked assessments, and curricular materials, future studies can characterize the construct of ELP—that is, the essential language knowledge and skills that EL students may need to acquire to meaningfully participate and succeed in academic learning and assessment. We anticipate that the findings of such studies can help improve the education of EL students.

Acknowledgments

The work presented here was supported in part by the William T. Grant Foundation grant ID187863 (An Investigation of the Language Demands in Standards, Assessments, and Curricular Materials for English Learners) to Educational Testing Service and UCLA. The opinions expressed are those of the authors and do not represent views of the Foundation.

Note

1 In this chapter, we use English language proficiency (ELP) standards to refer to both ELP standards and English language development (ELD) standards. Both terms are in use by the different states, with California and the WIDA consortium retaining ELD standards to refer to their most recent revisions of English language standards (2012 and 2015, respectively), whereas the ELPA21 Consortium, for example, refers to the standards as ELP standards.

References

Bailey, A., Butler, F., & Sato, E. (2007). Standards-to-standards linkage under Title III: Exploring common language demands in ELD and science standards. *Applied Measurement of Education*, 20(1), 53–78.

Bailey, A., & Wolf, M. K. (2012). *The challenge of assessing language proficiency aligned to the Common Core State Standards and some possible solutions*. Commissioned paper by the Understanding Language Initiative. Stanford, CA: Stanford University. Retrieved from http://ell.stanford.edu/papers/policy

Bailey, A. L. (2007). *The language demands of school: Putting academic English to the test*. New Haven, CT: Yale University Press.

Bailey, A. L. (2017). Progressions of a new language: Characterizing explanation development for assessment with young language learners. *Annual Review of Applied Linguistics*, 37, 241–263.

Bailey, A. L., & Durán, R. (2020). Language in practice: A mediator of valid interpretations of information generated by classroom assessments among linguistically and culturally diverse students. In S. M. Brookhart & J. H. McMillan (Eds.), *Classroom assessment and educational measurement* (pp. 46–62). New York, NY: Routledge.

Bailey, A. L., & Heritage, M. (2014). The role of language learning progressions in improved instruction and assessment of English language learners. *TESOL Quarterly*, 48(3), 480–506.

Bailey, A. L., & Huang, B. H. (2011). Do current English language development/proficiency standards reflect the English needed for success in school? *Language Testing*, 28(3), 343–365.

Black, P. J., Wilson, M., & Yao, S.-Y. (2011). Road maps for learning: A guide to the navigation of learning progressions. *Measurement*, 9(2–3), 71–123.

Boals, T., Kenyon, D. M., Blair, A., Cranley, M. E., Wilmes, C., & Wright, L. J. (2015). Transformation in K–12 English language proficiency assessment changing contexts, changing constructs. *Review of Research in Education*, 39(1), 122–164.

Brantmeier, C., Schueller, J., Wilde, J. A., & Kinginger, C. (2007). Gender equity in foreign and second language learning. In S. S. Klein (Ed.), *Handbook for achieving gender equity through education* (pp. 305–334). Mahwah, NJ: Lawrence Erlbaum Associates.

Bunch, G. C., Kibler, A., & Pimentel, S. (2012). *Realizing opportunities for English learners in the common core English language arts and disciplinary literacy standards.* Stanford, CA: Stanford University. Retrieved from https://ell.stanford.edu/papers/practice

California Department of Education. (2015). *English language arts/English language development framework for California public schools: Kindergarten through grade twelve.* Sacramento, CA: Author.

Council of Chief State School Officers. (2012). *Framework for English language proficiency development standards corresponding to the Common Core State Standards and the next generation science standards.* Washington, DC: Author.

Council of Chief State School Officers. (2013). *English language proficiency (ELP) standards with correspondences to K–12 English language arts (ELA), mathematics, and science practices, K–12 ELA standards, and 6–12 literacy standards.* Washington, DC: Author. Retrieved from https://elpa21.org/wp-content/uploads/2019/03/Final-4_30-ELPA21-Standards_1.pdf

DiCerbo, P. A., Anstrom, K. A., Baker, L. L., & Rivera, C. (2014). A review of the literature on teaching academic English to English language learners. Review of Educational Research, 84(3), 446–482.

Elementary and Secondary Education Act of 1965. Public Law 89-10.

Ellis, R. (2008). *The study of second language acquisition.* Oxford: Oxford University Press.

Every Student Succeeds Act (2015). Public Law 114–95 § 114 Stat. 1177.

Frantz, R. S., Bailey, A. L., Starr, L., & Perea, L. (2014). Measuring academic language proficiency in school-age English language proficiency assessments under new college and career readiness standards in the U.S. *Language Assessment Quarterly, 11*(4), 432–457.

Haas, A., Grapin, S., & Lee, O. (2018). How the NGSS science instructional shifts and language instructional shifts support each other for English learners: Talk in the science classroom. In A. L. Bailey, C. Maher, & L. Wilkinson (Eds.), *Language, literacy, and learning in the STEM disciplines: How language counts for English learners* (pp. 53–70). New York, NY: Routledge.

Hakuta, H. (2017, May). *Meditations on language and learning: ESSA in policy and practice.* New York, NY: William T. Grant Foundation.

Halliday, M. A. (1989). Some grammatical problems in scientific English. *Australian Review of Applied Linguistics. Supplement Series, 6*(1), 13–37.

Halliday, M. A. K. (1978). *Language as social semiotic: The social interpretation of language and meaning.* London: Edward Arnold.

Hoff, E. (2013). Interpreting the early language trajectories of children from low-SES and language minority homes: Implications for closing achievement gaps. *Developmental Psychology, 49*(1), 4–14.

Larsen-Freeman, D., & Long, M. (1991). *An Introduction to second language acquisition research.* London: Longman.

LaRusso, M., Kim, H. Y., Selman, R., Uccelli, P., Dawson, T., Jones, S., … Snow, C. (2016). Contributions of academic language, perspective taking, and complex reasoning to deep reading comprehension. *Journal of Research on Educational Effectiveness, 9*(2), 201–222.

Lee, O. (2017). Common Core State Standards for ELA/Literacy and Next Generation Science Standards: Convergences and discrepancies using argument as an example. *Educational Researcher, 46*(2), 90–102.

Lee, O. (2018). English language proficiency standards aligned with content standards. *Educational Researcher, 47*(5), 317–327.

Lee, O., Quinn, H., & Valdés, G. (2013). Science and language for English language learners in relation to next generation science standards and with implications for Common Core State Standards for English language arts and mathematics. *Educational Researcher, 42*(4), 223–233.

Mislevy, R. J., & Durán, R. P. (2014). A sociocognitive perspective on assessing EL students in the age of common core and Next Generation Science Standards. *TESOL Quarterly, 48*(3), 560–585.

National Academies of Sciences, Engineering, and Medicine. (2017). *Promoting the educational success of children and youth learning English: Promising futures.* Washington, DC: The National Academies Press.

National Academies of Sciences, Engineering, and Medicine. (2018). *English learners in STEM subjects: Transforming classrooms, schools, and lives.* Washington, DC: The National Academies Press.

National Governors Association Center for Best Practices, Council of Chief State School Officers. (2010). *Common Core State Standards.* Washington, DC: Author.

National Research Council. (2011). *A framework for K–12 science education: Practices, cross-cutting concepts, and core ideas.* Washington, DC: The National Academies Press.

NGSS Lead States. (2013). *Next generation science standards: For states, by states.* Washington, DC: The National Academies Press.

No Child Left Behind Act (2001). Public Law 107–110. Stat. 6319.

Plakans, L. (2009). The role of reading strategies in integrated L2 writing tasks. *Journal of English for Academic Purposes, 8*(4), 252–266.

Sato, E., & Thompson, K. (2020). Standards-based K–12 English language proficiency assessments in the U.S.A: Current policies and practices. In M. K. Wolf (Ed.), *Assessing English language proficiency in U.S. K–12 schools.* New York, NY: Routledge.

Schleppegrell, M. J. (2012). Academic language in teaching and learning: Introduction to the special issue. *The Elementary School Journal, 112*(3), 409–418.

Truckenmiller, A. J., Park, J., Dabo, A., & Wu Newton, Y. C. (2019). Academic language instruction for students in grades 4 through 8: A literature synthesis. *Journal of Research on Educational Effectiveness, 12*(1), 135–159.

Tsagari, D., & Cheng, L. (2016). Washback, impact, and consequences revisited. In E. Shohamy & I. Or (Eds.), *Language testing and assessment: Encyclopedia of language and education* (3rd ed., pp. 1–14). Berlin: Springer Press.

van Lier, L., & Walqui, A. (2012). *How teachers and educators can most usefully and deliberately consider language.* Commissioned paper by the Understanding Language Initiative. Stanford, CA: Stanford University. Retrieved from https://ell.stanford.edu/papers/language

Wetherell, M., Taylor, S., & Yates, S. (2001). *Discourse theory and practice: A reader.* London: Sage.

WIDA. (2004). *WIDA English language proficiency standards.* Madison, WI: Board of Regents of the University of Wisconsin System.

WIDA. (2007). *English language proficiency standards for English language learners in Pre-Kindergarten through Grade 12* (2007 ed.). Madison, WI: Board of Regents of the University of Wisconsin System.

WIDA. (2012). *Amplification of the English language development standards, kindergarten-grade 12.* Madison, WI: Board of Regents of the University of Wisconsin System.

WIDA. (2018). *Announcing the WIDA instructional framework for ELD standards.* Retrieved from www.wida.us/standards/2019Standards/WIDA_ELDstandards_Announcement.pdf

Wolf, M. K., & Butler, Y. G. (2017). An overview of English language proficiency assessments for young learners. In M. K. Wolf & Y. G. Butler (Eds.), *English language proficiency assessments for young learners* (pp. 3–21). New York, NY: Routledge.

Wolf, M. K., Everson, P., Lopez, A., Hauck, M., Pooler, E., & Wang, J. (2014). *Building a framework for a next-generation English language proficiency (ELP) assessment system* (ETS research report no. RR-14-34). Princeton, NJ: Educational Testing Service.

Wolf, M. K., Farnsworth, T., & Herman, J. L. (2008). Validity issues in assessing English language learners' language proficiency. *Educational Assessment, 13*(2), 80–107.

Wolf, M. K., & Faulkner-Bond, M. (2016). Validating English language proficiency assessment uses for English learners: Academic language proficiency and content assessment performance. *Educational Measurement: Issues and Practice, 35*(2), 6–18.

Wolf, M. K., Guzman-Orth, D., & Hauck, M. C. (2016). *Next-generation summative English language proficiency assessments for English learners: Priorities for policy and research* (ETS research report no. RR-16-08). Princeton, NJ: Educational Testing Service.

Wolf, M. K., Oh, S., Wang, Y., & Tsutagawa, F. (2018). Young adolescent EFL students' writing skill development: Insights from assessment data. *Language Assessment Quarterly, 15*(4), 311–329.

Wolf, M. K., Wang, Y., Huang, B. H., & Blood, I. (2014). Investigating the language demands in the Common Core State Standards for English language learners: A comparison study of standards. *Middle Grades Research Journal, 9*(1), 35–51.

4

INNOVATIONS AND CHALLENGES IN K–12 ENGLISH LANGUAGE PROFICIENCY ASSESSMENT TASKS

Ahyoung Alicia Kim, Mark Chapman, and Heidi Liu Banerjee

Students in kindergarten through Grade 12 (K–12) identified as English learners (ELs) made up 9.6% of U.S. public school enrollments in fall 2016, and this proportion is expected to continuously increase in the foreseeable future (National Center for Education Statistics, 2019). ELs are students whose native language is not English and who require language-related program support, such as English as a second language instruction, to participate in regular classroom activities and learn the academic content taught in school. In the United States, ELs have a legal right to receive appropriate Language Instruction Education Program (LIEP) support as they learn academic English under the *Every Student Succeeds Act* (ESSA; see Section 3102(3)), the reauthorized *Elementary and Secondary Education Act*. The ultimate goal of any LIEP is to support ELs so that they can meet the same challenging content demands and academic achievement standards as their non-EL peers (Linquanti & Cook, 2013).

To protect ELs' rights to receive appropriate LIEP support, each state is mandated to annually assess, place, and monitor the progress of EL students' English language proficiency (ELP) levels (see ESSA Section 1111(b)(2)(G)). To this end, states have either developed their own ELP assessments (e.g., Arizona, California, New York, Texas) or joined one of the two ELP assessment consortia: the WIDA consortium or the English Language Proficiency Assessment for the 21st Century (ELPA21) consortium. In the 2018–2019 school year, WIDA's ELP assessment, ACCESS for ELLs (hereafter, ACCESS), served over 2 million students across 40 U.S. states and territories (WIDA, 2018b), and ELPA21's summative ELP assessment was administered to over 350,000 students across eight states (ELPA21, 2019c). California, which serves the largest EL population in the United States (approximately 1.2 million), has recently developed a new statewide ELP assessment called the English Language Proficiency Assessments for California (ELPAC) on the basis of new standards (California Department of Education [CDE], 2014).

Notwithstanding multiple ELP assessments currently in use, a common goal of these assessments is to "develop next generation ELP assessments aligned with new academic standards," which are described in more detail in the next section (Wolf et al., 2016, p. 158). To this end, innovative assessment features, such as technology-enhanced items and scaffolding, have been explored and implemented in computer-based ELP assessments to elicit student performances that can meaningfully reflect their real language abilities. The aim of this chapter is to provide a review of the innovative features currently implemented in K–12 ELP assessment tasks and to discuss the challenges associated with these features. This review focused on three major ELP assessments: ACCESS, ELPA21, and ELPAC. These three assessments were selected for their large-scale administration across the nation; collectively, these tests serve K–12 EL students from the majority of states in the United States. This chapter first presents an overview of these three major ELP assessments. Then, the innovative features identified in the ELP assessment tasks are described with sample items. Finally, the challenges associated with the innovative features as well as future directions are discussed.

Overview of Three Major K–12 ELP Assessments in the United States

ACCESS, ELPA21, and ELPAC are high-stakes, large-scale, standards-based ELP assessments administered annually to K–12 ELs in the United States. These assessments are developed to primarily measure ELs' social and academic English skills in the four language domains of listening, reading, speaking, and writing. In addition, the assessments reflect the language skills ELs need for college- and career-readiness as defined in the Common Core State Standards (CDE, 2014; ELPA21, 2014; WIDA, 2012). Each assessment is also aligned to specific language standards (see Table 4.1).

Table 4.1 summarizes the main characteristics and features of the three assessments, as well as their tasks we identified, drawing upon existing theories on assessment tasks (e.g., "Bachman & Palmer, 1996"; Scalise & Gifford, 2006; Wolf, Shore, & Blood, 2014). These include information on the structure of the assessment (e.g., grade-level clusters, number of items), content (e.g., measurement of integrated skills, inclusion of multimedia), and innovative features (e.g., technology-enhanced items, scaffolding, and universal tools).

Publicly available test design blueprints and sample tasks or items of the four language domains (reading, writing, listening, and speaking) were collected for analysis. Specifically, for ACCESS, WIDA's annual technical report

TABLE 4.1 Summary of Three ELP Assessments.

Assessment	ACCESS	ELPA21	ELPAC
Member states, territories, and federal agencies[1]	40 members: AL, AK, BIE, CO, DC, DE, DODEA, FL, GA, HI, ID, IL, IN, KY, ME, MD, MA, MI, MN, MO, MP, MT, NV, NH, NJ, NM, NC, ND, OK, PA, PR, RI, SC, SD, TN, UT, VT, VA, WI, WY	8 members: AK, IA, LA, NE, OH, OR, WA, WV	CA
Aligned standards	WIDA English Language Development Standards	ELPA21 English Language Proficiency Standards	California 2012 English Language Development Standards
Proficiency levels	1. Entering 2. Emerging 3. Developing 4. Expanding 5. Bridging 6. Reaching	Level descriptors for individual language skills: 1. Beginning 2. Early Intermediate 3. Intermediate 4. Early Advanced 5. Advanced Level descriptors for combined language skills: 1. Emerging 2. Progressing 3. Proficient	1. Minimally developed 2. Somewhat developed 3. Moderately developed 4. Well developed
Mode of delivery	Online (Grades 1–12) and paper (K; Grades 1–12; Grades 1–3 writing)	Online	Online and paper (K–2 writing)
Grade clusters	1, 2–3, 4–5, 6–8, 9–12 (Online) K, 1, 2, 3, 4–5, 6–8, 9–12 (Paper)	K, 1, 2–3, 4–5, 6–8, 9–12	K, 1, 2, 3–5, 6–8, 9–10, 11–12
Number of items or tasks per domain (varies per grade level)	Varies for individuals due to the semi-adaptive nature of the assessment: • Listening: 18–24 items • Reading: 24–30 items • Speaking: 3–6 tasks • Writing: 3 tasks	• Listening: 20 items • Reading: 21–22 items • Speaking: 11–12 tasks • Writing: 10–11 tasks	• Listening: 20–22 items • Reading: 14–26 items • Speaking: 9–12 tasks • Writing: 6–8 tasks

[1]Numbers from the 2018–2019 school year.

(WIDA, 2018a) and online sample assessment items (https://wida.wisc.edu/) were examined. For ELPA21, test specifications and sample assessments published by the Oregon Department of Education (ODE, 2019) were reviewed. Likewise, for ELPAC, test blueprints (CDE, 2019b) and sample items available on the California Department of Education website (www.cde.ca.gov/ta/tg/ep/) were examined. Note that only the computer-based versions of the assessments were analyzed, including ELPAC, which is scheduled to be administered online for the first time in the 2019–2020 school year.

As seen in Table 4.1, the online versions of the three assessments offer variations for specific grade-level clusters to provide content that is age-appropriate for the students: Grades 1, 2–3, 4–5, 6–8, and 9–12 (ACCESS); Grades K, 1, 2–3, 4–5, 6–8, and 9–12 (ELPA21); Grades K, 1, 2, 3–5, 6–8, 9–10, and 11–12 (ELPAC). Although ACCESS and ELPAC are delivered to ELs either using an online platform or a paper-and-pencil format, depending on state policy or students' needs, this chapter focuses on online assessments only. The number of items or tasks included in each of the four language domains varies slightly across the three assessments depending on the grade-level cluster, generally with the greatest number of items in the reading domain and the least in writing (see Table 4.1). In ACCESS, the number of items for each grade–level cluster has additional variation due to the semi-adaptive nature of the assessment; ACCESS uses a tier system to group assessment items into different difficulty levels (Tiers A-C with Tier C being the most difficult; Tier Pre-A is available only in Speaking for new incoming students). In addition to the variation of item numbers, the number of proficiency levels measured by each assessment differs from three (ELPA21) to six (ACCESS).

While the ELP assessments measure each of the four language domain skills separately, the incorporation of integrated skills can be found in the speaking and writing domains. For instance, for speaking tasks, students are often asked to first use their listening skills to listen to a conversation, a story, or an academic presentation; then, they respond to the speaking prompt based on what they heard. Writing tasks, on the other hand, may involve students' listening skills (e.g., listen to an announcement) as well as reading skills (e.g., read an email) as part of the response process. The complexity in the incorporation of integrated skills increases by grade level.

The introduction of the computer-based assessment system has allowed for the implementation of a range of task features that cannot be operationalized in traditional paper-and-pencil assessments. For example, the three assessments incorporate a variety of multimedia components. Components such as colored static images, audio recordings, and animated videos are commonly used across the assessments to provide task instructions, serve as prompts or selected-response options, or contextualize the tasks. These multimedia components further enhance the innovative features of the tasks, as discussed in more detail in the subsequent section.

Innovations in K–12 ELP Assessment Tasks

In our analysis of the tasks on the ACCESS, ELPA21, and ELPAC assessments, we identified three key innovative features: (1) technology-enhanced items, (2) scaffolding, and (3) universal tools. These features are "innovative" because they are made possible by a computer-based assessment delivery system or because they have been reconceptualized in the digital context.

The Inclusion of Technology-Enhanced Items

Broadly speaking, technology-enhanced items can be categorized into "items that contain media that cannot be presented on paper" and "items that require test takers to demonstrate knowledge, skills, and abilities using response inter-actions," such as dragging an appropriate picture to a designated area (Russell, 2016, p. 20). Similarly, Bryant (2017) defines technology-enhanced items as "computer-based items that make use of formats and/or response actions not associated with conventional MCs and constructed response items" (p. 2). By drawing upon the literature, this chapter defines technology-enhanced items as items delivered via computer-based assessments that incorporate media for item stimuli and/or responses, which are different from traditional selected-response or constructed-response items.

When designed appropriately, technology-enhanced items can offer several advantages over conventional selected-response or constructed-response items, including broadening the measured construct, presenting heightened authenticity, reducing random guessing, increasing measurement opportunities, and promoting test-taker engagement (Bryant, 2017).

ACCESS and ELPA21 include a variety of technology-enhanced items, such as *drag-and-drop* (test takers move an image to a certain location within a larger picture or response area) and *hot spot* (test takers click areas of a picture). In ACCESS, technology-enhanced items are embedded in the listening and reading domains. As displayed in the sample hot spot item in ACCESS reading (Figure 4.1), to respond to the prompt "Where does Ava like to work?" students click on one of the pre-defined areas within the larger image.

ELPA21 implements technology-enhanced items in all four language domains. As reported by Huang and Flores (2018), technology-enhanced items account for approximately 20% of ELPA21 items. Figure 4.2 illustrates a sample drag-and-drop item on ELPA21. In this Grade 1 sample reading item, test takers are asked to read the prompt ("Read about Mr. Bear. Move the things Mr. Bear needs to the picture. Follow the directions."), and then drag the pictures into the boxes to respond to the prompt. These innovative items are intended to make the assessment more engaging and interactive.

While technology-enhanced items have many advantages, they also have a number of potential limitations (Bryant, 2017; Parshall & Harmes, 2014),

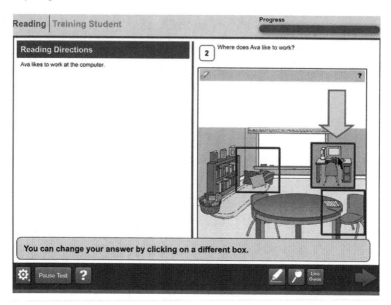

FIGURE 4.1 ACCESS for ELLs sample technology-enhance item (hot spot). Reproduced with permission.

Source: WIDA, n.d.

Read about Mr. Bear. Move the things Mr. Bear needs to the picture. Follow the directions.

It is hot and sunny outside today. Mr. Bear is going to swim in the pool. He needs his sunglasses, flippers, and a hat.

Move the things Mr. Bear needs onto his towel.

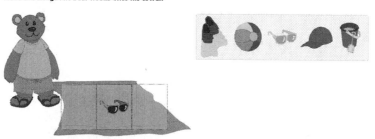

FIGURE 4.2 ELPA21 sample technology-enhanced item (drag and drop). Reproduced with permission.

Source: ELPA21, 2019b.

particularly in relation to construct representation, psychometric properties, and test-taker performance characteristics. Moon, Sinharay, Keehner, and Katz (2019) examined the relationship between test takers' cognition and the psychometric properties of technology-enhanced items embedded in a math assessment; they found that what test developers perceive as "subtle variations of item design"

(p. 1) can significantly affect test takers' cognitive processes and performance outcomes. Since this study was not conducted in a K–12 ELP assessment context but rather in the context of a mathematics assessment for a general population, its generalizability to language proficiency assessments is uncertain. To date, there is very limited research on the impact of technology-enhanced items on ELs' performance, particularly in the context of ELP assessments. In a recent study, Kim, Tywoniw, and Chapman (2019) examined Grades 1–12 ELs' performance on technology-enhanced items as compared to traditional multiple-choice items, using ACCESS reading data. Preliminary findings indicate that technology-enhanced items were slightly more difficult and took a longer time to complete than comparable multiple-choice items. Yet, the technology-enhanced items provided more item-level information for select grade levels, suggesting their usefulness. Therefore, empirical evidence to support the specific benefits of technology-enhanced items in K–12 ELP assessments remains to be established.

The Provision of Scaffolding in Tasks

Scaffolding, an instructional strategy to assist students until they can complete a given task independently, has been increasingly adopted in assessments with the goal of better measuring students' knowledge, skills, and abilities. As Wolf and López (2014) suggested, incorporating scaffolding strategies in ELP assessments can provide useful information for both learning and teaching because the degree and types of scaffolding students need reveal nuances of their actual language proficiency (see also Hauck, Pooler, Wolf, Lopez, & Anderson, 2017). Wolf et al. (2016) further proposed that the implementation of scaffolding strategies has the potential to improve the measurement opportunities of ELP assessments, allowing them to better align with the new academic standards.

Varying degrees of scaffolding are provided across ACCESS, ELPA21, and ELPAC. In ACCESS, scaffolding is provided at both the assessment level and the item level. For example, ACCESS items in the listening and reading domains are delivered to students in thematically linked folders of three items. The items within each folder are based on the same content theme to avoid rapid cognitive shifts, which are inappropriate for young learners; the items are independent from each other yet build upon each other in complexity. The difficulty of the folders delivered to students depends on the students' performance on previous folders, with the adaptive engine selecting a folder rather than individual items. Then, based on their listening and reading scores, test takers are given appropriate forms of the writing and speaking test: Tiers A to C for writing and Tiers Pre-A to C for speaking (WIDA, Data Recognition Corporation, and the Center for Applied Linguistics [CAL], 2015). This item arrangement by folder and tier can be considered scaffolding at the assessment level. At the task level in the writing domain, test takers who are placed in Tier A start with items that measure word-level knowledge and gradually progress to items that assess sentence- and paragraph-level ability. Tier

A test takers are also provided with scaffolded assistance in the form of sample writing, sentence starters, or word boxes. However, test takers who are placed in Tiers B or C are presented with different types of support that are more appropriate for their proficiency level. Specifically, they are provided with checklists to plan or check their written responses.

Meanwhile, speaking tasks in ACCESS employ model responses as a type of scaffolding, indicating to test takers the length and complexity expected in a proficient response. This innovative design allows ELs to maximally demonstrate their ELP and may ultimately yield more meaningful interpretations with respect to ELs' progress. Figures 4.3a and 4.3b illustrate a sample ACCESS Grade 1 speaking task with a prompt for a model response from a virtual student as a type of scaffolded assistance for test takers.

As Figures 4.3a and 4.3b show, in this Tier B/C Grade 1 sample speaking task, test takers interact with two characters: the virtual teacher, Ms. Lee, and a virtual student, Nina. After providing the context of the task, Ms. Lee states the prompt. However, instead of instructing test takers to respond, she asks Nina to respond first. The response provided by Nina serves as a model response for test takers. Afterwards, test takers are presented with a different prompt that is very similar to Nina's in terms of the expected length and complexity of the spoken response. The incorporation of this type of scaffolding could reduce erroneous responses due to unfamiliarity with the assessment format or anxiety and consequently minimize construct-irrelevant variance.

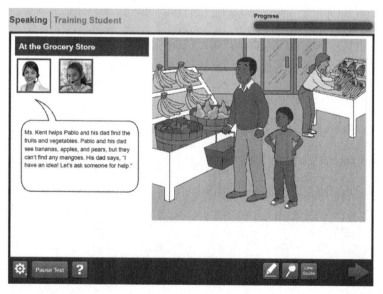

FIGURE 4.3a ACCESS for ELLs Grade 1 sample speaking task prompt. Reproduced with permission.

Source: WIDA, n.d.

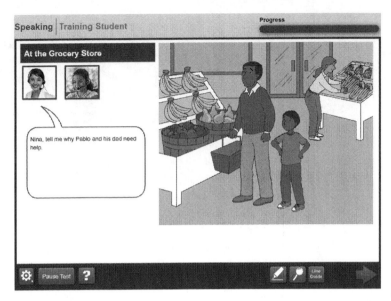

FIGURE 4.3b   ACCESS for ELLs Grade 1 sample speaking task with scaffolding. Reproduced with permission.
Source: WIDA, n.d.

ELPA21 also puts much emphasis on implementing scaffolding support in the assessment, as explicitly highlighted in the ELP Standards (Council of Chief State School Officers, 2014) that guide the development of ELPA21. As Hauck et al. (2017) indicate, scaffolding can be especially beneficial for ELs with low proficiency or young EL students. Some of the scaffolding techniques that have been operationalized or are in the process of being operationalized in ELPA21 include modeling responses; breaking down a task into steps; providing key words; and providing sentence frames, sentence starters, or graphic organizers. For example, for conversation-type speaking tasks in ELPA21, model responses are sometimes provided for EL test takers at low grade levels.

Similar to ACCESS and ELPA21, ELPAC incorporates scaffolding in the design of the assessment tasks. Although ELPAC is administered online, the speaking portion requires one-on-one administration to students across all grade levels. This administration setting introduces human support and standardized prompting by the test administrator. When a student does not answer or needs to hear the question again, the test administrator can repeat the prompt. Online scaffolding is also provided in domains other than speaking. For example, in the Grades 3–5 writing sample in Figure 4.4, the prompt is presented using a graphic organizer. Test takers can use the information presented in the graphic organizer when responding to the item. However, this scaffolding feature has limited benefit in that students cannot manipulate the content in the supplied graphic organizer.

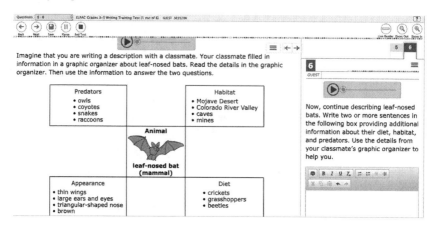

FIGURE 4.4 ELPAC Grades 3–5 sample writing item with scaffolding. Reproduced with permission.

Source: CDE, n.d.

As Hauck et al. (2017) cautioned, given the large-scale, standardized nature of these K–12 ELP assessments, the field needs to explore how to effectively incorporate scaffolding while, at the same time, maintaining standardization. It is challenging to ensure that the students who could benefit from scaffolding receive the appropriate support, considering the large-scale nature of the assessment. The field needs more research evidence that the provided scaffolding is actually benefiting students.

Universal Tools Embedded in Assessment

The use of computer-based assessment delivery platforms has allowed a variety of universal tools, also known as *accessibility features*, to be embedded in addition to non-digital universal tools (e.g., providing scratch paper) in ACCESS, ELPA21, and ELPAC. By definition, universal tools are "selectable embedded features or hand-held instruments used to carry out a particular purpose. Universal tools may either be embedded in the online test or provided to [ELs] by test administrators for online or paper tests" (Shafer Willner & Monroe, 2016, p. 3). Thanks to online assessment platforms, test takers can simultaneously use multiple features (e.g., highlighter, line guide, magnifier, or notepads), which increases the accessibility of the assessment content.

In general, all three assessments provide universal tools at the assessment level, with the same features available in all items across all four language domains. In addition, ELPA21 and ELPAC provide *designated* features for test takers who are identified in advance to have such needs; test administrators can make these designated features available to a group of or specified students prior to the assessment (CDE, 2019a; ELPA21, 2019a; WIDA et al., 2015). The three assessments also provide *accommodation* features that are available for test takers identified as having one or more disability. Table 4.2 provides a summary of online universal and designated tools available in the three ELP assessments.

As shown in Table 4.2, the three assessments have a number of digital universal tools in common. In general, efforts have been made to ensure that test takers who need certain types of assessment presentation to perform adequately have access to those tools, under the condition that the tools do not lead to construct misrepresentation (CDE, 2019a; ELPA21, 2019a; WIDA et al., 2015). For instance, in ELPAC, some of the universal tools (e.g., line reader, zoom out, zoom in; see upper right corner in Figure 4.5) are available at the overall assessment level, whereas others (mark for review, notepad, and strikethrough; see upper right corner of *Item 2* in Figure 4.5) can be used at the item level. In the example (*Item 2* in Figure 4.5), using these item-level universal tools, test takers can flag this item to review at a later time, make notes using the notepad feature, or strike through an option they think is incorrect.

TABLE 4.2 Summary of Main Embedded Universal Tools.

Universal tools	Description	ACCESS	ELPA21	ELPAC
Answer choice eliminator	Cross out answer options		U	U
Audio aids	Amplify or decrease sound.	U	U	D
Color contrast/overlay	Change the text and background color.	U	D	D
Digital notepad/Sticky notes	Make notes about item	U	U	U
Expandable item/passage	Expand item/passage to take up larger portion of screen		U	U
Flag for review	Flag items for review		U	U
General masking	Block off content that is distracting or not immediately needed		D	D
Highlighter	Mark text with color	U	U	U
Keyboard navigation	Navigate through the assessment using a keyboard in place of a mouse	U	U	U
Line reader	Assist in tracking each line of text	U	D	U
Magnifier/Zoom	Make text/graphic larger or smaller	U	U	D
Turn off universal tools	Turn off universal tools that might be distracting		D	D
Writing tools (e.g., cut and paste)	Editing tools for writing	U	U	U

Note. U = universal tools, D = designated features. Note that this list is not exhaustive and the actual names of the features embedded in the three assessments may differ slightly from those presented in the table.

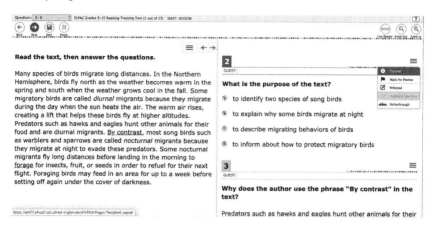

FIGURE 4.5 ELPAC Grades 9–10 sample reading item with accessibility features. Reproduced with permission.

Source: CDE, n.d.

The universal tools discussed so far are embedded in assessments to enhance ELs' access to content. As individual students are unique in their needs, research suggests that ELs vary in the use of the features. Kim, Yumsek, Chapman, and Cook (2019) examined the universal tools embedded in ACCESS and found that ELs used the line guide, highlighter, and magnifier more frequently than other features; in addition, advanced learners and ELs with disabilities used the features more often, suggesting that the universal tools might provide the intended support to test takers. Yet such research is limited, particularly in the context of K–12 ELP assessments, suggesting the need for more investigation in the future. Overall, the three major K–12 ELP assessments optimize their computer-based delivery platforms by implementing a number of innovative features that could not have been possible in the traditional, paper-based assessment format. Nevertheless, challenges remain in developing innovative items, as discussed in the following section.

Challenges and Suggestions for Innovative K–12 ELP Assessment Tasks

ACCESS, ELPA21, and ELPAC include many innovative and novel features, such as technology-enhanced items, scaffolding, and universal tools. However, innovative assessment and task designs, particularly those that are relatively new to the K–12 ELP assessment field, result in a variety of challenges for test developers and point to the likely need for including additional test development procedures. For example, the use of cognitive laboratories to ensure that assessment tasks are at an appropriate level of cognitive load for young learners should be considered during the assessment development process. Other considerations include the development of appropriate test administration procedures, addressing the challenges of appropriate administration, and response modes for young learners. Technology and innovative task designs open up many exciting opportunities for test developers, but innovative assessments must be delivered to students in age-appropriate formats with which students can engage and to which students can respond in ways that allow them to fully demonstrate their knowledge, skills, and abilities. Finally, we consider the potential need for enhanced scoring protocols for computer-delivered constructed response tasks. We discuss in the following section the associated challenges and further considerations in the development, administration, and scoring of innovative tasks.

Developing Age-Appropriate Innovative Tasks

Assessment tasks for K–12 ELs must be developmentally appropriate for the age of the target population. Rigorous task development processes have been documented in a number of publications (e.g., Alderson, Clapham, & Wall, 1995; Bachman & Palmer, 1996; Davidson & Lynch, 2002; Weigle, 2002). While these fundamental processes are necessary for the development of valid assessments, they are not necessarily sufficient for the development of age-appropriate and innovative tasks for young learners. The innovative nature of assessment tasks described in this chapter and the associated delivery platforms necessitate additional test development procedures to ensure that the interactions of task design and delivery method are age appropriate. We argue that such steps should include cognitive laboratories (or cognitive labs), tryouts (for constructed response tasks), and a field-test design that takes advantage of the computer-based environment.

A key step that should be taken relatively early in the development of new task types is to conduct cognitive labs (Beatty & Willis, 2007; Szpotowicz & Campfield, 2016; see also Wolf, Guzman-Orth, Still, & Winter2020, in this volume). Cognitive labs are designed to identify "possible problems with interpretations of instructions and questions, evaluating tasks and the level or sources of difficulty to complete the test" (Szpotowicz & Campfield, 2016, p. 124). A typical cognitive lab involves the administration of a task by an experienced test administrator or researcher to a representative student or a small group of students. The task should be administered in the same assessment environment and on the same platform that will be used in an operational administration, so that the cognitive lab environment replicates an authentic testing experience. Following the administration of the task, the researcher asks each student a series of questions to evaluate the appropriateness of the task for the target population, as well as whether the student can engage with and understand the associated technology features of the task design. For example, in creating technology-enhanced items for ACCESS, cognitive labs were conducted to examine students' performance and perception of the innovative features noted in this chapter (CAL, 2015). Interview questions used in the cognitive labs addressed whether students could understand instructions, whether they could process graphic supports and found those graphics to be appealing, and how difficult students found the task and using the technology features. Findings from such cognitive labs can be used to determine whether test tasks within the computer-based environment present students with an appropriate cognitive challenge and whether students can meaningfully engage with the assessment.

Computer-delivered assessments present both opportunities and challenges to tryout and field-test designs. For instance, the computer-based environment allows multiple field-test tasks to be delivered to students without printing and delivering a large number of different test booklets, a process that adds complexity and cost to test development. While computer-delivered assessments afford some advantages in this aspect of field-test design, computer-adaptive test designs, where students are presented with test items that are appropriately targeted to the students' ability level, based on their test performance, make field-test item placement somewhat complex. In the case of ACCESS, as students navigate through the computer-adaptive listening and reading domain tests, test takers receive content based on their cumulative performance on prior items. Students who perform well are presented with assessment content that is more difficult, consistent with the skill level they have demonstrated on previous tasks. Such adaptive design aims to maximize accurate measurement information as students engage with tasks that are tailored to their abilities. However, despite the advantages offered in measurement precision, the adaptive design results in many different permutations of the paths individual students take through the assessment. If developers wish to present field assessment content to students at the appropriate ability level and optimal position within the assessment, a complex field-test design will be required. For example, to guard against position effects, field-test items should be delivered to students as near as possible to the position in which these items would be delivered operationally. Determining where and when within an assessment to deliver field-test items can be challenging and time consuming. This drawback applies not only to formulating the field-test path but also to validating the field-test results. These hurdles are not insurmountable, but they do add considerable complexity to the test development process.

Developing Appropriate Test Administration Procedures for Innovative Tasks

Just as test development processes need to be tailored for innovative tasks, test administration procedures should be customized. Test administration procedures should consider the cognitive and social development of the target student population along with the more typical considerations of ensuring administration standardization and test security. Test administration procedures that can support innovative tasks for the age and development of the target population include ensuring (1) an appropriate number of students in a test session, (2) appropriate administration and response modes, and (3) test practice opportunities.

Regarding the number of students in a test session, tailored guidance should be provided to test administrators on the number of students in a test session. The recommended group size will vary with the age and proficiency of the students and the language domain being measured. A major advantage of computer-delivered assessments is the ability to assess students at different ability levels and grade levels in the same test session. Instructions and practice items can be administered via the computer. That is, test administrators might need only to monitor and troubleshoot, rather than having to deliver scripted instructions that might not be appropriate for an entire group of students at different ability and grade levels. This advantage makes it tempting to administer computer-delivered assessments to large groups of students concurrently, but there can be many reasons that doing so is not appropriate. It might be inadvisable, if not impossible, to assess the youngest learners (Grades K–2) in a group setting. In some such cases, speaking tasks are administered in a one-on-one setting, as in ELPAC, which allows for human support, as discussed earlier. Regardless of language domain, young students and low-proficiency students will benefit from relatively small test sessions. The guidance provided to ACCESS test administrators, for example, is no more than five students in a group.

Regarding administration and response modes, contemporary ELP assessments can be developed as both computer-delivered and more traditional, paper-and-pencil assessments. Test developers should consider whether it is feasible for students of all ages to engage with a computer-delivered assessment. Access to technology, familiarity with computers, and keyboarding skills are all factors that contribute to a decision as to whether students can successfully take or respond to a computer-delivered ELP assessment. In fact, recent research (Kim, Lee, Chapman, & Wilmes, 2019) indicates that Grades 1 and 2 students might perform better on writing tasks if they handwrite rather than type their responses. Similar issues need to be considered for computer-delivered speaking assessments. Not all students can demonstrate their true speaking ability when responding to computer-delivered tasks. Therefore, it might be beneficial to have one-on-one administration as in ELPAC. However, individual administrations add logistical challenges when teachers have a large number of ELs to assess. Some students might simply prefer a speaking assessment that is delivered by a human and familiar test administrator, and these students might feel uncomfortable or restricted when speaking into a computer microphone. Developers should carefully consider how students will be provided relevant scaffolding to help ensure computer-delivered speaking tasks elicit a response representative of a student's full ability.

As young learners might not be familiar with taking computer-based assessments with innovative features, it is advisable to offer a range of practice opportunities to students both before and during the test administration. These opportunities include (1) test demos, such as video-delivered explanations of how to engage with the test content; (2) sample assessment tasks, which provide students the opportunity to engage with authentic tasks under test conditions; and (3) test practice items, which are unscored but are embedded at the beginning of an operational test administration to introduce students to the test environment. Without such tools, students might be disadvantaged by the unfamiliar computer-based test environment or the tools available within the test platform. For instance, without test demos on universal tools, students might not fully grasp the variety of features that are embedded in ELP assessments. They need prior exposure to some of the features, such as using magnifiers or highlighters on practice items, so that they can engage with the content during the actual test administration session. Without such practice sessions, encountering universal tools during the assessment could be a distraction rather than a scaffold, hindering students rather than helping them perform their best.

Scoring Innovative Constructed-Response Tasks

The scoring of innovative constructed-response tasks can be particularly challenging. The linguistic features of speaking and writing responses elicited from innovative, computer-delivered tasks might not be comparable with those elicited by more traditional tasks. The challenges of developing appropriate scoring protocols for speaking are different from those for the writing domain.

Protocols for scoring students' speaking responses to computer-based assessment tasks must take into account the administration mode, supports provided to test takers, and the test taker's grade and proficiency level. The EL population, with its broad diversity in ability level and cognitive development, is not suited to a one-size-fits-all approach to scoring, and a balance needs to be struck between developing a suite of rubrics that are tailored to particular segments of the population and the practical constraints of producing meaningful and interpretable scores within a limited time frame. Finally, responses to computer-delivered tasks are scored centrally by trained raters who award scores after listening to an audio recording of students' performances. Rubrics, scoring criteria, and scoring descriptors should be developed based on the linguistic features of these audio-recorded responses, and scoring protocols should be consistent for each proficiency and age level within the target population.

Test developers face different challenges when determining scoring protocols for responses to computer-delivered writing tasks. First, they must consider appropriate response modes for students based on their ages and readiness to type responses. Scoring rubrics and protocols for typed responses might not be appropriate for handwritten responses, particularly for young students in kindergarten and elementary school grades. Regardless of response mode, raters of young learners' written language must be trained in the characteristics of emerging literacy, such as letter reversals, creative spelling, and lack of punctuation. As with speaking, it might not be appropriate to use a single scoring rubric and set of scoring protocols to rate students' written responses across K–12. Considerations of age and response mode will impact the development of appropriate scoring rubrics and protocols, which must meaningfully discriminate between different levels of performance across the target population.

In summary, the development of innovative tasks and test designs creates many opportunities for test developers and test takers, yet there are associated challenges and additional test development steps, including the enhancement of administration procedures and scoring protocols, compared to traditional language assessments. These challenges and associated new processes mean that developers need to reconsider assessment development timelines and carefully plan the development phases. It is likely that test development timelines will be longer and more complex than with traditional paper-and-pencil assessments.

Conclusion

This chapter described the innovations and challenges in K–12 ELP assessment tasks, focusing specifically on three major K–12 ELP assessments that are administered in the United States—ACCESS, ELPA21, and ELPAC. These assessments include tasks that have been carefully crafted to measure academic English as it is outlined in corresponding English language development standards. Moreover, the assessment tasks include innovative features—technology-enhanced items, scaffolding, and universal tools—to effectively support students' test taking. For example, traditional multiple-choice items with three to four options have been modified to include drag-and-drop or hot spot items to increase test takers' engagement in assessments. New methods of scaffolding have been developed, and a wide range of universal tools have been embedded in the three ELP assessments to help test takers better access the content.

However, the use of technology comes with caveats. Computer-based assessments in general are costly and require districts and schools to have sufficient computers and the infrastructure to administer online assessments. For example, online assessments require high-speed internet to deliver content. Test administrators also typically need extensive training to ensure that the administration proceeds smoothly. Furthermore, ELs need to have a certain level of computer literacy to demonstrate their ELP. For example, in order for students to provide responses in the writing domain, they need not only basic familiarity with computers but also adequate typing skills. As demonstrated in existing research, this could pose a challenge, particularly to young learners in Grades 1 and 2 (Kim, Lee, et al. (2019)). If schools do not provide instructional support for ELs to build computer familiarity, the online platform will create barriers for test takers.

The future for K–12 ELP assessments remains hopeful despite the challenges in designing and developing innovative assessment tasks. Along with the advancements in technology, ELP tasks have already begun to include animated video input (e.g., ELPA21), which could make the tasks more engaging to young learners. Some assessments are offered on tablets (e.g., ACCESS), allowing test takers to interact with touch screens. Furthermore, implementing automated scoring of productive domains can mean more efficient scoring of test-taker responses, enabling stake-holders to receive score reports in a timely fashion. Considering these benefits, the field should continuously explore ways to further enhance and implement innovative assessment tasks in K–12 ELP assessments.

References

Alderson, J. C., Clapham, M. C., & Wall, D. (1995). *Language test construction and evaluation*. Cambridge, UK: Cambridge University Press.

Bachman, L. F., & Palmer, A. S. (1996). *Language testing in practice*. Oxford, UK: Oxford University Press.

Beatty, P. C., & Willis, G. B. (2007). Research synthesis: The practice of cognitive interviewing. *Public Opinion Quarterly, 71*, 287–311.

Bryant, W. (2017). Developing a strategy for using technology-enhanced items in large-scale standardized tests. *Practical Assessment, Research, & Evaluation, 22*(1), 1–10.

California Department of Education. (2014). *California English language development standards: Kindergarten through grade 12*. Sacramento, CA: Author.

California Department of Education. (2019a). Matrix four: English language proficiency assessments for California accessibility resources. Retrieved from www.cde.ca.gov/ta/tg/ep/documents/elpacmatrix4.docx

California Department of Education. (2019b). *Test blueprints for the summative English language proficiency assessments for California*. Retrieved from www.cde.ca.gov/ta/tg/ep/documents/elpacsummativebluprt.pdf

California Department of Education. (n.d.). *Practice and training test resources*. Retrieved from www.elpac.org/resources/practicetests/

Center for Applied Linguistics. (2015). *Enhanced item types cognitive labs: Summary of findings*. Washington, DC: Author.

Council of Chief State School Officers. (2014). *English language proficiency (ELP) standards*. Retrieved from https://ccsso.org/sites/default/files/2017-11/Final%204_30%20ELPA21%20Standards%281%29.pdf.

Davidson, F., & Lynch, B. K. (2002). *Testcraft: A teacher's guide to writing and using language test specifications*. New Haven, CT: Yale University Press.

English Language Proficiency Assessment for the 21st Century. (2014). *Theory of action*. Retrieved from https://ucla.box.com/s/xrvipt6inhgfwq6786vkezig7409r2l8

English Language Proficiency Assessment for the 21st Century. (2019a). *Accessibility and accommodations manual*. Retrieved from https://ucla.box.com/s/ukpkuk05wamrpiwr5nont1ejcys6mzcz.

English Language Proficiency Assessment for the 21st Century. (2019b). *ELPA21 summative assessment [measurement instrument]*. Los Angeles, CA: Author.

English Language Proficiency Assessment for the 21st Century. (2019c). *The May insider newsletter*. Retrieved from http://mailchi.mp/elpa21/elpa21-insider-may.edition.

Hauck, M. C., Pooler, E., Wolf, M. K., Lopez, A., & Anderson, D. (2017). Designing task types for English language proficiency assessments for K–12 English learners in the U.S. In M. K. Wolf & Y. G. Butler (Eds.), *English language proficiency assessments for young learners* (pp. 79–95). New York, NY: Routledge.

Huang, B. & Flores, B. (2018). The English language proficiency assessment for the 21st century (ELPA21). *Language Assessment Quarterly, 15*(4), 1–10.

Kim, A., Lee, S., Chapman, M., & Wilmes, C. (2019). The effects of administration and response modes on grade 1–2 students' writing performance. *TESOL Quarterly, 53*(2), 482–513.

Kim, A., Tywoniw, R. L., & Chapman, M. (2019, October). *Technology enhanced items and young English learners: What construct are we measuring?* Poster presented at the meeting of the Midwest Association of Language Testers (MwALT) Conference, Bloomington, IN.

Kim, A., Yumsek, M., Chapman, M., & Cook, H. G. (2019). *Investigating K–12 English learners' use of universal tools embedded in online language assessments* (WIDA technical report 2019–2). Madison, WI: WIDA.

Linquanti, R., & Cook, H. G. (2013). *Toward a "common definition of English learner": Guidance for states and state assessment consortia in defining and addressing policy and technical issues and options.* Washington, DC: Council of Chief State School Officers.

Moon, J. A., Sinharay, S., Keehner, M., & Katz, I. R. (2019). Investigating technology-enhanced item formats using cognitive and item response theory approaches. *International Journal of Testing*, Advance online publication. doi: 10.1080/15305058.2019.1648270.

National Center for Education Statistics. (2019). *English language learners in public schools.* Retrieved from https://nces.ed.gov/programs/coe/indicator_cgf.asp.

Oregon Department of Education. (2019). *ELPA21 test specifications 2017–2018 grade 1.* Retrieved from www.oregon.gov/ode/educator-resources/assessment/Pages/English-Language-Proficiency.aspx.

Parshall, C. G., & Harmes, J. C. (2014). Improving the quality of innovative item types: Four tasks for design and development. *Journal of Applied Testing Technology, 10*(1), 1–20.

Russell, M. (2016). A framework for examining the utility of technology-enhanced items. *Journal of Applied Testing Technology, 17*(1), 20–32.

Scalise, K. & Gifford, B. (2006). Computer-Based Assessment in E-Learning: A Framework for Constructing "Intermediate Constraint" Questions and Tasks for Technology Platforms. Journal of Technology, Learning, and Assessment, 4(6).

Shafer Willner, L., & Monroe, M. (2016). *The WIDA accessibility and accommodations framework: Considerations influencing the framework development.* Madison, WI: WIDA.

Szpotowicz, M., & Campfield, D. E. (2016). Developing and piloting proficiency tests for Polish young learners. In M. Nikolov (Ed.), *Assessing young learners of English: Global and local perspectives* (pp. 109–138). New York, NY: Springer.

Weigle, S. C. (2002). *Assessing writing.* Cambridge, UK: Cambridge University Press.

WIDA. (2012). *2012 amplification of the English language development standards kindergarten–grade 12.* Madison, WI: Board of Regents of the University of Wisconsin System.

WIDA. (2018a). *Annual technical report for ACCESS for ELLs 2.0 online English language proficiency test, series 401, 2016–2017 administration.* Madison, WI: Board of Regents of the University of Wisconsin System.

WIDA. (2018b). *WIDA Consortium report, July 1, 2017 – June 30, 2018.* Retrieved from https://wida.wisc.edu/sites/default/files/Website/Memberships/Consortium/Annual-Reports/2018WIDAAnnualReport.pdf.

WIDA. (n.d.). *QuickStart guide for preparing students for ACCESS online.* Retrieved from https://wida.wisc.edu/assess/access/preparing-students.

WIDA, Data Recognition Corporation, and the Center for Applied Linguistics. (2015). *ACCESS for ELLs 2.0 grades 1–12 online test administration manual*. Madison, WI: Board of Regents of the University of Wisconsin System.

Wolf, M. K., Guzman-Orth, D., López, A. A., Castellano, K., Himelfarb, I., & Tsutagawa, F. S. (2016). Integrating scaffolding strategies into technology-enhanced assessments of English learners: Task types and measurement models. *Educational Assessment, 21*(3), 157–175.

Wolf, M. K., Guzman-Orth, D., Still, C., & Winter, P. (2020). Examining students' response processes in a computer-based English language proficiency assessment. In M. K. Wolf (Ed.), *Assessing English language proficiency in U.S. K–12 schools*. New York, NY: Routledge.

Wolf, M. K., & López, A. A. (2014). *The use of scaffolding strategies in the assessment of English learners*. Paper presented at the 3rd Teachers College Columbia University Roundtable in Second Language Studies, New York, NY.

Wolf, M. K., Shore, J. R., & Blood, I. (2014). *English Learner Formative Assessment (ELFA): A design framework*. Princeton, NJ: Educational Testing Service. Retrieved from www.ets.org/s/research/pdf/elfa_design_framework.pdf.

5

A REVIEW OF VALIDITY EVIDENCE ON K–12 ENGLISH LANGUAGE PROFICIENCY ASSESSMENT

Current State and Future Direction

Timothy Farnsworth

The No Child Left Behind Act of 2001 (NCLB, 2002) was groundbreaking educational reform legislation in many respects, not least of which was the explicit demand that attention and resources be devoted to the assessment of English learner (EL) students' English language proficiency (ELP). NCLB mandated that states develop ELP standards, measure EL students' progress toward these standards, and provide evidence of the validity and measurement qualities of the relevant assessments. The goal of this mandate, of course, was to improve educational outcomes for students, with a particular focus on this previously underserved, and historically underprivileged, minority group. Despite mixed evidence regarding the overall effectiveness of these reforms (Chalhoub-Deville, 2009a, 2009b; Dee & Jacob, 2010; Koretz, 2017), and considerable protestation from school professionals, scholars, and in the popular press about negative impacts of the testing-based accountability requirements on teaching and learning (Au, 2013; Ravitch, 2016), the central provisions of the law were retained in the most recent reauthorization of the law, now called the Every Student Succeeds Act (ESSA, 2015).

In the early years of NCLB, states rushed to meet the provisions of the law and assessments were rapidly produced, often without sufficient time allotted to the collection of comprehensive technical and overall quality evidence for those assessments (Rabinowitz & Sato, 2005; Wolf, Farnsworth, & Herman, 2008). In many cases, states banded together into consortia, with varying levels of success at developing ELP assessments that would satisfy federal requirements (National Research Council, 2011). As the two-decade mark of the original legislation approaches, however, the work needed to ensure high quality ELP assessments has come into much clearer focus.

With this context in mind, the purpose of this chapter is twofold: (1) to review validation work and evidence that are currently available and (2) to identify the areas of further validation needed for ELP assessments. By doing so, this chapter is intended to describe the various validation challenges that assessment developers have addressed and must continue to address when developing and conducting ongoing work on ELP assessments. First, I briefly describe the validation frameworks that test developers and government agencies have used to guide work in this area. Next, using federal regulatory guidance as a main organizing principle, I describe types of validation work that have been conducted. Finally, I identify areas of ELP assessment validation in which evidence and/or a theoretical basis is lacking, and I offer a few suggestions for future research directions. In most cases, I focus on work conducted during the past decade, as much has changed in ELP assessment during that time. Wolf et al. (2008) conducted a review of validation evidence covering the early years of NCLB. The work reviewed in this chapter both shows advancements in the field since then and highlights areas in need of further work.

Background and Theoretical Frameworks for ELP Assessment Validation

The complexity and scope of the various ELP assessment systems in use across states should be noted here to help the reader contextualize the problem. There are currently eight ELP assessment systems in use in K–12 public schools across the United States. Each assessment system is designed as a series or group of assessments organized by grade band cluster, starting with young learners' assessments (kindergarten, roughly age five) through to secondary school assessments (high school, roughly age 18). In addition, states use modified versions of these assessments, or additional assessments, for the purpose of initial EL identification. This poses significant reporting, equating, and validation challenges as the construct and target language use domain (Bachman & Palmer, 1996) of ELP needed for success in an English-language school environment is radically different across the ages and developmental ranges being assessed.

These assessments are extremely large in scale—in 2016, 1.8 million learners across 35 U.S. states took the ELP assessment called the ACCESS for ELLs assessment developed by the WIDA consortium (Center for Applied Linguistics, 2018), and in California alone approximately 1.2 million learners took the states' ELP assessment, the English Language Proficiency Assessments for California (ELPAC). The scale and complexity of these ELP assessments mean that significant attention to validation efforts is crucial to ensuring beneficial outcomes for millions of learners.

As discussed here and at length elsewhere in this volume (e.g., Kim, Chapman, & Banerjee; Sato & Thompson), states have chosen one of three approaches to ELP test development. Over the years since NCLB passage, there has been significant change with regards to state participation in consortia and individual states' efforts to develop their own ELP assessments; the discussion here concerns only the state of affairs as of 2019. The first approach has been to form consortia in order to develop common ELP standards and then ELP assessments. This consortium work was typically conducted in collaboration with industry and academic partners. Currently the two consortia are WIDA and the English Language Proficiency Assessment for the 21st Century (ELPA21). As mentioned briefly earlier, WIDA produces the ACCESS assessment, which is currently used in the majority of U.S. states and was the first and largest ELP test initiative in this area. ELPA21's ELP assessments are in use for eight states. Another approach has been for individual states to develop their own unique ELP assessments, as seen in Arizona, California, New York, and Texas. States that have pursued this independent approach have typically been those with large numbers of EL students, and the states have partnered with test-development agencies to produce their assessments. The final approach has been to use a pre-existing commercial assessment, as currently seen in the cases of Connecticut and Mississippi. These states use the LAS Links, 2nd edition, published by CTB/McGraw-Hill (2006).

Over the past decade or more, language assessment theorists have come to general consensus on a model of validation originally formulated by theorists such as Kane (2006, 2012, 2013), Mislevy, Almond, and Lukas (2004), Bachman (2005), and Bachman and Palmer (2010). This model, or general approach, discussed in detail elsewhere in this volume (see Chalhoub-Deville, 2020, in this volume), conceives of validation work as a set of evidence-based arguments around which a case for—or against—test use can be made. Conceptually then, validation evidence is collected in support of assessment use in the form of a series of claims to be made in support of test use. A clear benefit of this approach is that it brings the intended consequences of test implementation into focus, and thus we may say that it is not the test that is validated but rather the use or application of a test to a specific context (American Educational Research Association, American Psychological Association, & National Council on Measurement in Education [AERA, APA, & NCME], 2014; Bachman and Palmer, 2010; Mislevy, Almond, & Lukas, 2004).

The U.S. Department of Education (2018) requires that states submit evidence to support the quality and validity of their assessment systems, including ELP assessments. The submitted evidence is evaluated for its adequacy. This process is formally established as "Peer Review" by the U.S. Department of Education, wherein a panel of experts reviews evidence and provides recommendations for further validation or documentation, if needed (U.S. Department of Education, 2018). To facilitate this Peer Review process, the U.S. Department of Education has used as a guiding framework for their regulatory guidance the *Standards for Educational and Psychological Testing* (AERA, APA, & NCME, 2014; the *Standards*, henceforth). This framework is applied across the broader group of federally mandated statewide assessments of mathematics, reading/language arts, and science, in addition to the ELP assessments. The *Standards* and the Peer Review guidance document (U.S. Department of Education, 2018) discuss several types of evidence that must be collected to support validation efforts.

This state of affairs with regards to ELP assessments is a fruitful place to explore how differing theoretical approaches to validation may affect the work of test developers and researchers and the conclusions they are able to draw. It is reasonable to ask to what extent the *Standards*, the federal regulatory guidance (i.e., Peer Review guidance), and approaches such as Bachman and Palmer's (2010) Assessment Use Argument (AUA) are congruent, where they differ, and to what extent validity evidence collection and interpretation might differ depending on which approach is considered primary. Chapelle, Enright, and Jamieson (2010) assert that an argument-based approach can be useful in explicating the claims and types of evidence needed to support these claims.

While language assessment experts have moved toward an AUA-based approach, federal regulatory guidance uses the validation categories outlined in the *Standards* as an organizing principle (with some noteworthy changes), delineating validity evidence by its type or source: evidence based upon test content, evidence based on response processes, evidence based on internal structure, and evidence based on relations to other variables. The final category of evidence described in the *Standards*, evidence for validity and consequences of testing, is not included in the Peer Review guidance documentation. This is a noteworthy omission that will be discussed later in this chapter. Therefore, it is unsurprising that of the eight ELP assessments currently in use as of this writing, only two of them—ACCESS and ELPA21—have produced publicly available validity frameworks situating their test development and validation work using a version of an AUA conceptual framework (Center for Applied Linguistics, 2018; Hansen & Cai, 2013). Other available reports describe their development and validation work with a presumed eye to the *Standards* and federal regulators and do not articulate an overall validity framework (beyond the evidence categories described earlier) on which to organize and guide the various validation activities undertaken.

As we discuss ELP assessment validation, it is important to remember that there are three primary intended uses of this group of assessments: (1) identifying learners in need of English language support services, (2) tracking the progress of these learners as they acquire ELP, and (3) determining when these learners are prepared to meet the challenges of coursework without additional language support (this decision is commonly referred to as an exit or reclassification decision). Each of these broadly stated purposes is linked to specific actions that must be taken at the level of the individual child (e.g., the decision to designate a child as an EL), the school or district (decisions about allocation of teachers and other resources), and the state and federal level (decisions about schools and teacher professional development work). The number of EL students identified in a school district and in a state will affect resource allocation decisions about the number of trained professionals needed, amount and types of professional training that in-service teachers receive to support these learners, state incentive-based programs to increase the number of EL-certified teachers in the workforce, and so on. Each of these intended uses of ELP assessment presents unique challenges to the collection of validity evidence.

In order for test developers and other stakeholders to both maintain high standards of practice and satisfy federal guidance, a variety of ELP assessment validation efforts are needed. The assessment consortia and individual states have produced ELP assessments using somewhat different approaches and collected evidence in somewhat different ways, in addition to validation evidence and research produced by individual scholars. As described earlier, the U.S. Department of Education has provided Peer Review of the assessments using the *Standards* as an organizing principle with some changes (U.S. Department of Education, 2018). In the next section, I describe and organize various validation activities following the approach taken by the federal Peer Review guidance framework and the *Standards*.

Validity Evidence Collection and Regulatory Guidance

What follows is a brief description of selected validation work that has been conducted by the various states, consortia, and other researchers. A comprehensive description of all of the publicly available studies and analyses was not practical in this space. I have attempted to draw upon published technical reports of current ELP assessments and other documentation provided by developers, which also form the basis for the Peer Review requirement. In the cases of Connecticut and Mississippi, which use the LAS Links, I have consulted the 2006 technical report (CTB/McGraw-Hill, 2006).

The validation activities may be grouped as a collection of the following types of evidence, adopting the *Standards* and federal Peer Review approaches:

- Evidence based on test content
- Evidence based on response processes
- Evidence based on internal structure
- Evidence based on relations to other variables

As mentioned earlier, a noteworthy omission from the Peer Review framework is the absence of the need to provide evidence for "validity and the consequences of testing," which is the final major validity evidence category in the *Standards*.

Additional required evidence is also described in the Peer Review framework. Under the heading of "Technical Quality—Other" (U.S. Department of Education, 2018, p. 29), Peer Review guidance specifically requires evidence that

- Assessments are reliable,
- Assessments are accessible and alternative versions comparable for learners with disabilities,
- The full performance continuum has been measured,
- Multiple forms of assessments have been implemented, and
- Technical analyses and ongoing maintenance are performed.

These additional "Technical Quality—Other" categories do not fit neatly into the *Standards* approach or other approaches to validation—it can be inferred that these specific components are enumerated in order to show their importance to federal regulators. Finally, we may consider validation activities that are not specifically called for by the Peer Review guidance, including evidence of beneficial consequences for test use. Specifically, they might include

- Evidence that classification of learners into and re-designation out of EL status leads to a positive benefit to learners and
- Evidence that decisions made about teachers, such as teacher tenure, and about schools, such as their public rating, made in part on the basis of ELP assessment records are adequately supported (Chalhoub-Deville, 2020, in this volume).

In the next section, publicly available technical reports and the federal Peer Review response documents for the collection of evidence submitted by states on ELP assessments are analyzed in terms of which of the above types of evidence are more, and which are less, adequately provided at the current time. This analysis is intended to identify future validation work as these assessments are replaced or continuously improved.

Evidence Based on Test Content

Under NCLB and later under ESSA, states are required to develop ELP standards and to demonstrate that the content of their ELP assessments aligns to these standards, though the law says little about the required standards themselves (ESSA, 2015). States and state consortia have therefore created new ELP standards and collected validity evidence of alignment between the new assessments and the new standards. Standards themselves appear to vary significantly in level of specificity and in format among states and consortia (Wolf et al., 2016), posing challenges in alignment methods and comparability across assessments.

Cook (2007) describes an alignment study conducted to investigate the degree of alignment between the WIDA standards and ACCESS assessment, concluding that the test content aligned appropriately with standards. Yet, no public information is available regarding the alignment for the revised ACCESS assessment with revised WIDA standards (WIDA, 2012). Other available technical reports, to greater or lesser degrees, describe the process of examining ELP assessment alignment with state ELP standards. In some instances, alignment was claimed, but evidence that a study was conducted was not provided. For example, in Arizona, test developers claimed that their efforts "provide a solid rationale for having confidence in the content and design of the Arizona English Language Learner Assessment (AZELLA) as a tool from which to derive valid inferences about Arizona students' proficiency in English" (Arizona Department of Education, 2019, p. 66). However, no alignment study evidence was presented to support this claim.

Evidence Based on Response Processes

Available technical reports list relatively little information that fits neatly into the category of evidence based on response processes. This category concerns the examination of test takers' cognitive processes while engaging in assessment tasks to evaluate the appropriateness of tasks to measure the intended construct. Wolf, Guzman-Orth, and Wain (2015) conducted a cognitive laboratory study, investigating both EL and non-EL students' test-taking processes in a computer-based ELP assessment (i.e., ELPA21 assessment). The findings of the study informed further modifications of the assessment items and administration methods, as the study was conducted during the assessment development stages.

Evidence Based on Internal Structure

As for validity evidence based on internal structure, a variety of evidence was provided in all available documentation from test developers. Researchers have also conducted validity studies especially regarding the factor structure or dimensionality of ELP assessments. In one published study, Cai and Hansen (2018) used ELPA21 score data to explore multivariate IRT approaches to analyzing test structure. In another, Römhild, Kenyon, and MacGregor (2011) utilized a factor analytic approach to examine whether domain-specific language knowledge could be said to constitute an ability factor on the ACCESS assessment. They found that domain-general knowledge was the prevalent dimension but that for higher proficiency levels domain-specific knowledge was a salient contributor.

For another example of how states have analyzed tests based on their internal structures, the New York State English as a Second Language Achievement Test (NYSESLAT) developers report intercorrelations of modality subscores as one type of validity evidence in this category (New York State Department of Education, 2019). The state claimed that the correlations supported the overall validity of the test as well as the validity of subscore reporting requirements. The state of Arizona performed a similar analysis (Arizona Department of Education, 2019) and came to the same conclusions about its assessments.

Evidence Based on Relations to Other Variables

The *Standards* support the use of traditional validation work that relates the measure under study or under construction to other measures of the same or different constructs. This has been called criterion-related validity and is further subdivided into predictive and concurrent validity evidence—respectively, evidence that current performance on the measurement of interest predicts future outcomes of interest, or that current performance on the measurement of interest predicts contemporaneous and related measures or scores.

Test developers and other researchers have made criterion-related validity a key component of validation work, and ample evidence supporting the current group of ELP assessments has been collected. For example, Kong, Powers, Starr, and Williams (2012) used ELP assessment and state reading assessment scores to predict subsequent student achievement. The researchers found that overall the test scores were highly predictive of future academic performance of EL students, lending support to the validity of the ELP assessment scores. In another example, Parker, Louie, and O'Dwyer (2009) conducted an analysis of ACCESS scores in fifth and eighth grades and compared students' scores on this ELP assessment to scores on students' state-mandated content-area assessments of reading and writing (English language arts) and mathematics. The authors found significant and substantial correlations between the ELP assessment and content-area assessment scores. Correlations were highest in areas theorized to be most closely related (reading and writing domain scores from ELP and language arts assessment scores) and lower in areas theorized to be less closely related (ELP and mathematics assessments). The authors concluded this was evidence of construct validity for the ACCESS assessment for those grade bands.

Evidence for Validity and Consequences of Testing

The *Standards* require test developers to consider the intended and unintended consequences of testing. In addition, the *Standards* direct test developers to collect evidence of the overall beneficial impact of an assessment upon "components of the system that will go beyond the interpretation of test scores as a valid measure of student achievement" (AERA, APA, & NCME 2014, p. 19). The extent to which this work has been addressed by ELP test developers up to now is in question. Available evidence suggests that little has been done by test developers and states to validate the consequences, both intended and unintended, of ELP assessment use in schools. This is perhaps unsurprising given that this particular section of the *Standards* is not mentioned in the federal Peer Review guidance provided to states (U.S. Department of Education, 2018).

The Texas English Language Proficiency Assessment System (TELPAS) technical manual (Texas Department of Education, 2019a), alone among the publicly available technical reports, contains a section detailing the need for validation of consequences but does not cite any specific activity performed by developers to support consequential validity. Instead, a second document (Texas Department of Education, 2019b) is mentioned. This document describes a pattern of gradually increasing TELPAS scores, with a dip in average scores in 2013 when new standards were introduced, followed by another period of gradual increase, as evidence of beneficial consequential validity. Interestingly, this pattern—which is widespread in U.S. accountability testing—is precisely described by Koretz

(2002, 2017) as evidence of *negative* consequential validity in accountability testing. Koretz (2002) explains this pattern as a predictable outcome of teaching to the test and narrowing the curriculum—as educators learn about a new assessment, they adapt their teaching to the new test, resulting in modest average score increases for several years, until the "effectiveness" of this approach wanes. Then, a new assessment and new standards are created, and the cycle begins anew. Yet TELPAS cites this exact pattern of score increase as evidence that implementation of the test itself is promoting learning, with a premise that the new TELPAS assessment measures higher and more rigorous language skills. Increasing scores on an educational measurement, by themselves and without concurrent evidence of learning gains (such as that provided by an independently developed assessment), do not seem to be convincing evidence of beneficial consequential validity.

Little in the other available technical reports list any type of validity evidence that might fit into this category. Further, the federal Peer Review guidance documents (U.S. Department of Education, 2016, 2017, 2018) nowhere lists consequential validity evidence as a type of validity evidence that should be collected, nor note this as an area for states to work in the future. In reading the guidance documents, one would be forgiven for thinking that consequential validity evidence was not an explicit element of the *Standards,* elsewhere in the Federal guidance documents so carefully held up as an accepted standard of best practice.

Reliability and Other Technical Quality

The Peer Review guidance document groups some other elements of test development and analysis under the heading of "Technical Quality—Other" as described earlier. Here I describe some efforts relating to test score reliability that developers have included in technical reports. Developers and state agencies generally provide detailed evidence of test score consistency by documenting internal consistency reliability, interrater and parallel forms reliability estimates, and much more, as test design principles dictate. Developers report high levels of internal consistency reliability. For example, the ACCESS technical report includes Cronbach's alpha over 0.93 for each grade cluster (Center for Applied Linguistics, 2018).

Both the Arizona and Texas state ELP assessments (Arizona Department of Education, 2019; Texas Department of Education, 2019a) utilize machine scoring algorithms for the speaking portion of their assessments, using technology derived from the Versant family of assessments, and they report machine-human interrater reliability as a part of validity evidence, assuming that machine-derived scores measure the same constructs as human scores of EL speaking. Arizona reports Cronbach's alpha values in the range of 0.68 to 0.94 for various permutations of human/machine scores, which the state presents as positive evidence of score reliability. Texas reports similar results for its automated scoring technology. One question test developers might investigate more is why lower inter-item correlations are observed in the test versions designed for the lower grades than for higher grades—this was true for both the Arizona and Texas state assessments—and how to improve internal consistency estimates for younger test takers without adversely impacting their educational experiences.

One subcategory in "Technical Quality—Other" concerns the need for evidence of "Fairness and Accessibility." A fuller discussion of states' issues meeting reporting requirements relating to learners with disabilities is further discussed in the next section. A common analysis that might be fit into this subcategory is the search for item bias. Multiple states and consortia have conducted studies to examine potential item-level bias in the form of Differential Item Functioning (DIF), Zieky, 1993). This approach compares performance on individual test items between two groups and seeks to determine whether one group under or overperforms the other beyond that predicted by test takers' overall test scores. For example, Arizona examined the AZELLA assessment for DIF by gender and by ethnicity and found very little evidence of differential item functioning across its grade bands (Arizona Department of Education, 2019). Similarly, the ACCESS technical report (Center for Applied Linguistics, 2018) describes DIF analyses conducted annually using gender and ethnicity as foci. In general, ACCESS also reported low levels of DIF.

Particular Challenges for Validating ELP Assessment Systems

It is clear from the above-described reports and available research evidence that a great deal of validation work has been conducted to support the uses of these assessments and that the field has made substantial progress in this area since the initial passage of NCLB. However, given the complex nature of these assessment systems, more work is needed in some particular areas.

Additional areas of further research and development are justified by the purpose and test-taker population of these assessments, in particular the need for more research and validation of standard-setting and consequences of reclassification cut scores and the design of assessment tasks for young learners. Furthermore, the Peer Review documents reviewed make clear that the U.S. Department of Education requires much more attention be paid to validation for EL students with disabilities (Center for Standard, Assessment and Implementation, 2019; U.S. Department of Education, 2017). Additionally, newer approaches to validation (e.g., Bachman & Palmer, 2010) and the *Standards* explicitly demand that attention be paid to collecting validity evidence relating to consequences of test use. In the next section, I discuss four major areas in which much more validation work is needed: (1) reclassification, (2) consequences, (3) young learners, and (4) EL students with disabilities.

Validation Research on Reclassification Decisions

One of the high-stakes decisions involved in ELP assessments is reclassification (i.e., exiting EL students from EL status). To provide validity evidence to support the use of ELP assessments for this particular decision, various types of evidence must be collected. They include, but are not limited to, evidence to defend cut scores established from a standard-setting procedure to determine students' different ELP levels including the level of being proficient. This is one of the most theoretically and technically challenging aspects of ELP assessment decision-making: where and how to set cut scores to make the decision to remove EL students from formal language support services and reclassify them as former ELs (Linquanti, 2001). Challenges with respect to this decision include the choice to include other metrics (e.g., other performance measures and teacher recommendations) as additional or support criteria, challenges regarding available test score data, and other issues. Similarly vexing are the standard-setting decisions around initial classification of learners as EL students (Bailey, Heritage, & Butler, 2014; Linquanti, Cook, Bailey, & Macdonald, 2016). With the initial passage of NCLB, many states were challenged by the lack of capacity to adequately address the theoretical, practical, and measurement challenges posed by the standard-setting problem for ELP assessments; over the ensuing years, researchers have worked to identify data-based best practices in this area. Still, much remains to be done.

Promising is the growing research on guidance and methods to validate ELP levels for reclassification. Linquanti, Cook, Bailey, and Macdonald (2016) lay out a series of four policy papers on the issue that illustrate the fields' emerging understanding of the dilemmas inherent in these high-stakes decisions and provide much-needed guidance for states seeking to improve decision-making in this area. As for some empirical research, Cook, Linquanti, Chinen, and Jung (2012) conducted a study with three states using EL students' content area (reading and mathematics) state assessment scores and their relationships with ELP assessment scores. This work was based on the hypothesis that ELP and content assessment scores would be less closely related at higher levels of ELP, indicating that ELP was no longer a major contributor to content area assessment scores, and that this could be an indication that EL services were no longer required. Baron, Linquanti, and Huang (2020, in this volume) describe work done to facilitate standard setting for California's ELPAC exam, including both the use of content-area assessment scores as criterion measures and teacher judgments in a contrasting groups approach. Further, using the ACCESS assessment, Kenyon, Ryu, and MacGregor (2013) also exploited quantitative methods followed by teacher surveys to help move the ACCESS cut scores from a single score per grade "band" encompassing multiple grades to a per-grade cut score approach.

While this recent work in standard setting and criteria to determine reclassification is clearly needed, much more can and must be done at a theoretical level to define threshold levels of language proficiency across various grade levels and to operationalize this in the form of test items and tasks. Moreover, empirical research to examine consequences of this reclassification decision based on ELP assessments is currently lacking but critically needed.

Attention to Consequences of ELP Assessment Use

As mentioned, in addition to validation work suggested by the *Standards* and requested by regulatory agencies, an AUA approach to validation suggests additional activities that should fall to assessment experts. As discussed in more detail in this volume (Chalhoub-Deville, 2020, in this volume), attention to the consequences of test use appears to be critically missing, both from federal guidance and from the work undertaken by test developers and state agencies. It is here that the *Standards* approach and that of regulatory agencies (i.e., Peer Review guidance) part ways with assessment theorists such as Kane (2006) and Bachman and Palmer (2010).

The federal regulatory approach to the topic of consequential validity limits itself to discussions of accessibility, Universal Design for Learning, and equal access to assessments. No regulatory guidance suggests that test developers be held to account for overall positive educational outcomes, and in fact such outcomes are not defined in guidance documents as a basis for validation efforts. Therefore, it comes as no surprise that test developers, state educational agencies, and researchers have not more actively sought to include evidence of beneficial outcomes in their validation efforts to date. Two consortia assessments (ELPA21 and ACCESS) explicitly claim to be based upon an argument-based validity framework and clearly discuss the importance of evaluating consequences in their own literature. Nevertheless, they do not describe validation activities related to outcomes in available technical documentation or elsewhere, even though such work is explicitly called for in their published theoretical frameworks. Examples of relevant validation work would include examinations of how educators use ELP assessment results in their daily work with ELs or comparisons of educational outcomes for students whose parents "opt out" of EL services after being identified as potential ELs against outcomes for students included in services.

Assessing Young English Learners

In the past decade or more, assessment theorists and researchers have worked to address some of the significant challenges with regards to assessing young school age learners (Bailey et al., 2014; McKay, 2006; Wolf & Butler, 2017). In particular, the nature of the young learner "academic" ELP construct vis-a-vis typical non-EL language growth needs to be better understood. In addition, issues of task design and young learner needs and abilities with regards to attention, motivation, and other variables must all be taken into account (Wolf & Butler, 2017; Wolf et al., 2016).

In fact, young learners represent the largest segment of the EL population in the United States, and so addressing their unique assessment challenges is a core issue for K–12 ELP assessment. While federal guidance documents do not point specifically toward the need to address these challenges, as noted above some of the reported validation evidence submitted by states supports the need for more attention to be paid to the best ways to assess young learners.

Inclusion of ELs with Disabilities in ELP Assessments

The Peer Review response documents for several states' ELP assessments contain one recurring recommendation, acknowledging the lack of evidence in this particular area. They all indicate a need for more extensive work to be done to support the validity of test scores for EL students with disabilities.

Each Peer Review response document differs somewhat with respect to evaluating evidence on students with disabilities, but in each case, the response letters express the need for test developers to pay more attention to EL students with disabilities in the development of ELP assessments. In some cases, this guidance related to technical qualities or highly specific alternative assessments. For example, in the case of New York's NYSESLAT (Department of Education, 2019, p. 5), the Peer Review response letter requires the state to provide:

Evidence that the NYSESLAT Braille versions in kindergarten and Grades 1–2:

> Followed a design and development process to support comparable interpretations of results for students tested across the versions of the assessments. Documented adequate evidence of comparability of the meaning and interpretations of the assessment results.

In other cases, the Peer Review response indicates more attention be paid to inclusive policies relating to learners with disabilities. The Peer Review guidance, taken all together, indicates the federal government's commitment to including all learners in ELP assessment. Clearly, this imposes considerable resource and technical burdens on test developers to include learners with disabilities' needs in the item and task design stages and the analysis of results and to create alternative assessments for learners with specific disabilities, such as visual impairment. The number of test takers for these alternative assessments may be quite limited. For example, the number of designated EL students in Grades 1–2 with a significant visual impairment in New York State is likely to be small. However, Peer Review guidance suggests that substantial validation efforts need still be conducted. This is a clear priority for policymakers and one that poses significant challenges for test developers and state agencies.

Conclusion

This chapter has described a wide variety of validity evidence collection that has been conducted for ELP assessments. Certainly, the field has made progress in establishing best practices for many of the challenging problems presented, including establishing a basis for standard setting, and documenting the technical qualities of the assessments. However, much work remains to be done. In particular, validation work on consequences is entirely absent.

Collection of validation evidence on the impact and consequences of ELP assessment programs on learners, educators, and school systems should be advocated by test developers as part of their work, as the *Standards* and other approaches mandate. While I have laid out some major areas for further consideration in ELP assessment development and use, the work should be done in collaboration of test developers, various stakeholders (e.g., policymakers, state and local agencies, educators), and researchers to promote validity and best practices in ELP assessment. Additionally, more work needs be done in the areas of standard setting and task design for young learners. Developers and state agencies have made great strides in understanding the best practices in ELP assessment over the past decade, particularly in relation to technical quality and to some extent in explicating the construct of ELP in this context. It is now time to begin in earnest to explore the consequences of ELP test use and to incorporate this work into our validation arguments.

References

American Educational Research Association, American Psychological Association, and National Council on Measurement in Education (AERA, APA, & NCME). (2014). *Standards for educational and psychological testing.* Washington, DC: Author.

Arizona Department of Education. (2019). AZELLA: Arizona English language learner assessment technical report 2016. Retrieved from https://www.azed.gov/assessment/technical-and-legal-resources/

Au, W. (2013). Hiding behind high-stakes testing: Meritocracy, objectivity and inequality in U.S. education. *The International Education Journal: Comparative Perspectives, 12*(2), 7–19.

Bachman, L. F. (2005). Building and supporting a case for test use. *Language Assessment Quarterly, 2*(1), 1–34.

Bachman, L. F., & Palmer, A. S. (1996). *Language testing in practice.* Oxford, UK: Oxford University Press.

Bachman, L. F., & Palmer, A. S. (2010). *Language assessment in practice.* Oxford, UK: Oxford University Press.

Bailey, A. L., Heritage, M., & Butler, F. A. (2014). Developmental considerations and curricular contexts in the assessment of young language learners. In A. J. Kunnan (Ed.), *The companion to language assessment* (pp. 1–17). Boston, MA: Wiley.

Baron, P., Linquanti, R., & Huang, M. (2020). Validating threshold sores for English language proficiency assessment uses. In M. K. Wolf (Ed.), *Assessing English language proficiency in U.S. K–12 schools.* New York, NY: Routledge.

Cai, L., & Hansen, M. (2018). Improving educational assessment: Multivariate statistical methods. *Policy Insights from the Behavioral and Brain Sciences, 5*(1), 19–24.

Center for Applied Linguistics. (2018). *Annual technical report for ACCESS for ELLs 2.0 English language proficiency test, series 401 online, 2016–2017 administration (WIDA consortium annual technical report no. 13B).* Washington, DC: Author.

Chalhoub-Deville, M. (2009a). The intersection of test impact, validation, and educational reform policy. *Annual Review of Applied Linguistics, 29,* 118–131.

Chalhoub-Deville, M. (2009b). Standards-based assessment in the U.S.: Social and educational impact. In L. Taylor & C. J. Weir (Eds.), *Language testing matters: Investigating the wider social and educational impact of assessment* (pp. 281–300). *Studies in Language Testing 31.* Cambridge, UK: Cambridge University Press and Cambridge ESOL.

Chalhoub-Deville, M. B. (2020). Toward a model of validity in accountability testing. In M. K. Wolf (Ed.), *Assessing English language proficiency in U.S. K–12 schools.* New York, NY: Routledge.

Chapelle, C. A., Enright, M. K., & Jamieson, J. (2010). Does an argument-based approach to validity make a difference? *Educational Measurement: Issues and Practice, 29*(1), 3–13.

Cook, H. G. (2007). *Alignment study report: The WIDA consortium's English language proficiency standards for English language learners in Kindergarten through Grade 12 to ACCESS for ELLs® Assessment.* Madison, WI: WIDA Consortium.

Cook, H. G., Linquanti, R., Chinen, M., & Jung, H. (2012). *National evaluation of Title III implementation supplemental report: Exploring approaches to setting English language proficiency performance criteria and monitoring English learner progress.* Washington, DC: US Department of Education, Office of Planning, Evaluation and Policy Development. Retrieved from www2.ed.gov/rschstat/eval/title-iii/implementation-supplemental-report.pdf

CTB/McGraw-Hill. (2006). LAS links technical report. Retrieved from https://dese.mo.gov/sites/default/files/asmt-tac-ell-las-links-tech-manual.pdf

Dee, T., & Jacob, B. A. (2010). The impact of no child left behind on students, teachers, and schools. *Brookings Papers on Economic Activity, 2,* 149–207.

Every Student Succeeds Act. (2015). Public Law No. 114–354.

Hansen, M., & Cai, L. (2013). *A quality assurance plan for ELPA21: Gathering the evidence to evaluate validity, reliability, fairness and utility.* Los Angeles, CA: National Center for Research on Evaluations, Standards, and Student Testing (CRESST).

Kane, M. (2006). Validation. In R. Brennan (Ed.), *Educational measurement* (4th ed., pp. 17–64). Westport, CT: American Council on Education and Praeger.

Kane, M. (2012). Validating score interpretations and uses. *Language Testing, 29*(1), 3–17.

Kane, M. (2013). Validating the interpretations and uses of test scores. *Journal of Educational Measurement, 50,* 1–73.

Kenyon, D. M., Ryu, J. R., & MacGregor, D. (2013). *Setting grade level cut scores for ACCESS for ELLs* (WIDA consortium technical report no. 4). Washington, DC: Center for Applied Linguistics.

Kim, A. A., Chapman, M., & Banerjee, H. (2020). Innovations and challenges in K–12 English language proficiency assessment tasks. In M. K. Wolf (Ed.), *Assessing English language proficiency in U.S. K–12 schools.* New York, NY: Routledge.

Kong, J., Powers, S., Starr, L., & Williams, N. (2012). *Connecting English language learning and academic performance: A prediction study.* Paper presented at the Annual meeting of the American Educational Research Association, Vancouver, British Columbia. Retrieved from https://eric.ed.gov/?id=ED576686

Koretz, D. (2002). Limitations in the use of achievement tests as measures of educator's productivity. *The Journal of Human Resources, 37*(4), 752–777.

Koretz, D. (2017). *The testing charade: Pretending to make schools better.* Chicago, IL: University of Chicago Press.

Linquanti, R. (2001). *The redesignation dilemma: Challenges and choices in fostering meaningful accountability for English learners.* Berkeley, CA: University of California Linguistic

Minority Research Institute. Retrieved from https://escholarship.org/uc/item/2hw8k347

Linquanti, R., Cook, H. G., Bailey, A. L., & Macdonald, R. (2016). *Moving toward a more common definition of English learner: Collected guidance for states and multi-state assessment consortia.* Washington, DC: Council of Chief State School Officers.

McKay, P. (2006). *Assessing young language learners.* Cambridge, UK: Cambridge University Press.

Mislevy, R. J., Almond, R. G., & Lukas, J. F. (2004). A brief introduction to evidence-centered design (*CSE report 632*). Los Angeles, CA: National Center for Research on Evaluation, Standards, and Student Testing (CRESST).

National Research Council. (2011). *Allocating federal funds for state programs for English language learners.* Washington, DC: The National Academies Press.

New York State Education Department. (2019). *New York State English as a second language achievement test (NYSESLAT) technical report 2018.* Retrieved from http://p12.nysed.gov/assessment/nyseslat

No Child Left Behind. (2002). Act of 2001, Pub. L. No. 107–110, 115 Stat. 1425.

Parker, C. E., Louie, J., & O'Dwyer, L. (2009, November 20). New measures of English language proficiency and their relationship to performance on large-scale content assessments (*issues & answers report, REL 2009–no. 066*). Washington, DC: U.S. Department of Education, Institute of Education Sciences, National Center for Education Evaluation and Regional Assistance, Regional Educational Laboratory Northeast and Islands. Retrieved from https://files.eric.ed.gov/fulltext/ED504060.pdf

Rabinowitz, S., & Sato, E. (2005). *The technical adequacy of assessments for alternate student populations.* San Francisco, CA: WestEd.

Ravitch, D. (2016). *The death and life of the great American school system: How testing and choice are undermining education.* New York, NY: Basic Books.

Römhild, A., Kenyon, D. M., & MacGregor, D. (2011). Exploring domain-general and domain specific linguistic knowledge in the assessment of academic English language proficiency. *Language Assessment Quarterly, 8,* 213–228.

Sato, E., & Thompson, K.D. (2020). Standards-based K–12 English language proficiency assessments in the United States: Current policies and practices. In M. K. Wolf (Ed.), *Assessing English language proficiency in U.S. K–12 schools.* New York, NY: Routledge.

Texas Department of Education. (2019a). *Texas English language proficiency assessment (TELPAS) technical digest 2017–18.* Retrieved from http://tea.texas.gov/Student_Testing_and_Accountability/Testing/TELPAS

Texas Department of Education. (2019b). TELPAS validity evidence based on the consequences of testing (proficiency-level trends). Retrieved from https://tea.texas.gov/sites/default/files/TELPAS_Consequential_Long_Term_032119_FORWEB_0.pdf

United States Department of Education (2019). Decision Letter on New York Final Assessment System. Retreived from https://www2.ed.gov/admins/lead/account/nclbfinalassess/index.html

U.S. Department of Education. (2016). *Non-regulatory guidance: English learners and Title III of the Elementary and Secondary Education Act (ESEA), as amended by the Every Student Succeeds Act (ESSA).* Retrieved from www2.ed.gov/policy/elsec/leg/essa/essatitleiiiguidenglishlearners92016.pdf

U.S. Department of Education. (2017). *Resource guide: Accountability for English learners under the ESEA.* Retrieved from www2.ed.gov/programs/sfgp/eseatitleiiiiresourceaccountelsguide.pdf

U.S. Department of Education. (2018). *A state's guide to the U.S. Department of Education's assessment peer review process*. Washington, DC: Author. Retrieved from www2.ed. gov/admins/lead/account/saa/assessmentpeerreview.pdf

WIDA. (2012). *2012 Amplification of the English language development standards, Kindergarten through Grade 12*. Madison, WI: Board of Regents of the University of Wisconsin System.

Wolf, M. K., & Butler, Y. G. (2017). An overview of English language proficiency assessments for young learners. In M. K. Wolf & Y. G. Butler (Eds.), *English language proficiency assessments for young learners* (pp. 3–21). New York, NY: Routledge.

Wolf, M. K., Farnsworth, T., & Herman, J. (2008). Validity issues in assessing English language learners' language proficiency. *Educational Assessment, 13*(2), 80–107.

Wolf, M. K., Guzman-Orth, D., & Wain, J. (2015). *Investigating the usability of technology-enhanced assessment items during the ELPA21 development process: ELPA21 cognitive lab study report*. Final Deliverable to the English Language Proficiency Assessment for the 21st Century (ELPA21) Consortium. Retrieved from www.elpa21.org/resources/recdoSRr39KO7OvFC/

Wolf, M. K., Guzman-Orth, D. A., Lopez, A., Castellano, K., Himelfarb, I., & Tsutagawa, F. S. (2016). Integrating scaffolding strategies into technology-enhanced assessments of English learners: Task types and measurement models. *Educational Assessment, 21*(3), 157–175.

Zieky, M. (1993). Practical questions in the use of DIF statistics in test development. In P. Holland & H. Wainer (Eds.), *Differential item functioning* (pp. 337–347). Hillsdale, NJ: Lawrence Erlbaum Associates.

SECTION II

Empirical Research and Practical Considerations on the Development of K–12 ELP Assessments

6

COLLABORATING WITH EDUCATORS ON THE DEVELOPMENT OF ENGLISH LANGUAGE PROFICIENCY ASSESSMENTS

Maurice Cogan Hauck and Emilie Pooler

In the U.S. K–12 educational system, accountability requirements mandate that states administer standards-based summative assessments annually to measure the progress English learner (EL) students have made in attaining English language proficiency (ELP). The development of such assessments is a complex endeavor, involving a range of stakeholders including state Departments of Education (DOE), educational researchers, test publishers, and classroom educators, among others. Classroom educators are, of course, significantly impacted by the implementation of these assessments, as they need to ensure their instruction supports students' ELP development in a manner that is aligned with standards. While these classroom-level practitioners are often involved in the design and development of summative ELP assessments, relatively little documentation is available as to how their input is incorporated and what the impact of their input is.

The purpose of this chapter is twofold: (1) to offer a comprehensive description of classroom educators' involvement in the various stages of the development of K–12 English ELP assessments and (2) to consider the impact of educators' roles both on the validity of test score interpretations for such assessments and on the professional development of the educators themselves.

In discussing the educators' involvement in the development of ELP assessments, we use contexts in which a state chooses to design and develop its own K–12 ELP assessment program (rather than joining a consortium or adopting an existing assessment), and we focus primarily on the development of an annual summative ELP assessment to be used for accountability purposes. Most of the examples in the chapter are drawn from the K–12 ELP assessment program of the state of California entitled the English Language Proficiency Assessments for California (ELPAC).

The chapter begins with a summary of the roles of key parties involved in the design and development of such assessments: state DOE, test publishers, and classroom educators. An extended example of the role of classroom educators in the development of a representative K–12 ELP assessment, the ELPAC, is provided, followed by a discussion of the benefits to the involvement of educators, including both a possible increase in test score validity and benefits to the participating educators themselves. The chapter ends with a conclusion providing recommendations for future practice.

Key Parties Involved in the Design and Development of K–12 ELP Assessments

When a new assessment program for the K–12 students in a given state is to be developed, three parties play key roles. These parties are the state's DOE; a testing vendor, which may include one or more sub-contractors with special areas of expertise; and classroom educators. Given the focus of this chapter, the roles of the first two parties will be described briefly and the role of classroom educators will be covered in greater depth.

The state DOE is, in a real sense, the "author" of the assessment, the responsible and accountable party with the broadest authority for all aspects of the testing program. The state DOE typically initiates the test development process by releasing a Request for Proposals (RFP), which provides requirements for the major aspects of the testing program. Such RFPs commonly require that classroom educators be included in the development process, although states differ in the manner and degree of educator involvement called for. Once the contract has been awarded to a testing vendor, the state DOE provides oversight for all activities related to the testing program, including assessment design, test development, test administration, scoring, and score reporting.

Testing vendors are contracted by the state DOE and have primary responsibility for executing all requirements specified in the RFP (and in the resulting contract). They may also be called on to provide technical advice and solutions as needed to fill gaps in the RFP or to respond to changing needs and conditions. The requirements for the testing vendor cover a broad range of tasks from the highly conceptual (e.g., designing the assessment to ensure that meaningful, reportable evidence of students' abilities is gathered) to the very practical (e.g., printing and shipping large numbers of test books to test administration sites and then receiving them back for scoring). The testing vendor is also responsible for implementing the RFP's requirements for the involvement of classroom educators in various stages of the assessment design and development.

In the development of K–12 state assessments (including but certainly not limited to ELP assessments) asking classroom educators to participate in activities is common practice, although assessment programs vary in the type and number of stages in which educators are included. Classroom educators, by definition, work directly with students every day and provide instruction that constitutes the most practical interpretation and implementation of the state's educational standards into the students' education. As a result, they are well positioned to make informed judgments about grade-level appropriateness—a factor that is often referred to in state standards but rarely specified well enough in the standards to be directly operationalized in the assessment. Educators can be effective in representing the perspective of students in the test-development process because their specific knowledge of the classroom context enables them to make informed judgments about what constitutes appropriate evidence that students are (or are not) meeting the expectations described in the standards. This detailed knowledge of students and the classroom, which largely complements that of the DOE and the testing vendor, allows educators to help to ensure both that test items are well aligned with standards and instructional practice and that test items elicit evidence of student abilities at a variety of levels that will result in meaningful scores.

There are also significant benefits to educators in terms of professional development. A useful concept for analyzing the impact of involvement on classroom educators is assessment literacy (Popham, 2009; Stiggins, 1995, 1999) or more specifically language assessment literacy (Fulcher, 2012; Herrera & Macias, 2015; Inbar-Lourie, 2013; Malone, 2013; Taylor, 2013). Both assessment literacy (with a focus on assessment in general) and language assessment literacy (with a focus on language proficiency assessments in particular) define the knowledge, skills, and abilities necessary for classroom educators to successfully accomplish those parts of their roles that relate to assessment.

In this chapter, we will use Stiggins' (1999) model of assessment literacy (one that is relevant for the subcategory of language assessment literacy as well) to analyze the impact that participating in assessment development activities has on educators' professional development. Stiggins' model identifies seven content requirements or competencies that constitute a comprehensive foundation in assessment practices including:

1) Connecting assessments to clear purposes
2) Clarifying achievement expectations
3) Applying proper assessment methods
4) Developing quality assessment exercises and scoring criteria and sampling appropriately
5) Avoiding bias in assessment
6) Communicating effectively about student achievement
7) Using assessment as an instructional intervention

During the development of the ELPAC assessments, educators had opportunities to meaningfully develop their competencies in these seven areas, as will be discussed in the next section. This section will also illustrate the major impacts of the involvement of educators—their contributions to the validity of the tests and the professional development they receive—by means of an extended discussion of the role that classroom educators have played in the design and development of the state of California's ELPAC program.

Classroom Educator Involvement in the ELPAC

Designed to measure students' ELP based upon California's current English Language Development Standards (California Department of Education, 2014), the ELPAC program consists of two test titles: the Initial ELPAC test and the summative ELPAC test. The Initial ELPAC test is administered to students newly arrived in California schools who have been identified as potential ELs in order to determine whether they should be classified as English learners (ELs) or as Initially Fluent English Proficient (IFEP). The Summative ELPAC test is administered each spring to students who are classified as ELs. The purpose of the Summative ELPAC is to measure the progress of EL students' ELP from year to year and to provide input as to whether a student should be Reclassified Fluent English Proficient (RFEP), that is, exited out of the EL support programs.

Both ELPAC assessments measure the listening, speaking, reading, and writing skills of students from kindergarten to Grade 12 (with different test forms provided at a range of grades or grade spans). The ELPAC development process began in 2015 with the first operational administrations of both the Summative ELPAC and the Initial ELPAC in 2018. On the launch of the ELPAC, the tests were administered in paper-and-pencil format. At the time of writing the present chapter, work is underway to transition the ELPAC to a computer-based format beginning with the spring 2020 administration.

The California DOE has made educator involvement a priority in the development of the ELPAC, with classroom educators playing key roles in both the design and the ongoing annual development of new test forms. The selection of qualified educators for such roles is done thoughtfully. For the ELPAC, the recruitment criteria called for educators who have at least five years of experience in a role related to instructing ELs, who are familiar with and incorporate the English Language Development (ELD) Standards in their instruction and who instruct students who will take the ELPAC exam. Other considerations in selecting educators include geographic representation (i.e., from north, central, and southern sections of the state); representation from urban, suburban, and rural districts; ethnocultural diversity of educators; diversity of primary language groups taught; and representation from different roles (e.g., employees of county offices of education, teachers, and EL coaches). The emphasis placed on each of these criteria may vary based on the types of educator expertise needed for each particular task.

In the ELPAC development process, educators' involvement was centered on five stages, as illustrated in Figure 6.1: (1) Pilot Study of Task Types; (2)

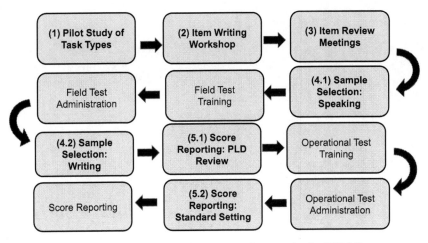

FIGURE 6.1 Overview of classroom educator involvement in the ELPAC.

Item Writing Workshop; (3) Item Review Meetings; (4) Sample Selection to Support Constructed Response Scoring; and (5) Support for Score Reporting: Performance Level Descriptor Review and Standard Setting. (Some key stages in which educators are not directly involved are also included in Figure 6.1 for context.) For each stage, consideration is given to the role played by educators, the ways in which the educators' involvement contributed both to the validity of the assessment, and with reference to Stiggins' model of assessment literacy, to the professional development of the educators.

Each of these stages represents a collaborative effort among the California Department of Education (CDE), ETS (as a testing vendor), and California classroom educators. For each stage, ETS planned the work in considerable detail; the ETS plans were reviewed and approved by the CDE; a large-scale meeting or other event was held at which the educators provide their input; and after the event, ETS and CDE resolved, integrated, and applied educator input. This model is an effective one because it allows the complementary knowledge and skills of the educators, the CDE, and ETS to be applied in a symbiotic manner to improve the quality of the assessments. The educators provide their on-the-ground knowledge of the students and how the standards are being implemented; ETS provides technical knowledge of assessment to ensure that educator input is applied in a standardized and systematic manner; and the CDE provides general oversight to make sure that the assessment is developed in a manner that meets the needs of California students, parents, educators, and other stakeholders.

In the remainder of this section, we describe the ways in which educators were involved at each stage of the test development process.

Pilot Study of Task Types

An important early stage in the ELPAC design process was a small-scale proto-type or pilot event that focused on evaluating and refining task types being considered for use on the ELPAC. Because the ELPAC was a new test being designed to assess a new set of standards (that were quite different from the previous state ELD standards), developing and validating appropriate task types to be used to measure those standards was a crucial precursor to the develop-ment of a test blueprint and test specifications. Work on this pilot study began with ETS, under the direction of the CDE, identifying, adapting, or designing new task types intended to capture evidence of students' ELP in relationship to the CA 2012 ELD Standards. ETS then drafted a test blueprint, constituting a proposal for how many of each task type should be administered in order to capture appropriate evidence given the scores to be reported. For each task type under consideration for inclusion on the ELPAC test blueprint, a few representative items were administered to a small population of students, stu-dent responses were reviewed, and the task types were evaluated to consider which were the most appropriate for large-scale development, field-testing, and operational use.

Classroom educators played central roles in administering the pilot, provid-ing input based on their experience administering the pilot, and evaluating the task types based both on the experience of administering the tasks and the evaluation of student responses. Some of this input was focused on logistics (e.g., providing guidance on, for example, how the student and the test exam-iner should be seated in relation to each other for lower-grades task types that require considerable interaction), while other input related to ensuring that the task types were pedagogically sound and consistent with how the standards are being implemented in the classroom.

One of the key ways in which the CA 2012 ELD Standards differ from Cali-fornia's previous ELD standards is in their strong emphasis on communication. In the CA 2012 ELD Standards, communicative skills are clearly foregrounded and labeled as, "Part I: Interacting in Meaningful Ways." The organization of the standards communicates that the rule-based, grammatically focused, less dir-ectly communicative standards (Part II: "Learning about How English Works") serve the other standards and are not meant to be taught in isolation.

The task types developed for the pilot were highly communicative and focused on the Part I standards. However, the educators, upon reviewing all of the writing task types, raised concerns about the omission of the Part II stand-ards. They noted that if the Part II standards are not visibly included in the assessment, there is a risk that teachers and students will not focus classroom instruction on these enabling skills that are critical to development of ELP (i.e., there was concern that the washback of the assessment would have a negative effect on classroom practices). To address this concern, the ETS item development team, in consultation with educators, revised a task type ("Writing—Describe a Picture" at Grades 3–12) by asking students to read a sentence and rewrite it with more details or to read a sentence containing two errors and rewrite it correctly.[1] As a result of the educators' input, the Writing tasks became more balanced. That is, the tasks retain the overall focus on communicative skills (the Part I standards), but also call for assessment of students' mastery of key enabling skills (the Part II standards) in the service of those communicative skills.

These decisions, and others made as part of the pilot process, strengthened the validity of the tests by ensuring that the ELPAC Test Blueprints (Educational Testing Service, 2017) and the Item Writing Guidelines for the ELPAC (Educational Testing Service, 2016)—two documents that played central roles in all subsequent aspects of design and development of the program—reflected the input of California educators.

In terms of professional development for the participating educators, the pilot provided broad experience in several of the competencies outlined in Stiggins (1999), most notably (1) Connecting assessments to clear purposes; (2) Clarifying achievement expectations; (3) Applying proper assessment methods; and (4) Developing quality assessment exercises and scoring criteria and sampling appropriately.

Item Writing Workshops

Once task types were finalized, the task of producing a sizable pool of test items to support the field test and operational launch of the ELPAC could get underway. Given their firsthand knowledge of how the standards are implemented in the classroom, educators are uniquely well positioned to provide input on how students are likely to respond to a given topic and what level of challenge certain test items might provide. All of this allows educators to provide unique and valuable insight into the item-writing process.

Item writing is a complex skill, and educators are generally not able to produce finished test items in the limited time available during an item-writing workshop. However, they usually are able to produce valuable draft items and proposed topics for listening and reading stimuli that can be refined through later review.

Soon after the development of the ELPAC Test Blueprint and the ELPAC Item Writing Guidelines, a large-scale item-development effort began to produce new test items to be field tested for use in both the Initial ELPAC and the Summative ELPAC. In that first year, 42 classroom educators participated in two-day Item Writing Workshops as part of an effort to ensure that a substantial proportion of the items in the pool of ELPAC items used for field-testing originated from educators. These educators received training in a range of Listening, Speaking, Reading, and Writing task types and generated draft items for later review and refinement.

In addition to this item production, a distinct additional value provided by the educators at the item-writing workshop could be described as general consulting on concepts and terminology for ELPAC test items. They provided expert judgment regarding grade-appropriate topics and text difficulty, and they generated lists of topics of interest and realistic scenarios for identified grades. They also provided clarification regarding terminology that would or would not be likely to be understood by students (e.g., confirming that the term "text" is used consistently to refer to reading passages, even at kindergarten and Grade 1, but that the term "graphic organizer" is not used consistently across the state).

Since the operational launch of the ELPAC in 2018, item-writing efforts have been conducted on an annual basis to generate new items to be field tested within operational test forms. While these annual efforts are much smaller in scale than the first one, item-writing workshops with California educators remain an essential part of the process, and the educators continue to provide valuable input both through drafting of new items and through providing general information about their students' interests and experiences.

Based on Stiggins' (1999) assessment literacy model, the most direct impact of participation in item-writing workshops on teachers' language assessment literacy is in (4) Developing quality assessment exercises and scoring criteria and sampling appropriately; this is experience they can directly apply to the writing of test items for their own formative and summative assessments. Additionally, the workshop experience provides, at least indirectly, opportunities for educators to gain knowledge and experience in other competences described in Stiggins' model, such as (1) Connecting assessments to clear purposes; (2) Clarifying achievement expectations; (3) Applying proper assessment methods; and (5) Avoiding bias in assessment.

Item Review Panels

Across K–12 educational assessments in the United States, item review committees are likely the most common opportunity for educators to be involved in assessment development. Such item-review panels are an efficient means of gathering educators' input, which allows states to make the important claim that all items on the assessment were approved by classroom educators from the state before being administered to students. On the ELPAC, representatives of the CDE conduct a substantive review of the test items before the item review panels and work with the testing vendor to review and resolve comments from the review panels before implementation.

At the item-review meetings themselves, each test item is reviewed before field testing by two separate panels of educators:

- A content review panel reviews each item for quality of content, with an emphasis on ensuring alignment to the state ELD standards and grade-level appropriateness.

- A bias-and-sensitivity panel reviews each item to ensure it is free from issues related to bias (i.e., items that may function differently for different groups within the testing population) and sensitivity (i.e., items that may be offensive or distracting to test takers).

Item-review panel meetings begin with a training session in which educators learn about principles of effective item review and about the place of their review in the overall test-development process. This training also prepares educators for the collaborative nature of the review panels' work: Their role, individually and as a group, is to look for opportunities to improve each item and the pool as a whole.

During the ELPAC development process, large-scale Content Review Panel and Bias & Sensitivity Review Panel meetings were first held in Sacramento, California, in August 2016. At this first meeting, over 2,000 items were reviewed and approved by committees totaling approximately 100 California educators. Subsequently, smaller-scale review panel meetings are held annually to review items developed for refresh of Summative ELPAC operational forms.

At the 2016 ELPAC Content Review panel, teams of educators reviewed and discussed each item carefully and provided a considered judgment about the content appropriateness of each item. In addition to reviewing the overall clarity and accuracy of item content, panel members ensured that each selected response item (e.g., multiple choice) has a single best correct answer and that other response options are plausible but incorrect. For constructed response items (e.g. writing prompts), panel members considered how well the prompt (in tandem with the relevant scoring rubric) elicits a response that would allow students to demonstrate their language abilities.

The panels' input resulted in adjustments to the design of task types. For example, the content review panel recommended a change to the mode of presentation for the speaking task type "Summarize an Academic Presentation." This task type features an aural stimulus that is fairly extensive and dense with academic content. The educators recommended that this stimulus be provided via professionally recorded audio, rather than read aloud by test examiners, in order to ensure standardization of presentation and to reduce the burden on administrators. This input from educators was implemented for the operational launch of the ELPAC, providing an instance in which educators, in addition to ensuring the quality of test items, also initiated an improvement in the test administration model.

Directly after the work of the content review panels was completed, the test items were handed over to a separate panel to ensure that the items, including any revisions recommended by the content review panel, were free from issues related to bias and sensitivity. The independent panel review provided value beyond the review for bias and sensitivity that is part of the standard internal ETS review process for all items. Educators on the panel often make recommendations for improvement of items that are reflective of their diverse experience working with EL students in California schools. For example, an observation related to potential bias was made regarding a passage on the topic of Native Americans. An educator pointed out that there are a number of Native American students classified as English learners in California, and that the events described in the passage were most likely specific to a Native American tribe from the plains states, but the tribe or region was not specified. A California student who is Native American and not from a tribe of plains origin would be likely to experience that passage as an overgeneralization.

This observation is an illustration of the fact that the English learner population is complex and ever changing. Educators who serve on bias and sensitivity committees play a crucial role because they are able to consider items from the perspective of their students, informing the test developers about who their students are, where they come from, and the challenges they face. The educators' input both helps to improve the items being reviewed and stays with the test developers, helping to inform their work as they develop the items and passages in the future.

In terms of opportunities to improve educators' language assessment literacy, the experience of serving on content review panels differs somewhat than that of serving on bias and sensitivity review panels. Per Stiggins' (1999) model, content review panelists can be expected to develop in (1) connecting assessments to clear purposes; (2) clarifying achievement expectations; (3) applying proper assessment methods; and (4) developing quality assessment exercises and scoring criteria and sampling appropriately. At the same time, they also receive some exposure to (5) avoiding bias in assessment. For bias and sensitivity review panelists, the emphasis is reversed: The primary experience is focused on (5) avoiding bias in assessment, while there is also secondary exposure to competencies (1) through (4).

Sample Selection to Support Constructed-Response Scoring

In the development of constructed-responses tasks (including all ELPAC Speaking and Writing tasks), the expectations for student performance are delineated both by the task itself and by the rubric used to assign scores to student responses. In the sample selection process, representative sample student responses (also commonly called benchmark samples or range-finding samples) are chosen as exemplars of student performance at each score point on the rubric. At this point, refinements in defining expectations of student responses and training raters on how to apply the rubrics take place. On the ELPAC program, classroom educators make important contributions during this process.

Sample selection for speaking tasks takes place before the operational administration (so that test examiners can be trained to score speaking responses in the moment) and after the operational administration for Writing. However, the role of the educators is similar: Teams of educators are selected to review student responses and to choose those that are appropriate for use as sample responses in training raters. This is a crucial task for the Constructed Response scoring process. The sample responses define and operationalize expectations for student performance on each task type at each grade or grade span, and they provide the basis for rater training. Educators are called upon to make concrete evaluations of how the rubric should be applied to the wide range of responses that students produce.

Because it is a relatively new testing program, educators participating in ELPAC sample selection, particularly on the field-test administrations, were able to provide recommendations for refinements to the rubrics. The process of refining rubrics is another good example of how the complementary skills of test development professionals and classroom educators can come together to improve the assessment. Before student responses are available, test development professionals can develop rubrics that consistently interpret the standards and will be suitable for evaluating a large percentage of student responses. However, the actual responses produced by students inevitably include interpretations of and reactions to the writing task that could not have been anticipated in advance. The feedback educators provide based on a review of these student response helps to ensure that the rubrics are suitable for the full range of student responses.

The impact on participating educators' language assessment literacy focuses on Stiggins' (1999) model of (2) Clarifying achievement expectations and on the "scoring criteria" part of (4) Developing quality assessment exercises and scoring criteria and sampling appropriately. It also offers some indirect exposure to (1) Connecting assessments to clear purposes; (3) Applying proper assessment methods; and (5) Avoiding bias in assessment.

Support for Score Reporting: Performance Level Descriptor Reviews and Standard Setting

In the area of score reporting, classroom educators played two major roles: (1) as reviewers of performance level descriptors (PLDs), statements that describe what students who score in identified score ranges on the test typically know and can do and (2) as judges in a standard-setting process, the process of defining threshold scores necessary to be included in each of the ELPAC performance ranges.

Performance Level Descriptors

A PLD is an essential part of score reporting as it provides a written explanation of what numerical scores mean in terms of what students know and can do. The involvement of classroom educators in PLD development was focused on the development of "Range" PLDs—those that are specific to each of the four domains (Listening, Speaking, Reading, and Writing) at each of the seven ELPAC grades or grade-spans (Kindergarten, Grade 1, Grade 2, Grades 3–5, Grades 6–8, Grades 9–10, and Grades 11–12). In addition to their role in score reporting, these Range PLDs were key inputs to the standard-setting process by helping to define the meaning of threshold scores and score ranges.

The panels of educators were charged with ensuring that the Range PLDs, drafts of which were produced for educator review by ETS, were accurate statements based on the evidence gathered by the test (as shown in the ELPAC task types and blueprints) and were phrased in a manner that would communicate effectively to the intended audience (educators, parents, students, etc.).

Educators provided substantive input that helped to ensure that the Range PLDs did not express expectations of ELs that surpassed expectations of native speakers in the same grade. For example, in the Speaking domain, the educators recommended adding text about expectations regarding students' pronunciation to make clear that EL students should be able to achieve the top score while retaining a non-native accent. This change helped to make sure that the Range PLDs, and therefore ELPAC score reporting, reinforced a key idea in the CA 2012 ELD Standards: Ability to communicate in English is the overall goal, rather than having pronunciation indistinguishable from that of a native English speaker. The educators also made similar recommendations for the PLDs for Writing at Grade 1, establishing the expectation that, based on age-appropriate literacy development, letters written by students could be considered representative of a high degree of English proficiency even if they contain reversals or inversions.

Standard Setting

Educators' role in standard setting, a process described in more detail in chapter 9 of this volume (Baron, Linquanti, & Huang, 2020), consisted primarily of working collaboratively to develop "borderline student definitions"—that is, descriptors of the language proficiency that typifies students who are just across the conceptual line between one performance level and another—and making judgments about what test items are most representative of the performance of such students. The outcome of the standard-setting process was that educators made recommendations to the CDE regarding what threshold scores should be implemented for each of the ELPAC performance levels, input that was directly related to supporting the validity of test-score interpretations.

In terms of Stiggins' (1999) assessment literacy model, the work on the PLDs provided educators with a fairly broad overview of the test development process: a focus on (1) Connecting assessments to clear purposes, (2) Clarifying achievement expectations, and (3) Applying proper assessment methods, and also some exposure to (4) Developing quality assessment exercises and scoring criteria and sampling appropriately, while also having some exposure to (5) Avoiding bias in assessment. The exposure to educators participating in the standard-setting study is somewhat narrower by focusing primarily on (2) Clarifying achievement expectations while also offering some exposure to (1) Connecting assessments to clear purposes and (3) Applying proper assessment methods.

Impact of the Involvement of Educators

As we hope this chapter has illustrated, classroom educators make significant contributions to the design and development of K–12 ELP assessments such as the ELPAC. Educators are able to make these contributions because of the depth of their firsthand knowledge about how standards are implemented in the classroom and because of their insights about what students in a given grade should know and be able to do. As a result, the involvement of classroom educators improves the validity argument for the assessment by providing substantial evidence to support a claim that the assessment reflects not simply student ELP in general, but more specifically student ELP as defined in the ELD standards and as those standards are implemented in the classroom.

Additionally, the experience of contributing to assessment development efforts provides meaningful professional development for educators, particularly in the area of assessment literacy or, more specifically, language assessment literacy. As detailed in the discussion of the ELPAC development process, the experience of participating in assessment development activities gives educators an increased understanding of the principles of assessment, of their application to K–12 ELP assessments, and of practical challenges in assessment design and development and how those challenges are being resolved. For such educators, involvement in assessment development efforts can make a state assessment such as the ELPAC feel less like something "dropped in out of the sky" (Hauck, Wolf, & Mislevy, 2016) and more like the product of a broad team of dedicated professionals making the best assessment they can within a range of practical constraints. Teachers are likely to put more faith in test results for an assessment they have helped create (or know that their colleagues have helped create).

A significant secondary impact of the involvement of educators is the reception of the new assessment among educators across the state. Those educators who have participated in assessment design and development events can, upon return to their schools and districts, improve understanding of the assessment program in the field by acting as "ambassadors," describing what they learned about the assessment program. Specifically, these educators can share information about the process by which the test is developed; share facts about the test (e.g., the location of resources such as rubrics and test blueprints); explain how the speaking and writing responses will be scored; and serve as ongoing sources of information for colleagues with questions about the test. It is important to note, however, that educators who participated in various item-review or administration training meetings are not allowed to talk to their colleagues about specific test items or about the specifics of discussions held while the panel was in session; these limits on what can and cannot be shared are emphasized in the training provided to educators at each event.

There are, of course, some costs, practical challenges, and limitations to the effectiveness of involving educators in the development of large-scale standardized assessments. Time and resources must be made available to hold meetings at which educators provide input, and the overall assessment development timeline must allow for both the execution of such educator-focused meetings and appropriate processes for integrating the educators' input. Additionally, it is worth noting that not all educator input can be integrated as provided. Educators in general, perhaps teachers of English learners in particular, often take on a role of advocacy for their students. While engaging in assessment-related activities, it is important that this tendency toward advocacy not extend to an assumption (stated or unstated) that appropriate test items are ones that can be answered correctly by most or all of their students. Instead, educators must see their role as helping to develop a rigorous test that will assess the standards faithfully and thereby provide good information about which students have attained a sufficient degree of English proficiency and which are still in the process of doing so. Similarly, there is some risk that educators may over-apply knowledge of the specific context of their own students (geographic, socioeconomic, etc.) to students across the state. There is a need for educators to consider that their context is one of many in which the test will be administered and to present input that will be appropriate across all of those contexts. Both of these risks can be mitigated through careful training of educators at the beginning of panel meetings and other events, training that emphasizes the overall goals of the assessment, the role of the educators in meeting those goals, and the appropriate processes for interacting and providing input during the educators' working sessions.

The primary limitations to the benefits to participating educators are practical and logistical. In a state as large as California, as many as 10,000 educators play a role in the administration of the ELPAC and even in a year in which large-scale design and development work is underway, there is space for only a few hundred educators to participate directly in events such as item writing workshops, item review panels, and PLD review committees. While care is taken to ensure that such committees reflect the diversity of educators across the state in order to be as representative as possible, the number of educators directly involved in design and development is necessarily a modest percentage of those impacted by the assessment.

Recommendations for Successful Involvement of Educators in Practice

We hope that this chapter has provided a number of useful examples of how including classroom educators at a range of key steps in the assessment development process can improve the quality of a K–12 ELP assessment program. We now provide some general and practical principles for the successful involvement of educators, based on our experience on ELPAC and other K–12 ELP assessment programs.

The involvement of educators requires significant planning from the onset of the assessment design effort, considering factors such as the following:

- The inclusion of educators must be intentionally planned from the early stages of a new assessment or new assessment cycle (and must be budgeted for). If the program is to be developed based on an RFP, the roles of educators should be specified to allow the testing vendor to budget appropriately and plan appropriate timelines for integration of their input.
- A recruiting effort must be planned and implemented considering thoughtful criteria for selecting educators to achieve appropriate representation of educators with appropriate qualifications and representing the diversity of the testing population (e.g., from a range of geographical areas, backgrounds, and teaching contexts).
- The testing vendor must devote appropriate resources to develop suitable training materials, to facilitate meetings with educators effectively, and to update test materials to reflect educators' input. Perhaps most prominent are the assignment of assessment developers with broad skills in the principles of test design and development and the ability to work effectively to train educators and facilitate their involvement through panel reviews and other means, ensuring that the input from educators is implemented in a thoughtful and consistent manner.
- Individuals representing each party involved in the assessment development process (the DOE, the testing vendor, and the educators) must enter into the work with a conscious attitude of professional collaboration. That is, they must all realize that they have valuable experience and opinions to impart; that the others have different but similarly valuable experiences and opinions; and that the test will be more valid if it reflects a considered and balanced blending of input from all who are participating.
- Appropriate steps must be taken to ensure security of test materials at all stages of development.

Finally, while educators' involvement in ongoing annual activities such as item-writing workshops and item-review panels are of significant value, it is worth noting that involving educators in test-design activities allows them to have a somewhat deeper and more lasting impact on the assessment program. Thoughtful advance planning to support the involvement of educators at key stages of assessment design and development can help to ensure that these efforts result in a more robust validity argument for the assessment and meaningful professional development for the educators themselves.

Note

1 See the ELPAC Practice Tests www.elpac.org/resources/practicetests/for representative samples of the ELPAC task types as they appeared when the test was launched operationally.

References

Baron, P., Linquanti, R., & Huang, M. (2020). Establishing an English-proficient perform-ance standard for English language proficiency assessment uses. In M. K. Wolf (Ed.), *Assessing English language proficiency in U.S. K–12 schools.* New York, NY: Routledge.

California Department of Education. (2014). *California English language development stand-ards: Kindergarten through grade 12.* Sacramento, CA: Author. Retrieved from www.cde.ca.gov/sp/el/er/documents/eldstndspublication14.pdf

Educational Testing Service. (2016). *Item writing guidelines for the ELPAC.* Unpublished document.

Educational Testing Service. (2017). *Summative assessment test blueprints for the English lan-guage proficiency assessments for California.* Sacramento, CA: California Department of Education. Retrieved from www.cde.ca.gov/ta/tg/ep/documents/elpacadoptedblueprints.pdf

Fulcher, G. (2012). Assessment literacy for the language classroom. *Language Assessment Quarterly, 9*(2), 113–132.

Hauck, M. C., Wolf, M. K., & Mislevy, R. (2016). *Creating a next-generation system of K–12 English learner (EL) language proficiency assessments* (ETS research report no. RR-16–06). Princeton, NJ: Educational Testing Service.

Herrera, L., & Macias, D. (2015). A call for language assessment literacy in the education and development of teachers of English as a foreign language. *Colombian Applied Linguis-tics Journal, 17*(2), 302–312.

Inbar-Lourie, O. (2013). Guest editorial to the special issue on language assessment literacy. *Language Testing, 30*(3), 301–307.

Malone, M. E. (2013). The essentials of assessment literacy: Contrasts between testers and users. *Language Testing, 30*(3), 329–344.

Popham, W. J. (2009). Assessment literacy for teachers: Faddish or fundamental? *Theory into Practice, 48*(1), 4–11.

Stiggins, R. J. (1995). Assessment literacy for the 21st century. *Phi Delta Kappan, 77*(3), 238–246.

Stiggins, R. J. (1999). Evaluating classroom assessment training in teacher education programs. *Educational Measurement: Issues and Practices, 18*(1), 23–27.

Taylor, L. (2013). Communicating the theory, practice and principles of language testing to test stakeholders: Some reflections. *Language Testing, 30*(3), 402–412.

7

EXAMINING STUDENTS' RESPONSE PROCESSES IN A COMPUTER-BASED ENGLISH LANGUAGE PROFICIENCY ASSESSMENT

Mikyung Kim Wolf, Danielle Guzman-Orth, Cathryn Still, and Phoebe Winter

With the increased use of computer technology in K–12 education, many state education agencies in the United States have begun to develop or adopt computer-based English language proficiency (ELP) assessments for English learner (EL) students. Two multistate ELP consortia called WIDA and the English Language Proficiency Assessment for the 21st Century (ELPA21) launched their respective computer-based ELP assessments in 2016. As of this writing, over 40 states have been implementing computer-based ELP assessments for EL students in kindergarten through Grade 12, using WIDA,[1] ELPA21, or individual states' own computer-based ELP assessments (e.g., Arizona, Texas) for the past few years.

Considering the characteristics of the EL population in terms of formal schooling experience (some with interrupted or limited formal education), socioeconomic status, computer familiarity, and ELP levels, it is crucial to ensure that the use of technology does not inadvertently introduce construct-irrelevant variance in assessing students' ELP. Of particular note are students in early primary grades, who are included in computer-based ELP assessments but not in standardized content assessments until Grade 3. EL students in kindergarten to Grade 2 (approximately ages five to seven) constitute a substantial portion of the EL population. For example, in California, approximately 40% of students who took the state ELP assessment in 2018 were from this grade span (based on the data extracted from the California Department of Education, www3.cde.ca.gov/elpac/). These young students, as well as students who are recently arrived EL students enrolling in any grade level, may have limited computer familiarity, raising an important validity concern related to computer-based ELP assessments, that is, whether students demonstrate their English ability without interference from their computer skills. Undeniably, computer-based ELP assessments should be designed and developed by incorporating empirical usability evidence from target EL students.

This chapter illustrates collaborative efforts undertaken among test developers and researchers during the development of a computer-based ELP assessment with a specific focus on garnering validity evidence based on students' response processes. Specifically, this chapter[2] reports on a small-scale usability study that was conducted during an early stage of developing the ELPA21's computer-based ELP assessment prior to its large-scale field test. At the time of the study in 2014, large-scale computer-based ELP assessments were being administered to K–12 EL students in only a few states; hence, little empirical research was available to illuminate K–12 EL students' computer usage and their interaction with computer-based assessments.

ELPA21 intended to utilize technology-enhanced (TE) assessment items in order to increase the authenticity of item types as well as students' engagement. To this end, ELPA21 was concerned with empirically examining how students would interact with the TE features to ensure that computer-based assessment items would appropriately measure students' ELP, not their computer skills. The findings of the study were anticipated to provide useful information to prepare for the administration guidelines as well as the design of the test platform for the large-scale field test and future operational administration.

In this chapter, we describe the study method, major findings, and ELPA21's actions taken based on the findings. We discuss how this type of usability study, followed by the enactment of the recommendations from the study findings, helps enhance the validity of computer-based ELP assessment interpretations. We also hope that the study design and method described in this chapter are instrumental for those interested in conducting a similar line of the study for K–12 ELP assessments.

Relevant Literature

Prior to describing the usability study, we provide a brief account of the literature on computer-based ELP assessments and validity evidence based on test-taking or response processes. These two areas of the literature offer theoretical groundings for the study design and our discussion points.

Advantages of Computer-Based ELP Assessments

The use of the computer technology for ELP testing is not new. Large-scale, standardized computer-based ELP assessments have been utilized with adult L2 learners for more than a decade (e.g., IELTS by the British Council and Cambridge Assessment English, PTE Academic by Pearson, and TOEFL iBT by

Educational Testing Service). A large body of literature has documented major advantages of computer-based testing, including efficiency in standardization, testing time (particularly in the case of adaptive testing), scoring, reporting, and data management (e.g., Bachman, 2000; Chalhoub-Deville, 2001; Douglas, 2013; Fulcher, 2003). The literature also establishes the benefits of using technology in terms of task design and construct representation by increasing authenticity and interactiveness (e.g., Bachman, 2000; Bennett, 2018; Chalhoub-Deville, 2001; Fulcher, 2003; Hauck, Wolf, & Mislevy, 2016). For example, computer-based language testing can integrate multimedia and enriched contexts to resemble target language use situations more readily than paper-based testing can (Bachman, 2000; Ockey, 2009).

Recently, the increased use of computer-based assessments in K–12 settings has added another benefit of technology use in assessment, that is, enhancing accessibility of assessments for a wide range of students (Almond et al., 2010; Thurlow, Lazarus, Albus, & Hodgson, 2010). Many states' computer-based content assessments have already embedded accessibility features in the testing platform. These features include text-to-speech for directions to be read aloud, pop-up glossary for construct-irrelevant words or phrases, and dual-language presentation, to name a few. All these features aim to support a valid assessment of EL students' knowledge and skills. Additionally, some researchers have demonstrated the ease of including scaffolding tasks in computer-based language assessments to better measure students' language ability (Poehner, Zhang, & Lu, 2017; Wolf et al., 2016).

In addition, technology can be used to generate innovative ELP assessments to foster students' engagement in testing, thereby increasing measurement accuracy. Yet, caution should be exercised during the development of innovative assessments, as students may have differing degrees of computer skills. Specific validity evidence regarding inferences to be made about students' language ability vs. computer skills should be examined to support the development and continued use of computer-based ELP assessments.

Validity Evidence Based on Response Processes for Computer-Based ELP Assessments

In discussing a host of validity issues concerning computer-based language assessments, Bachman (2000) stresses the reconceptualization of the construct to be assessed and the generalizability of inferences to be made about students' language ability from computer-based language assessments. Some of the questions he has raised include, for example, (1) the extent to which the reading skill construct as measured on paper differs from that measured on the computer screen and (2) the degree to which computer-based assessment tasks reflect real-life language use.

One way to address these kinds of validity issues is to examine test-takers' response processes. The *Standards for Educational and Psychological Testing* (American Educational Research Association, American Psychological Association, & National Council on Measurement in Education [AERA, APA, & NCME], 2014) explicitly call for validity evidence based upon response processes to support inferences about test takers' ability from the assessment results. For instance, the examination of test takers' behaviors during testing can reveal their strategies and reasoning in completing items and provide evidence of construct representation. The analysis of test takers' strategies may then be performed to distinguish construct-relevant from construct-irrelevant behaviors in order to better evaluate the validity of inferences of assessment scores (Cohen, 2006). The *Standards* also stress that validity evidence based upon response processes contributes to an improved understanding about the construct of interest and its representation through an appropriate task design.

The literature offers a variety of techniques to examine response processes, including verbal protocol analysis and cognitive laboratories (labs) (Ericsson & Simon, 1993; Leighton, 2017). Thanks to the advancement of technology, other process data such as response times, keystrokes, and eye movements have become more available (AERA, APA, & NCME, 2014). In particular, cognitive lab methods have gained popularity for investigating the interaction between diverse test-taker characteristics and assessment task characteristics (e.g., Martiniello, 2008; Winter, Kopriva, Chen, & Emick, 2006; Wolf, Kim, & Kao, 2012). This method entails systematic observation of individual students' test-taking processes with concurrent or retrospective interviews about the processes in one-on-one settings. These methods are especially useful for identifying any issues related to item/task characteristics during test development stages (Peterson, Peterson, & Powell, 2017). Improving assessment items and tasks to elicit test takers' skills can then help strengthen the validity of score interpretations.

Study Contexts and Research Questions

As described earlier, the present study was conducted in collaboration among ELPA21 leadership group members and a team of ETS assessment specialists and researchers. Employing a cognitive lab method, the study focused on students' interaction with new TE item types and use of technology features during computer-based testing. It also attempted to identify any possible sources of difficulties related to item quality such as the clarity of directions and the presentation of the items. For instance, the directions for TE items (e.g., selecting a specific zone, performing a drag-and-drop, and navigating a drop-down menu) should be clear for students who may be accustomed to traditional paper-based assessments.

The study dealt with three areas related to technology features: (1) clarity of directions for TE features, (2) students' interaction with TE items, and (3) students' use of accessibility features embedded in the preliminary test platform. In this chapter, we report on the first two areas because the accessibility features are discussed in detail in another chapter (see Guzman-Orth, Sova, & Albee, 2020 in this volume). This chapter presents the findings based on EL students *without* disabilities to increase clarity in the interpretation of the findings on students' interaction with TE features. Within each area, the study addressed the following research questions:

(1) Clarity of directions

- Are the directions clear enough for students to respond to items independently?
- What difficulties, if any, do students at different levels of English proficiency have in understanding the directions?

(2) Interaction with TE features

- To what extent can students complete new TE item types independently?
- What difficulties, if any, do students have in completing TE items?

Method

Participants

With the assistance of the Washington State Office of Superintendent of Public Instruction (OSPI), a total of 91 students (59 EL students without identified disabilities, 14 EL students with identified disabilities, and 18 non-EL students) in Grades K–3 and Grades 6–8 were recruited from two elementary schools and one middle school in two urban districts in Seattle. Although the original study included a sample of EL students with disabilities as noted ($n = 14$), this chapter reports on findings from the remaining 77 students (without disabilities). Due to time and resource constraints, not all of the grade levels were included in the study. Efforts were made to maximize the usability of the study findings by selecting younger grades rather than older grades for similar item types. For instance, since the TE item types for Grades 4–5 were similar to those for Grades 2–3, we focused on examining younger grade students' interactions with the TE item types with an assumption that younger grade students may have more difficulties with TE features. Similarly, Grades 9–12 were not included as their item types were similar to those for Grades 6–8.

To investigate the clarity of the directions and the use of technology features in specific item types, we included EL students at different ELP levels as well as fluent English speakers (i.e., native English speakers and reclassified EL students). For the purpose of this study, we categorized the latter group as non-EL in comparison to our focal group of EL students. The inclusion of non-EL students was important in determining whether the sources of difficulties students might have are related to EL-specific issues. For instance, if non-EL students who are fluent in English display some difficulty in understanding the directions, this would be an indication of the need to further clarify the directions. As a small-scale study, we limited our EL participants' home language background to Spanish, Vietnamese, and Russian. These were the top three languages spoken by the EL population in Washington and were commonly included in other ELPA21 states (U.S. Department of Education Office of English Language Acquisition, 2018). Table 7.1 summarizes the number of participants by grade and ELP levels.

With regard to students' computer experience, the cognitive interview data revealed that the sample of students in this study had prior experience with the computer except for some kindergarten and Grade 1 students. In the kindergarten sample, eight (40%) students had never used a computer prior to the present study and one EL student in Grade 1 had no prior computer experience.

Study Instruments

The research team developed a cognitive lab protocol to systematically collect interviewers' observations and verbal data from each student. The protocol contained a set of interview questions to examine students' understanding of the directions and any difficulties in using technology features. The protocol also included a set of rating scales to efficiently identify the areas of further examination by the interviewer (see the Appendix for the interview questions and rating scales). The interviewers were also asked to provide comments to justify their ratings based on their observations and interviews.

TABLE 7.1 The Number of Participants by Grade and ELP Levels.

Student Category	Grade or Grade Bands				
	Grade K	Grade 1	Grades 2–3	Grades 6–8	Total
Beginning EL	5	1	2	2	10
Intermediate EL	9	7	8	15	39
Advanced EL	0	3	7	0	10
Non-EL	6	4	5	3	18
Total	20	15	22	20	77

In addition, a student questionnaire was developed to collect participating students' background characteristics such as home language, EL status, ELP levels, and reading proficiency levels according to other testing measures, if applicable. The questionnaire was completed by the teachers from each school. All of the participants were assigned unique study IDs to maintain anonymity.

Item Types Included in the Study

Due to the limited time (i.e., one class period) for each cognitive lab, item types were purposefully selected from each listening, speaking, reading, and writing domain. The primary criterion for selection was to include the new item types with TE features (e.g., drag & drop, drop-down menu, zone selection, recording functions, etc.). Additionally, these item types were selected to examine the students' interactions with the computer, including a mouse and keyboard. Tables 7.2 and 7.3 present an entire set of ELPA21 item types as well as selected item types in elementary and middle school grades, respectively. In the tables, a checkmark ✓ denotes the selected item types.

Tutorial Development for the Study

At the time of this study, a tutorial or demo of sample items was not yet available. Since it was important to explain the test layout, major icons, and functions (e.g., recording buttons, audio buttons, and accessibility tools) to the test takers, the research team created a short tutorial video for the study. The Grade K and 1 version was 3:47 minutes long, and the Grade 2–3 and 6–8 version was 4:20 minutes long. The tutorial was necessary not only for demonstrating the item layout and features but also for standardizing the cognitive lab conditions.

Procedure

Nine interviewers (assessment specialists and researchers) received two 2-hour training sessions to facilitate the cognitive labs according to the protocol. The majority of the interviewers also had prior experience in conducting cognitive labs with K–12 students. Some interviewers were fluent speakers of Spanish, Russian, or Vietnamese in order to conduct interviews in those languages when needed. In total, 17 interviews were either conducted entirely in the students' home language (14 students) or assistance was provided in the home language when necessary (3 students).

The cognitive labs were conducted over three days in October 2014 at the school sites. Note that the study was conducted at an earlier time within the school year than the operational summative test would be administered. Thus, kindergarteners were still relatively new to school, and most of the Grade 1

TABLE 7.2 Item Types Selected for the Study, Grades K–3.

Domain	Item Type	Grade K	Grade 1	Grades 2–3
Listening				
	Listen and Match			
	Follow Instructions	✓	✓	✓
	Short Conversation			
	Long Conversation	✓	✓	✓
	Teacher Presentation	✓	✓	
	Read aloud Story			✓
Speaking				
	Classroom Tableau			
	Show and Share Questions	✓	✓	✓
	Show and Share Presentation	✓		
	Picture Description	✓	✓	✓
	Conversation			
	Observe and Report			
	Opinion			✓
Reading				
	Word Wall	✓		
	Read along Story	✓		
	Read and Match			
	Short Correspondence	✓		
	Read along Sentence		✓	✓
	Read for Details		✓	✓
	Informational Set			
	Literary Set		✓	
	Procedural Text			✓
Writing				
	Word Builder	✓	✓	✓
	Sentence Builder	✓	✓	✓
	Picture Caption			✓
	Write an Opinion			✓

students in the sample were still emergent readers and mostly could not yet read sentence-level text independently. These factors needed to be taken into consideration in interpreting the study results.

Each one-on-one cognitive lab was conducted with a laptop (14-inch screen) and a standard-sized mouse (except one interviewer who used a smaller-sized mouse). Each student used a headset with a microphone attached. Before beginning the test, each student watched the tutorial video showing how to use the accessibility features and the TE computer-interface features such as audio buttons, recording buttons, arrows, and scroll bar. Several questions pertaining to

TABLE 7.3 Item Types Selected for the Study, Grades 6–8.

Domain	Item Type	Grades 6–8
Listening		
	Listen for Information	✓
	Academic Lecture or Discussion	
	Interactive Student Presentation	✓
	Academic Debate	
Speaking		
	Compare Pictures	✓
	Analyze a Visual and a Claim	✓
	Language Arts Presentation	✓
	Analyze a Visual and a Claim	
Reading		
	Short Informational Set	✓
	Short Literature Set	
	Extended Informational Set	✓
	Extended Literature Set	✓
Writing		
	Storyboard	✓
	Discrete Editing Tasks	✓
	Writing Questions Tasks	
	Responding to a Peer E-mail	
	Construct a Claim	

the students' use of and familiarity with computers were asked prior to the item administration. The interviewer asked the questions from the cognitive lab protocol after each item type or each domain, depending on the student's pace of answering the items. During the test, the interviewer explained the TE features (e.g., the use of the audio buttons, recording buttons, arrow buttons, scroll bar, mouse, and item type functionality) when the student had difficulty understanding the features needed for answering the question.

All of the cognitive lab interviews were audio recorded. The interviewers rated the student's (1) understanding of directions, (2) degree of difficulty in the use of TE features, (3) independence in solving the questions, (4) engagement, and (5) use of accessibility tools. In this chapter, we report on the ratings of the four areas (excluding the use of accessibility tools) as they pertained to the research questions. The interviewers also took detailed notes following the protocol. After completing the cognitive labs each day, the interviewers debriefed to share their notes and the immediate patterns they had observed. The interviewers' notes and ratings were used as part of the data set, along with the students' responses.

Analysis

Descriptive statistics for the student background data and the interviewers' ratings were computed. Overall ratings in major categories on a three-point scale were analyzed (see the Appendix for the scales). For the areas that received low ratings, the student background, student responses, and interview notes were reviewed to determine the source of low ratings. The interviewers' detailed notes were qualitatively analyzed. Four researchers conducted multiple readings of the notes and categorized them according to the areas of interest in this study. Commonly identified patterns of student performance and areas of difficulty were then summarized.

Findings

As described above, based on their observation and interview notes, cognitive lab interviewers rated students' response processes regarding the following major categories in the protocol (see the rating scale in the Appendix): student's (1) understanding of directions, (2) degree of difficulty in the use of TE features, (3) independence in solving the questions, and (4) engagement. Figure 7.1 displays the average percentage of students by grade level or grade spans across the three rating scale points (0-no, 1-partially, and 2-entirely).

As shown in Figure 7.1 (Engagement in items), the vast majority of students were highly engaged with these TE items. In particular, students in kindergarten and Grade 1 expressed their enjoyment of interacting with technology features (e.g., advancing the computer screen, clicking certain zones, moving parts around on the screen). Some students remarked, "I liked moving the letters. I want more," "I like to press the buttons," "I like doing these activities," and "I want to do more. Can I start again?" In cases where a rating of 1 (partially engaged) was given, interviewers commented that some students were unable to read fluently yet and thus were unable to engage in the reading section items.

Despite the generally high engagement level, some issues were noted regarding certain directions and TE features, as indicated by a considerable portion of ratings of 2s (partial understanding of directions and partial difficulties in the use of TE features). Common patterns are described in the next session for each of the two research questions (clarity of directions and interaction with TE features).

Clarity of Directions and Types of Difficulties

As presented in Figure 7.1, across all grade levels, many students were found to have some difficulty understanding directions and completing items independently. The percentage of students with ratings of 0 (no) or 1 (partial) in these two areas was notably higher in kindergarten to Grade 3 than in Grades

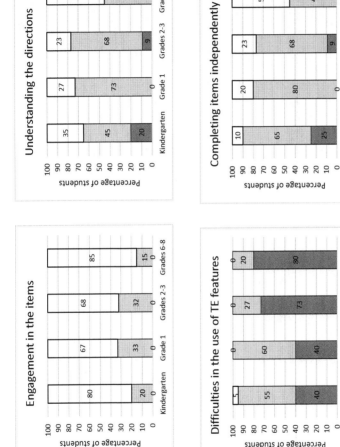

FIGURE 7.1 Percentage of students in each rating category across grade level/grade spans.

6–8. A closer look at the sample revealed that students in these ratings included non-EL students. The interviewers' notes revealed that this rating (0 or 1) was largely attributed to the following factors: (1) a lack of explicit directions about the test platform functions (e.g., arrow buttons used to progress to the next item, audio buttons, recording buttons), (2) students' (particularly from kindergarten to Grade 2) limited experience with testing and with a computer-based speaking test, and (3) some EL students' low English proficiency.

Due to the lack of explicit directions about how to advance to the next item, many students had some difficulty in the beginning of the test (i.e., moving on from the first item). The number of students experiencing this type of difficulty was substantial in kindergarten and Grade 1. It is interesting to note that the arrow buttons, which might be self-explanatory to experienced test takers or adult learners, were not obvious to younger students who had limited experience with computer programs. Once interviewers told the students how to progress to the next item, this issue was quickly resolved.

A similar issue was noted for the first item of the speaking section. Although some students were able to use the recording buttons independently, many students in kindergarten to Grade 3 needed reminding by the interviewers to press the recording button for the first speaking item. The interviewers observed that students quickly learned how to use all of the navigational buttons as the testing progressed.

One noteworthy finding was that kindergarten students had a strong tendency to check with the interviewer regarding their understanding of the directions in each item or ask for help with the use of TE features. There was also a frequent need for the interviewers to initially prompt the students in kindergarten to speak for the speaking items. These findings point out the importance of a test administrator's role.

Despite the video tutorial, the students in general appeared to need more explicit directions and opportunities to practice for new item types and items with TE features. The interviewers noted that some students (30%) in kindergarten and Grade 1 did not pay attention to the tutorial video as the tutorial content was perhaps more accessible to the upper grade students.

Related to clarity of directions, the interviewers' notes indicate that several students were not clear about the desired response format in a few items (e.g., the "Picture Description" item in speaking and the "Word Builder" item in writing), which involved clicking a zone or performing a drag-and-drop of the answer choices. Once directed by the interviewers, the students were able to figure out the rest of the items independently.

Another notable issue emerged from a combination of the ratings for direction clarity, item presentation, and students' reading proficiency in the "Reading for Details" item type. To illustrate this interaction between the test presentation and student characteristics, Figure 7.2 includes a screenshot of this reading item as it appeared at the time of the study. First, it was unclear to some students that

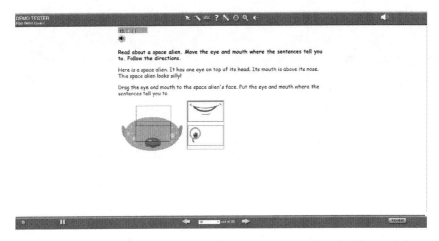

FIGURE 7.2   A sample "Reading for Detail" type item. Reproduced with permission.

they needed to read a passage in order to complete the item. Some students were confused that only the directions were read aloud and tried to complete the item without reading the given passage. The interviewers commented that the item presentation could be improved to clearly mark the reading passage section in addition to making the directions more pronounced. As is often the case at the beginning of the school year, some students at this grade level had yet to develop their reading skills regardless of their EL vs. non-EL status. Thus, those students could not identify the passage to read in order to complete this particular item.

As another example related to direction and item presentation issues, some students in Grades 6–8 were initially uncertain as to whether the given items were reading or speaking items due to the nature of the integrated language skills in the items (e.g., the "Language Arts Presentation" item type in reading). This was another example of the importance of explicit directions and students' opportunity to become familiar with new item types.

Students' Interaction with TE Features

With respect to TE features, students' use of drag-and-drop, zone selection, audio buttons for listening, recording buttons for speaking, and typing for writing was of particular interest in this study. In the kindergarten sample, 60% of the students were rated as having some difficulties with these TE features at least once across the items (see Figure 7.1). The interviewers' notes indicated that the standard-sized mouse was too big for students in kindergarten and Grade 1; this was the major obstacle to students performing a drag-and-drop. Students often had difficulties simultaneously pressing and holding the button and moving the mouse for the drag-and-drop, particularly when the object and the dropping zone were relatively long distance from each other (e.g., across the computer screen). One interesting observation was that some students in Grade 3 and above switched to using a track pad instead of a mouse during testing as they were more familiar with and accustomed to using track pads in their school. The use of a track pad made the drag-and-drop a little harder for these students compared to using a mouse.

In addition, the interviewers regularly commented that the younger students (kindergarten and Grade 1) were still developing their motor skills, let alone the ability to use a mouse adequately. For example, interviewers commented that the size of the clickable targets on the computer interface seemed too small for these young students who were not precise in their clicks of the mouse and had difficulties with a relatively small target size.

A similar problem was found in the "Literary Set" item type in reading. This item type included a relatively long passage, requiring the test takers to scroll down to view the entire text. Some interviewers considered this a TE feature issue and assigned a score point of 1 to the students who had difficulty using a mouse and grabbing the scroll bar. All interviewers reported that the scroll bar seemed too narrow and that the color was too discreet for these young students.

As presented in Figure 7.1, a significantly higher percentage of the sample in Grades 2–3 was rated "no" difficulties for the use of TE features (73%) than in Grades K and 1. The students in Grades 2–3 also demonstrated easy use of the audio buttons to replay the given listening stimuli in the listening items. The difficulties using the TE features in this grade band mainly concerned the recording buttons, which was commonly observed in other grades as well.

As described earlier, speaking to the computer and recording responses is, in general, a new type of assessment task for K–12 students in the United States. All students in the study needed to learn how to use the three recording buttons (i.e., record, stop, and playback) in the speaking items. Students' initial difficulty with the recording buttons seemed mainly due to a lack of practice or explicit directions on the use of the three buttons. The interviewers' notes were consistent in reporting that all students were able to use recording buttons independently after trying a couple of items. Some students were observed to replay their recorded responses to evaluate their own responses and then re-record their answers if desired.

As far as typing is concerned for extended writing items, many students in Grades 2–3 were noted to have substantial difficulties typing responses to the items. It was clear that the students in the sample were not accustomed to typing. The students often asked the interviewer for help locating letters on the keyboard. Most students were also noted to type using one or two fingers at a slow pace. Some students' response samples provided evidence that students were not able to fully demonstrate their writing skills when required to type their responses. For example, one advanced-level EL student wanted to type, "I want to be a police officer" for the "Write an Opinion" item type. However, her typed response on the computer was, "i wot to be a ples ofi sr. (sic)" It appeared that the problem was not only her writing skills (e.g., correct spelling being part of the construct) but also her difficulty in finding the letters on the keyboard.

To better disentangle the impact of typing a response versus writing a response, some students were offered the opportunity to write their responses on paper after spending some time typing on the computer. Figure 7.3 includes two examples comparing students' responses on the computer and paper after a similar length of time. It was apparent that these students' typing skills might have had an impact on students' ability to demonstrate their writing skills.

In contrast, the sample of Grades 6–8 students in this study had very little difficulty typing on the computer. Although only 13 students were able to complete the writing items due to the limited testing time, all students except one typed their responses to the "Storyboard" item without any typing issues. One

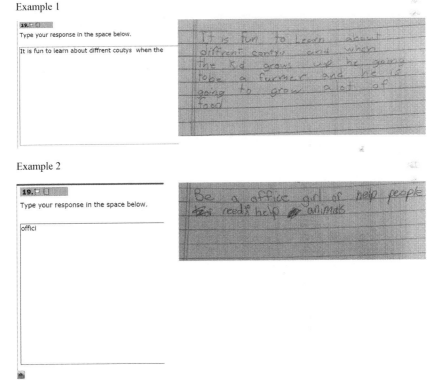

FIGURE 7.3 Examples of students' responses in Grades 2–3 on the computer vs. on paper.

student commented that she preferred to write on paper, but other students commented that they preferred to type on the computer due to the neatness of their written responses. In fact, the interviewers generally commented that they found a noticeable difference between the Grades K–3 and the Grades 6–8 samples in terms of the use of TE features. None of the students in Grades 6–8 sample had a problem with the drag-and-drop, zone selection, or drop-down menu features.

In summary, while the study sample students generally exhibited high engagement in the computer-based ELP assessment and TE items, a common problem emerged when students encountered TE features for the first time at the beginning of the assessment. In spite of the video tutorial, students' attention span and lack of hands-on experience seemed to have limited the impact of the tutorial. Although all students were able to learn how to handle TE features quickly during the testing, the need for explicit directions and opportunities for hands-on tutorial/practice was paramount.

It is important to note that this study was conducted with a small sample using a preliminary test platform when the directions and final design of the test platform were yet to be developed. While the study findings should be carefully interpreted, they provided useful information to enhance the quality of the ELPA21 assessment. In the next section, we describe how the study findings were utilized for further assessment development.

Recommendations and Actions Taken Based on Findings

The results of the study yielded important empirical evidence regarding areas of further improvement during the assessment development stages. The study team provided a set of practical recommendations and had a series of meetings to discuss them with test developers and the ELPA21 leadership group to inform future development as well as administrative considerations. Following are some major recommendations and ELPA21's efforts to address them (for a full list of recommendations and undertaken actions, see Wolf, Guzman-Orth, & Wain, 2015).

- Recommendation 1: Tutorials and sample practice items should be provided to students prior to testing. ELPA21 assessments include various, innovative TE item types on a computer-based test platform; thus, it is critical to provide opportunities for students to become familiar with the item types, including the TE features and other platform functions. This is essential to adequately elicit students' ELP skills, unimpeded by the familiarity with TE features. It is equally important that students have hands-on experience with technology features through practice items.

  - Actions taken: ELPA21 developed and provided an interactive item demonstration site for the field test, accompanied by detailed lesson plans for specific grade bands. Teachers were encouraged to demonstrate the items to their students and provide opportunities to practice with the items so that they are familiar with the testing environment.

- Recommendation 2: Clear and explicit directions must accompany each item type. The directions should clearly include what the students are expected to do in order to complete the given item types. For students whose ELP is too low to understand the directions, individual demonstrations of expected responses with sample items are desirable, in addition to prior exposure to sample practice items.

  o Actions taken: Each item type on the field test was accompanied by specific directions. ELPA21 also planned to examine student responses and reports from field-test administrators to determine the effectiveness of the instructions.

- Recommendation 3: Individual assistance should be provided during the test administration for lower grade students. The study results indicated that students in Grades K and 1 had limited testing experience and were accustomed to confirming understanding with the teachers. These students also tend to have limited experience with technology.

  o Actions taken: ELPA21 developed explicit guidelines about administrator-to-student ratios. For kindergarten to Grade 1, the recommended ratio for the computer-based testing is 1 to 5; for Grade 2 it is 1 to 8. ELPA21's *Accessibility and Accommodations Framework* also provides guidance on individual assistance.

- Recommendation 4: Item formatting should be clear and intuitive and should not require unnecessary use of technology navigation features. It is preferable that students can view an entire item without scrolling the screen so that students easily understand what they are expected to do. Yet, presenting a reading passage requiring students to scroll is often unavoidable. In that case, the directions should be clear and the scroll bar should be noticeable. The appropriate size of the font, graphics, and functional icons also need to be carefully determined.

  o Actions Taken: Improvements were made to the field-test platform based on the cognitive lab results.

- Recommendation 5: The construct measured by each item type should be clearly defined in order to determine any necessary accommodations or specific accessibility features for a computer-based test. This issue was a consideration particularly for some writing items that require students to provide an extended written response. In our study, some students at the elementary grades demonstrated a noticeable difference when writing on paper compared to writing on a computer. If the construct of interest in a writing item was to solely measure students' writing proficiency regardless of the test delivery mode, allowing students to write on paper should be an acceptable response format. An explicit definition of the construct for each item type would help test users determine appropriate methods for alternate response modes or accommodations to support student needs.

- ○ Actions Taken: The *Accessibility and Accommodations Framework* that guides ELPA21 takes the constructs being assessed into account; items and tasks were developed with available accommodations and accessibility tools in mind. ELPA21 also planned to regularly examine students' responses in the writing section of operational assessments.

Conclusion and Future Research

In this chapter, we demonstrated how a usability study conducted in an early stage of assessment development helped ELPA21 make evidence-based decisions on the assessment design and administration procedures. As the *Standards* (AERA, APA, & NCME, 2014) emphasize, fairness and validity need to be carefully considered throughout all stages of test development and use. From the larger perspective, considering K–12 EL students who are not familiar with large-scale, computer-based ELP assessments, interaction with technology features is a considerable validity concern. A close examination of students' response processes during the computer-based testing and ELPA21's immediate actions to address the issues certainly helped to enhance the validity for score interpretations and uses from the ELPA21 assessments.

Since the usability study was completed, ELPA21's ELP assessments have been widely used across eight states for four years. The use of technology in classroom and students' access to technology in general (e.g., computers, tablets, smart phones) have also grown rapidly. Bennett (2018) asserts that future assessments will be even more technology-based, measuring new constructs as well as including more innovative assessment tasks. As shown in the ELPA21's ELP assessment, this trend is already taking place. Yet, empirical research about how K–12 EL students from diverse backgrounds adequately demonstrate their English abilities in these innovative computer-based ELP assessments is relatively limited. Current available studies on this topic are mostly limited to small-scale cognitive lab designs. While more research is needed to examine various aspects via a close observation and verbal protocol analysis, large-scale research based on other sources of data (e.g., student scores at item and test levels, other process data) is an urgent need given the high-stakes uses of K–12 ELP assessments.

We also call for empirical research on the impact of computer-based K–12 ELP assessments in practice. These computer-based ELP assessments are intended to have a positive impact on teaching and learning. For example, the use of technology and TE item types were expected to better instantiate communicative language skills EL students should acquire while helping students prepare for college and careers. It will be important to investigate the extent to which technology use is implemented for EL students' ELP development (e.g., writing on the computer) in classroom, which in turn may affect the reconceptualization of the construct in this digital era. We anticipate that the ELP construct and real-life language use tasks may shift over time as technology standards are developed in K–12 education and technology use becomes more commonplace for instruction and assessment. As the nature of the construct and the technology evolve, there is increasing demand for empirical research to better understand best practices for computer-based ELP testing and their valid uses for EL students.

Notes

1 For WIDA's ELP assessments, students in kindergarten are administered the paper-based assessment while other grades are administered the computer-based assessment.
2 The present chapter is adapted from the ELPA21 cognitive lab study report (Wolf et al., 2015).

References

Almond, P., Winter, P., Cameto, R., Russell, M., Sato, E., Clarke-Midura, J., … Lazarus, S. (2010). Technology-enabled and universally designed assessment: Considering access in measuring the achievement of students with disabilities—A foundation for research. *Journal of Technology, Learning, and Assessment, 10*(5). Retrieved from www.jtla.org

American Educational Research Association, American Psychological Association, & National Council on Measurement in Education (AERA, APA, & NCME). (2014). *Standards for educational and psychological testing.* Washington, DC: Author.

Bachman, L. F. (2000). Modern language testing at the turn of the century: Assuring that what we count counts. *Language Testing, 17*(1), 1–42.

Bennett, R. (2018). Educational assessment: What to watch in a rapidly changing world. *Educational Measurement: Issues and Practice, 37*(4), 7–15.

Chalhoub-Deville, M. (2001). Language testing and technology: Past and future. *Language Learning & Technology, 5*(2), 95–98.

Cohen, A. D. (2006). The coming of age of research on test-taking strategies. *Language Assessment Quarterly, 3*(4), 307–331.

Douglas, D. (2013). Technology and language testing. In C. A. Chappelle (Ed.), *The encyclopedia of applied linguistics* (pp. 1–7). Oxford, UK: Blackwell Publishing, Ltd.

Ericsson, K. A., & Simon, H. A. (1993). *Protocol analysis: Verbal reports as data* (Revised edition). Cambridge, MA: MIT Press.

Fulcher, G. (2003). Interface design in computer-based language testing. *Language Testing, 20*(4), 384–408.

Hauck, M. C., Wolf, M. K., & Mislevy, R. (2016). *Creating a next-generation system of K–12 English learner language proficiency assessments* (ETS Research Report No. RR-16-06). Princeton, NJ: Educational Testing Service.

Leighton, J. P. (2017). *Using think-aloud interviews and cognitive labs in educational research.* New York, NY: Oxford University Press.

Martiniello, M. (2008). Language and the performance of English language learners in math word problems. *Harvard Educational Review, 78*(2), 333–368.

Ockey, G. J. (2009). Developments and challenges in the use of computer-based testing for assessing second language ability. *The Modern Language Journal, 93*(s1), 836–847.

Peterson, C. H., Peterson, N. A., & Powell, K. G. (2017). Cognitive interviewing for item development: Validity evidence based on content and response processes. *Measurement and Evaluation in Counseling and Development, 50*(4), 217–223.

Poehner, M. K., Zhang, J., & Lu, X. (2017). Computerized dynamic assessments for young language learners. In M. K. Wolf & Y. G. Butler (Eds.), *English language proficiency assessments for young learners* (pp. 214–233). New York, NY: Routledge.

Thurlow, M., Lazarus, S. S., Albus, D., & Hodgson, J. (2010). *Computer-based testing: Practices and considerations* (Synthesis Report 78). Minneapolis, MN: University of Minnesota, National Center on Educational Outcomes.

U.S. Department of Education, Office of English Language Acquisition. (2018). *Fast facts: Languages spoken by English learners (ELs).* Retrieved from https://ncela.ed.gov/files/fast_facts/FastFacts-Languages-Spoken-by-ELs-2018.pdf

Winter, P. C., Kopriva, R. J., Chen, C., & Emick, J. E. (2006). Exploring individual and item factors that affect assessment validity for diverse learners: Results from a large-scale cognitive lab. *Learning and Individual Differences, 16*(4), 267–276.

Wolf, M. K., Guzman-Orth, D., Lopez, A., Castellano, K., Himelfarb, I., & Tsutagawa, F. (2016). Integrating scaffolding strategies into technology-enhanced assessments of English learners: Task types and measurement models. *Educational Assessment, 21*(3), 157–175.

Wolf, M. K., Guzman-Orth, D., & Wain, J. (2015). *Investigating the usability of technology-enhanced assessment items during the ELPA21 development process: ELPA21 cognitive lab study report.* Final Deliverable to the English Language Proficiency Assessment for the 21st Century Consortium. Retrieved from www.elpa21.org/resources/recdoSRr39KO7OvFC/

Wolf, M. K., Kim, J., & Kao, J. (2012). The effects of glossary and read-aloud accommodations on English language learners' performance on a mathematics assessment. *Applied Measurement in Education, 25*(4), 347–374.

APPENDIX
Cognitive Lab Interview Questions and Rating Scales

Computer Questions

1. Have you used a computer before?   Yes: _____ No: _____
2. How often do you use a computer? (1) never, (2) once a month, (3) two to three times a month, (4) at least two to three times a week
3. Did you do any activities on the computer in school?   Yes: _____ No:_____
4. What activity did you do? How often did you do it? _____

Questions and Probes

Ask the following questions after each set of questions (i.e., each item type). Adjust your language as needed for the student you interview.

- **Clarity of Directions:** Check student's understanding of directions

  o   Did you understand the directions? What did you need to do?
  o   Can you tell me what you were asked to do?
  o   Were there any parts that you did not understand?
  o   Were there any words that you did not understand?

- **Difficulty**: Check any difficulties the student had.

  o   Were these questions easy to answer or hard to answer?
  o   (Very easy, A little bit easy, A little bit hard, Very hard)
  o   Why do you think it was easy/hard? Which part?
  o   Why did you choose that as an answer?

  [For speaking items]

  o   Did you have any difficulty in using the headset and microphone? Why?
  o   Did you have any difficulty in recording your response in the speaking question? Why? (i.e., play, pause, stop, listen, replay)

- **Question Presentation**: Check student's understanding of how the question was presented.

  ○ Did you understand this picture? Can you tell me what this picture is of?
  ○ Was the picture/letter/word big enough for you to understand?
  ○ Can you tell me where you looked first on the screen? Where did you look next?
  ○ Were you able to scroll up and down the screen?
  ○ Were there any parts that you did not understand on this screen?

- **TE Features in Question**: Check student's ability to use TE features.

  ○ Were you able to move [the picture/object]? Did you have any difficulty with moving (drag-and-drop) the picture? Why? [ask the same question for other features such as hotspot and multiple sections]
  ○ Was it clear where you needed to click?

General Follow-up Questions

- What did you mean by _____?
- Can you tell me more?

After the Test

- **Usability of Other Technical Functions:** Record student's difficulties in interacting with the test question or the testing interface (computer, mouse, keyboard, recording, navigational pane).

  ○ Did you have any difficulty in using the mouse? Clicking? Why?
  ○ Did you have any difficulty using the scroll bar to see the full screen?
  ○ Did you have any difficulty in using the headset and microphone? Why?
  ○ Did you have any difficulty in recording your response in the speaking question? (i.e., play, pause, stop, listen, replay) Why?

- **Any Specific Difficulty:** Record student's difficulties with any specific questions.

  ○ Which one was most difficult for you? Why?
  ○ Were there any words you did not understand?
  ○ Were there any parts of the computer that were not easy to use? Give me examples.
  ○ Which one was easiest for you? Why?
  ○ Which one did you like the most? Why?

- **Accessibility Features:** Record student's difficulties in using the available accessibility features (including universal and designated supports).Note: show a screen shot of accessibility features tool bar when asking these questions.

  ○ Did you understand what these pictures were? Go over each tool.
  ○ (If the student didn't use them) Why did/didn't you use them?
  ○ (If the student used the features) Were these helpful? Why/why not?
  ○ Was anything confusing or hard to understand?

Rating Scale

The Interviewer completes the following ratings for each item type and overall test performance.

Topic	Rating & Comments		
Did the student understand what he or she was supposed to do based on the question directions? **(Directions)**	0 (no)	1 (partially)	2 (yes, entirely)
	Comments:		
Did the student understand the layout of the question? **(Question Presentation)**	0 (no)	1 (partially)	2 (yes, entirely)
	Comments:		
Were there any issues or difficulties with use of the TE features (e.g., drag-and-drop, zone selection, hot spot, writing tools—cut, copy, paste)? **(TE Questions)**	0 (no)	1 (partially)	2 (yes, entirely)
	Comments:		
Did the student have any issues in using the equipment (keyboard, mouse, recording, headphones, microphone)? **(Equipment)**	0 (no)	1 (partially)	2 (yes, entirely)
	Comments		
Did the student have any issues or difficulties in making use of the accessibility features (universal and designated features)? **(Accessibility- Usability)**	0 (no)	1 (partially)	2 (yes, entirely)
	Comments		
To what extent was the student engaged? **(Engagement)**	0 (no)	1 (partially)	2 (yes, entirely)
	Comments		
Was the student able to complete the item(s) independently without difficulties? **(Difficulty/Independence)**	0 (no)	1 (partially)	2 (yes, entirely)
	Comments		

8

GENERATING SCORE REPORTS

Psychometric Issues to Consider

Hanwook Yoo, Joyce Wang, David P. Anderson, and Eric Zilbert

Large-scale, standards-based English language proficiency (ELP) assessments in Grades K–12 are designed to provide scores that support interpretations for purposes such as identifying students as English learners (ELs), monitoring students' progress, and reclassifying students as English proficient. To meet federal accountability requirements, as in the Every Student Succeeds Act (2015), states' ELP assessments should report students' proficiency levels derived from the four domains of listening, speaking, reading, and writing. Also, state ELP assessments should measure students' annual progress to monitor their growth in achieving ELP.

Communicating test results to stakeholders is one of the critical components of large-scale educational assessments, including ELP assessments, and the development of adequate score reports entails a number of technical as well as practical considerations impacting the test design (Goodman & Hambleton, 2004; Zenisky & Hambleton, 2012). Score reports should be easily understood by the intended audiences and provide technically accurate score information. Key psychometric issues must be thoroughly considered in generating reliable and meaningful test scores in the reports (Educational Testing Service [ETS], 2009). For example, ELP assessments must include appropriate numbers of items to generate valid and reliable overall scores and subscores. Reliability coefficients of scores are required to investigate whether reported scores are precise and sufficiently reliable to support their intended uses and interpretations. In addition, the internal test structure and intended/unintended test consequences should be evaluated as part of validity evidence in support of intended score interpretation (American Educational Research Association [AERA], American Psychological Association [APA], & National Council on

Measurement in Education [NCME], 2014). While high-quality psychometric analyses are essential for generating valid and reliable test scores, the results of the analyses need to be considered together with practical concerns to create final score reports for operational testing.

In this chapter, we discuss how to develop technically sound and practically useful score reports for K–12 ELP assessments with an emphasis on a psychometric perspective, which is a general issue for newly developed assessments in K–12 contexts. The chapter focuses on two empirical psychometric analyses used to address the principal issues of score reporting: (a) a dimensionality analysis to evaluate the internal test structure of four language skills as well as the overall ELP construct and (b) a vertical scaling analysis that yields scale scores (from kindergarten through Grade 12) that are used to monitor the students' annual ELP progress. The score report development procedures are demonstrated based on the Summative Assessment of the English Language Proficiency Assessments for California (hereafter, Summative ELPAC, www.elpac.org). The Summative ELPAC measures student progress toward meeting the *California English Language Development Standards, Kindergarten through Grade 12* (*CA ELD Standards*, for short henceforth), California Department of Education, 2014). The *CA ELD Standards* describe the English language skills that students in California need to succeed in school. As a successor to the previous California ELP assessment (California English Language Development Test, CELDT), the Summative ELPAC was launched for the school year 2017–2018. The authors of the present chapter were involved in the development of the Summative ELPAC including the field testing process (See Chapter 6 of this volume for more details about the ELPAC development).

In this chapter, we first provide a description of the test structure of the Summative ELPAC and its hierarchical score reporting structure, which explains the relationship between the overall test scale score and specific language domain scores. Second, we provide an overview of two psychometric analyses we conducted with the Summative ELPAC field test data: the dimensionality analysis and the vertical scaling analysis. Some key psychometric and practical issues involved in each analysis are discussed. We also discuss the types of validity evidence provided from our analyses and further psychometric considerations for developing ELP assessment score reports.

The Summative ELPAC Test Structure and Score Report

The Summative ELPAC measures four language skills: listening, speaking, reading, and writing, in order to meet federal requirements pertaining to ELP assessments. As described earlier, the Summative ELPAC is aligned with the *CA ELD Standards*, which emphasize the communicative use of language. One of the important features of the *CA ELD Standards* is to consider students'

ELP holistically, including a focus on integrated language skills to reflect the multidimensional nature of language proficiency (Wolf, Guzman-Orth, & Hauck, 2016). The Summative ELPAC brings this feature into the assessment by including integrated skill task types, which are test items that incorporate two language skills, such as listening and speaking. Measuring integrated language skills enhances the authenticity of an assessment because real-life communication frequently involves the integration of language skills.

Since the ELPAC must be aligned with the *CA ELD Standards*, the task types, test blueprint, reporting hierarchy, and score reports need to reflect the integrated nature of language skills as described by the standards. Task types indicate the types of activities that students perform when taking the ELPAC. Although the *Summative Assessment Test Blueprints for the ELPAC* (California Department of Education, 2017) are divided into the four domains of listening, speaking, reading, and writing, the document notes whenever a task type requires the use of integrated language skills. For example, the task type "Summarize an Academic Presentation" is noted as a speaking with listening task type since a student listens to a presentation and then gives a spoken summary. Another example is the task type called "Write about Academic Information" (writing with reading) in which the student reads a pie chart or a bar graph and then writes responses to questions about the chart or graph.

A hierarchical reporting structure was developed for the Summative ELPAC to properly report scores based on integrated language skills that were suggested by *CA ELD Standards*. The ELPAC contains five task types that measure integrated skills. Table 8.1 provides a list of the integrated tasks in the Summative ELPAC, a description of the integrated skills assessed, and the language domain to which each item is mapped. For a full list of Summative ELPAC task types and their alignment with the *CA ELD Standards*, see the *Summative Assessment Test Blueprints for the ELPAC* (California Department of Education, 2017). Of the five integrated task types, two are speaking with listening and two are writing with reading. As a result, one option for the score reporting hierarchy was a model that combined listening and speaking scores to obtain an oral language score and a second scale that combined reading and writing scores to produce a written language score. After psychometric analyses of different options and consideration of practical issues, this score reporting hierarchy was eventually selected. Figure 8.1 illustrates the hierarchical structure of reported score on the Summative ELPAC.

The development of an overall scale score spanning kindergarten to Grade 12 is a recommended feature of state ELP assessments. This feature allows students' ELP progress to be evaluated by comparing annual summative assessment scores (Kenyon, MacGregor, Li, & Cook, 2011). Instead of deriving an overall scale score from four scale scores (from listening, speaking, reading, and writing) as the CELDT did, the ELPAC derives the overall scale score from

TABLE 8.1 Summative ELPAC Integrated Task Types and Skill Mapping.

Task Type	Description of Integrated Skills	Domain Mapping
Retell a Narrative (Grades K–5)	Speaking with Listening: This item assesses a student's ability to listen to a story while viewing related pictures and to provide a clear and detailed retelling of the story with the assistance of the pictures.	Speaking
Present and Discuss Information (Grades 6–12)	Speaking with Reading: A student interprets information from a graph/chart. The first question assesses the student's ability to present information from the graph/chart. The second question assesses the ability to state whether or not a claim is supported based on the information in the graph/chart.	Speaking
Summarize an Academic Presentation (Grades K–12)	Speaking with Listening: This item assesses a student's ability to listen to an academic presentation while viewing supporting images and to provide a spoken summary of the main points and details of the presentation with the assistance of the images.	Speaking
Describe a Picture (Grades 1–12)	Writing with Reading: At Grades 1–2, the student looks at a picture and writes a description about what is happening. At Grades 3–12, the student views an image and reads a paragraph that another student has written about the image. The paragraph may contain errors. A set of items assesses the student's ability to add details to a sentence, correct errors in a sentence, condense ideas from two sentences, or express what might happen next.	Writing
Write About Academic Information (Grades 3–12)	Writing with Reading: The student reads information in a graphic organizer that has notes about a topic such as a story. The first question assesses the student's ability to use relevant details from the graphic organizer to write text. The second question assesses the student's ability to use relevant details from the graphic organizer to justify an opinion in writing.	Writing

the oral language and written language scale scores. The overall scale score is a weighted average of the oral and written language scale scores and is reported as a scale score divided into four performance levels. Information about student performance for each language domain (listening, speaking, reading, and writing) is reported as a performance level without a scale score. This decision was made because the number of operational items in the speaking and writing domains (6 to 13 items) does not allow for the calculation of precise scale scores.

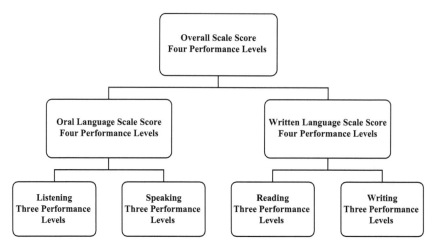

FIGURE 8.1 Reporting hierarchy of summative ELPAC, Kindergarten through Grade 12.

While the reporting hierarchy needed to satisfy psychometric demands to meet the needs of the ELPAC program, practical considerations regarding test length also contributed to its selection. Developing a stable continuous scale and reliable scores for each of the four language domains would have required a relatively large number of items in each language domain, which could be a burden to test takers. Lengthy testing time, especially for younger ELs, was one of the disadvantages of the CELDT. The ELPAC's reporting hierarchy (using oral and written language scale scores) offered a practical way to reduce the number of test items needed and thus keep testing time relatively short. Combining two pairs of language domains in psychometric scoring and scaling analyses allowed the test length to be minimized while maintaining reliable scores and a stable continuous scale. Reduced testing time minimizes the burden on students, schools, and local educational agencies and preserves time for instruction. The ELPAC score report was designed to convey the score reporting hierarchy along with student scores in a format that is easy to interpret. Figure 8.2 shows a sample Summative ELPAC student score report with fictional student information.

The score report reflects the score reporting hierarchy by showing overall score information at the top of the report, information about the oral and written language scores at the middle of the report, and then information about performance in the four language domains at the bottom of the report. The information is visually presented to indicate that listening and speaking scores contribute to the oral language score and that reading and writing scores contribute to the written language score. The Overall Score History at the upper right-hand corner of the first page shows overall scale scores for the current year and up to two prior years, making it easy to compare the student's performance

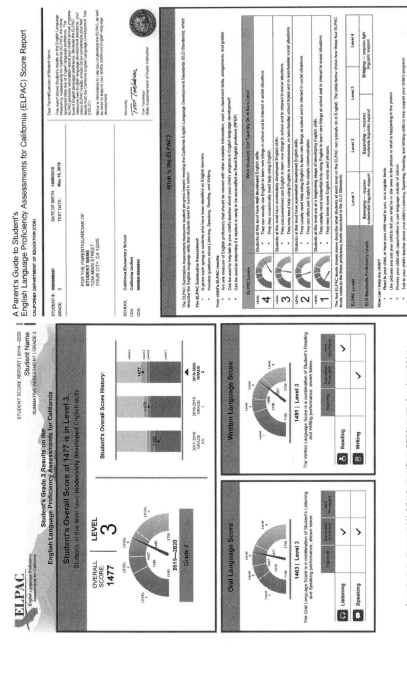

FIGURE 8.2 Example of a Summative ELPAC Student Score Report. Copyright 2018 by the California Department of Education. Reproduced with permission.

across years. The continuous vertical scale allows for direct comparison of the overall scores.

Psychometric Analyses to Generate Score Scales

To develop the Summative ELPAC score report as shown in Figure 8.2, two types of psychometric analyses were conducted. First, a dimensionality analysis based on the multidimensional item response theory (MIRT) framework was conducted to validate the test construct of the Summative ELPAC. Once the dimensionality of the Summative ELPAC was established, an IRT-based vertical scaling analysis using the separate linking approach was conducted to generate the continuous scale across grades/grade spans. In addition, the challenges and limitations of using measures of reading and writing to distinguish between young ELs (e.g., kindergarten) and native speakers were considered during the vertical scaling analysis. Both unidimensional and multidimensional non-compensatory two-parameter logistic model (2PLM) and generalized partial credit model (GPCM) were selected to conduct the psychometric analyses.

Overview of Dimensionality Analysis

Historically, researchers in language testing have evaluated several competing models of language proficiency that include multiple language skills that are distinct, correlated, or hierarchically related to an overall proficiency (Bachman & Palmer, 1982; Kunnan, 1995; Sawaki, Stricker, & Oranje, 2008). Although researchers have concluded that multiple language skills comprise language proficiency, there was no consensus on the exact nature of the relationship among the skills (see Hunsaker, 1990 for the historical backgrounds of oral language skill). Previously, state ELP assessments that contain four language skills, each measuring related but distinct latent factors, are commonly encountered in practice. In the past, item response modeling of such tests has proceeded either by applying a unidimensional model to each of the scales of listening, speaking, reading, and writing separately, or by ignoring the multidimensionality and treating the test as a unidimensional measure of ELP.

As mentioned in the previous section, the current *CA ELD Standards* demonstrate movement away from standards focusing on discrete language skills to standards that call for the integration of language skills (Faulkner-Bond, Wolf, Wells, & Sireci, 2018; see Bailey & Wolf, 2020, in this volume for changes in the construct of ELP assessments). Thus, evaluating dimensionality is an essential subject of psychometric analyses to ensure that the newly developed test measures the redefined ELP construct(s) as intended. Additionally, collecting validity evidence based on internal structure is stressed by the Standards for Educational and Psychological Testing, which noted that "evidence concerning the internal structure of the test should be provided if the rationale for test score interpretation depends on premises about the relationships among test items" (AERA, APA, & NCME, 2014, pp. 26–27).

Another purpose of this dimensionality analysis was to interpret the interrelationship among the four language domains, the two combined language scores (oral language and written language), and the overall test score, so that the scores from the reporting hierarchy were consistent with the construct(s) being assessed. The results from the dimensionality study informed the measurement model and scaling of the Summative ELPAC. The dimensionality analysis was used to explore whether the interrelationship among scores was consistent across grades/grade spans.

Overview of Vertical Scaling Analysis

The purposes of vertical scaling are straightforward: (a) to allow scale scores obtained from different grades/grade spans to have a consistent meaning and (b) to compare differences between scores to gauge student growth (Yen, 2009). This process provides estimates for student growth across years. In the case of ELP assessments, assessing and monitoring student progress with continuous scales is essential to provide accurate information that can be used to make decisions regarding the reclassification status of EL students (Kenyon et al., 2011; Llosa, 2012; Wolf et al., 2008).

The results of the vertical scaling analysis of the Summative ELPAC established the range of scale scores for both oral and written language scores as well as the overall test score for each grade/grade span, which led to the development of the Student's Overall Score History on the Summative ELPAC score report. The score differences in the continuous scale from non-adjacent grades cannot be assumed to have the same meaning, as the construct of ELP as defined in the *CA ELD Standards* changes somewhat with grade level.

Analysis of the Summative ELPAC Field Test Results

In spring 2017, a field test of the Summative ELPAC was conducted prior to its operational launch in 2018. The Summative ELPAC was divided into seven grades/grade spans targeting kindergarten and Grades 1, 2, 3–5, 6–8, 9–10, and 11–12. Both the dimensionality analysis and the vertical scaling analysis were conducted using the data from the field test, which included a sample of approximately 41,000 ELs. The sampling plan was made to provide a demographically and geographically representative sample of students even if participation in the field test was voluntary. Demographic information such as gender, race/ethnicity, disability status, socio-economic status, home language, and English acquisition status were used to evaluate the representativeness of the realized student sample.

Table 8.2 displays the demographic characteristics of the ELPAC field test sample compared to all K–12 ELs recorded in the California Longitudinal Pupil Achievement Data System (CALPADS). The field test sample data were close to the demographic composition of the population of ELs in California. Table 8.3 shows the number of examinees, the number of field test items and score points by grades/grade spans and by the four language domains.

Study One: Dimensionality Analysis

Three psychometric issues were considered to evaluate the internal test structure of the Summative ELPAC. First, the number of dimensions (also known as latent factors or language skills) were analyzed to see whether they reflect the number of skills that the items measure. Goodness of model fit indices were used to evaluate the number of dimensions. In this study, two dimensions representing oral and written language skills were expected based on hierarchical score reporting structure. Two dimensions representing receptive (listening and reading) and productive (speaking and writing) language skills were also evaluated to find the best way of demonstrating the dimensionality of the Summative ELPAC.

TABLE 8.2 Demographic Information for Summative ELPAC Field Test Sample.

Subgroup Category		ELPAC FT Sample	CALPADS Total Data
Total ELs		41,942	91,639
Gender	Male	53.7%	54.8%
	Female	46.3%	45.2%
Ethnicity	Hispanic or Latino	83.3%	85.1%
	Asian	9.2%	7.9%
	White	4.5%	4.1%
	Black or African American	0.3%	0.3%
	Native Hawaiian or Pacific Islander	0.3%	0.3%
	American Indian or Alaska Native	0.1%	0.1%
	Two more races	0.3%	0.3%
Other Subgroups	Students with disabilities	9.9%	16.6%
	Economically disadvantaged	84.4%	85.8%
Home Language	Spanish	84.0%	85.6%
	Chinese	2.6%	2.1%
	Vietnamese	1.8%	1.7%
	Arabic	1.6%	1.5%
	Hmong	0.6%	0.6%

Note. Students with limited English proficiency (LEP) status = Yes from CALPADS data obtained on January 4, 2017, when the Summative ELPAC field test sample roster was selected.

TABLE 8.3 Number of Items, Score Points by Grade/Grade Span and by Four Language Skills.

Number of Items (Points)	Grade/Grade Span						
	K	1	2	3–5	6–8	9–10	11–12
	N=5,338	N=6,368	N=6,338	N=6,013	N=5,646	N=6,015	N=5,142
Total	139 (194)	152 (209)	175 (243)	182 (260)	173 (254)	174 (255)	174 (255)
Listening	48 (48)	41 (41)	48 (48)	53 (53)	52 (52)	55 (55)	55 (55)
Speaking	30 (65)	29 (61)	35 (73)	33 (72)	36 (78)	34 (73)	34 (73)
Reading	37 (45)	52 (52)	64 (64)	72 (72)	61 (61)	60 (60)	60 (60)
Writing	24 (36)	30 (55)	28 (58)	24 (63)	24 (63)	25 (67)	25 (67)

The second issue was how dimensions were correlated with each other. The correlational relationship between dimensions was considered as an important criterion in the dimensionality evaluation because of its implications for the meaningfulness of each domain score and total score (as combined domain scores) in the multidimensional scale. For example, a high correlation between dimensions (e.g., higher than 0.9) indicates that the dimensions are not distinct from each other (Bagozzi & Yi, 1988). In this study, we expected that the two dimensions representing oral and written language skills were distinct but moderately correlated (around 0.7–0.8).

The third issue was how to interpret the meaning of the identified dimensions. The hypothetically defined dimensions that underlie the observed item responses were evaluated by the significance of item parameter estimates (i.e., factor loading estimates in terms of factor analytic approach). The meaning of each dimension was important because a clear understanding of the scores' meaning is necessary for the proper interpretation of scale scores and ultimately for the choice of scoring methods in psychometric analysis.

Analysis

In this study, the MIRT-based item-level factor analytic approach was used to evaluate four models that represent the hypothesized factor structure of the Summative ELPAC. These four models were:

1. Model 1: A correlated four-factor model in which listening, speaking, reading, and writing items are considered *unique language skills* (shown in Figure 8.3a)
2. Model 2: A correlated two-factor model in which listening and speaking items are considered *oral language skills* and reading and writing items are considered *written language skills* (shown in Figure 8.3b)

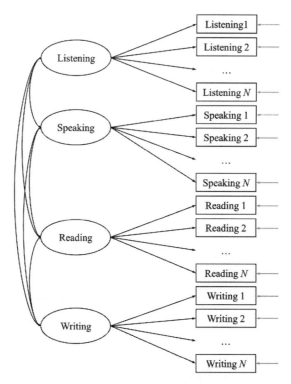

FIGURE 8.3a Correlated four-factor model (listening, speaking, reading, writing).
Note. Squares and ellipse(s) represent observed items and latent factor(s) respectively.

3. Model 3: A correlated two-factor model in which listening and reading items are considered *receptive language skills* and speaking and writing items are considered *productive language skills* (shown in Figure 8.3c)
4. Model 4: A single-factor model in which all four language skills are psychometrically indistinguishable from one another (shown in Figure 8.3d)

As illustrated in Figure 8.3, the current study used the simplified factor structure models for practical reasons (i.e., score interpretation issues). These models strongly assumed that each ELPAC test item was associated with a single language skill (listening, speaking, reading, or writing), although items from integrated task types measure multiple language skills. It was the best practice in score reporting to associate each test item to one reporting category; the factor structures tested in this study followed this principle. In instances in which a test item assessed integrated skills, the test item was mapped to the language skill that the student used to provide a response. For example, the task type called Summarize an Academic Presentation assessed a student's ability to

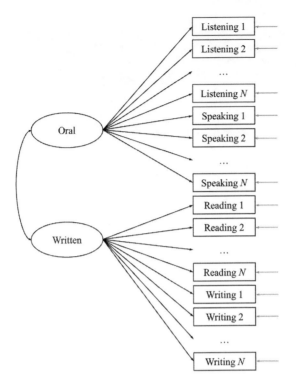

FIGURE 8.3b   Correlated two-factor model (oral and written).

listen to a presentation while viewing supporting images and then provide a spoken summary of the main points and details of the presentation with the assistance of the images. While the item assessed a student's ELP in the skills of listening and speaking, the item was mapped to the speaking domain because the student's response was spoken (e.g., Sawaki et al., 2008).

All analyses were conducted using software FlexMIRT (Cai, 2013). Due to the mixed response type data for the ELPAC (i.e., multiple choice and constructed response items), both the unidimensional and multidimensional versions of the 2PLM and GPCM were used. The unidimensional model, which was the most parsimonious, was used as a baseline for comparison with the results from the multidimensional models. In total, 28 factor models (4 factor models x 7 grades/ grade spans) were evaluated to identify the best-fitting test structure of the Summative ELPAC.

Three goodness of model fit indices were used for evaluating the factor models: Akaike information criterion (AIC), Bayesian information criterion (BIC), and -2 log-likelihood (-2 LL). AIC and BIC are comparative measures of fit, which can be used to compare either nested or non-nested models, so

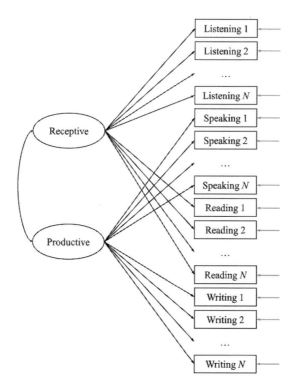

FIGURE 8.3c Correlated two-factor model (receptive and productive).

they are useful in comparing multiple competing models. The model with the lowest AIC and BIC is the best-fitting model. The difference of -2 LL and the ratio of -2 LL to the degree of freedom were also evaluated.

Despite considerable advances in the estimation of confirmatory factor models, there is no rule of thumb or perfect fit index for factor-model acceptance. In general, the more complex factor model tends to fit better than the model with fewer factors. Thus, model parsimony and the reasonableness of individual parameter estimates (statistical significance) as well as correlations among the latent factors were considered in the evaluation of competing models to select the most useful structure.

Results

Table 8.4 presents the summary of model fit indices for all grade levels. The best-fitting model was the correlated four-factor model and the least-fitting model was the single factor model across all grades. The oral and written

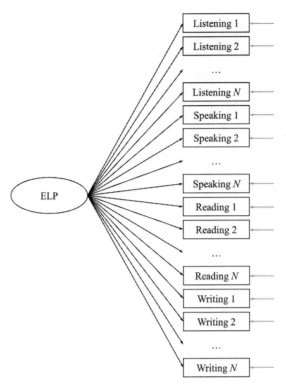

FIGURE 8.3d   Unidimensional model (ELP: English language proficiency).

factor model also fit reasonably well across all grades, while the receptive and productive factor model only fit well for Grades 6–12.

Factor loadings, which are the regression slopes of test items weighted by latent factor(s), are reported in Tables 8.5 through 8.7 and indicate how distinctively each hypothesized factor contributes to test structure.

The values higher than 0.3 are assumed reasonable factor loading. The results show that reasonable factor loadings were derived from all three multi-factor models. Tables 8.6 and 8.7 also provide the correlations between two pairs of latent factors (oral and written; receptive and productive) respectively. Correlations between receptive and productive language skills for kindergarten and Grades 1, 2, and 3–5 tests ranged from 0.80 to 0.84 (Table 8.6), while such correlations were lower for Grade 6 and up. So, the receptive and productive language skills were not as distinct at kindergarten through Grade 5 as they were at Grades 6–12. Table 8.8 shows the correlation across language skills in listening, speaking, reading, and writing. The results showed that reading and writing language skills were more highly correlated in the lower grades than in the higher grades (0.68 to 0.87). The correlation between listening and speaking

TABLE 8.4 Summary of Model Fit Statistics (Kindergarten through Grade 12).

Grade/ Grade Span	Model	df	-2 Log Likelihood	AIC	BIC	Order of Lowest Fit Value
K	1F	333	367,779	368,445	370,637	4
	2F (O+W)	334	353,507	354,175	356,374	2
	2F (R+P)	334	364,232	364,900	367,099	3
	4F (L+S+R+W)	339	347,407	348,085	350,316	1
1	1F	361	336,648	337,370	339,810	4
	2F (O+W)	362	328,357	329,081	331,528	2
	2F (R+P)	362	335,013	335,737	338,184	3
	4F (L+S+R+W)	367	324,944	325,678	328,158	1
2	1F	418	408,755	409,591	412,414	4
	2F (O+W)	419	400,133	400,971	403,801	2
	2F (R+P)	419	406,056	406,894	409,724	3
	4F (L+S+R+W)	424	394,676	395,524	398,387	1
3–5	1F	442	455,579	456,463	459,426	4
	2F (O+W)	443	452,188	453,074	456,043	2
	2F (R+P)	443	453,443	454,329	457,298	3
	4F (L+S+R+W)	448	448,248	449,144	452,147	1
6–8	1F	427	466,630	467,484	470,319	4
	2F (O+W)	428	463,530	464,386	467,228	3
	2F (R+P)	428	463,336	464,192	467,033	2
	4F (L+S+R+W)	433	458,802	459,668	462,543	1
9–10	1F	429	505,500	506,358	509,233	4
	2F (O+W)	430	500,863	501,723	504,605	3
	2F (R+P)	430	499,019	499,879	502,761	2
	4F (L+S+R+W)	435	492,963	493,833	496,749	1
11–12	1F	429	429,173	430,031	432,839	4
	2F (O+W)	430	426,355	427,215	430,029	3
	2F (R+P)	430	424,588	425,448	428,263	2
	4F (L+S+R+W)	435	420,489	421,359	424,206	1

Note. 1F denotes the single-factor model; 2F (O+W) denotes the correlated two-factor model with oral and written language skills; 2F (R+P) denotes the correlated two-factor model with receptive and productive skills; 4F (L+S+R+W) denotes the correlated four-factor model. AIC and BIC denote Akaike and Bayesian Information Criteria, respectively.

language skills was also moderately high (0.59 to 0.69) across all grades/grade spans but more highly correlated in the lower grades.

Test length as well as ease of score scale maintenance over future administrations were two practical issues considered during the factor model evaluation. Although the correlated four-factor model had a slightly better model fit, it would require a greater number of items to implement than either the receptive and productive

TABLE 8.5 Correlations and Factor Loadings from Oral and Written Language Skills.

Grade/ Grade Span	Mean (and SD) of Non-zero Factor Loadings		Correlations across Latent Factors
	Oral	Written	
K	.55 (.14)	.61 (.23)	.62
1	.54 (.14)	.66 (.09)	.62
2	.51 (.11)	.67 (.13)	.58
3–5	.47 (.12)	.45 (.15)	.70
6–8	.47 (.18)	.39 (.12)	.72
9–10	.50 (.19)	.46 (.13)	.75
11–12	.48 (.18)	.43 (.14)	.77

TABLE 8.6 Correlations and Factor Loadings from Receptive and Productive Language Skills.

Grade/ Grade Span	Mean (and SD) of Non-zero Factor Loadings		Correlations across Latent Factors
	Receptive	Productive	
K	.53 (.12)	.64 (.18)	.82
1	.59 (.15)	.58 (.11)	.82
2	.61 (.18)	.51 (.14)	.84
3–5	.44 (.15)	.47 (.10)	.80
6–8	.39 (.14)	.53 (.12)	.71
9–10	.45 (.14)	.59 (.13)	.69
11–12	.43 (.15)	.57 (.12)	.69

TABLE 8.7 Factor Loadings from Four Language Skills (Listening, Speaking, Reading, and Writing).

Grade/ Grade Span	Mean (and SD) of Non-zero Factor Loadings			
	Listening	Speaking	Reading	Writing
K	.57 (.12)	.70 (.07)	.54 (.14)	.85 (.06)
1	.56 (.14)	.66 (.11)	.70 (.09)	.67 (.10)
2	.58 (.15)	.59 (.08)	.71 (.14)	.67 (.10)
3–5	.48 (.11)	.60 (.11)	.46 (.18)	.52 (.10)
6–8	.43 (.15)	.66 (.09)	.40 (.13)	.51 (.09)
9–10	.48 (.14)	.72 (.09)	.48 (.15)	.56 (.09)
11–12	.44 (.15)	.70 (.07)	.46 (.16)	.55 (.10)

TABLE 8.8 Correlations across Four Language Skills (Listening, Speaking, Reading, and Writing).

Grade/Grade Span	Domains	Correlations among Latent Factors			
		Listening	Speaking	Reading	Writing
K	Listening	1			
	Speaking	.69	1		
	Reading	.79	.68	1	
	Writing	.57	.52	.81	1
1	Listening	1			
	Speaking	.69	1		
	Reading	.65	.55	1	
	Writing	.59	.55	.87	1
2	Listening	1			
	Speaking	.61	1		
	Reading	.71	.48	1	
	Writing	.57	.43	.84	1
3–5	Listening	1			
	Speaking	.60	1		
	Reading	.74	.54	1	
	Writing	.59	.54	.78	1
6–8	Listening	1			
	Speaking	.59	1		
	Reading	.75	.49	1	
	Writing	.61	.60	.68	1
9–10	Listening	1			
	Speaking	.61	1		
	Reading	.78	.49	1	
	Writing	.65	.69	.70	1
11–12	Listening	1			
	Speaking	.61	1		
	Reading	.78	.48	1	
	Writing	.69	.68	.68	1

factor model or the oral and written factor model. Test length was an important consideration in this situation in which the Summative ELPAC would be administered to over 1.2 million students per year. Not only do longer tests increase the burden of test administration and scoring, they also reduce the amount of instructional time, since paper-based tests were administered by local test examiners, who were often ESL classroom teachers. At kindergarten and Grade 1, all domains were administered one-on-one between a test examiner and a student, and the speaking domain was delivered as a one-on-one administration at all grades/grade spans. The small advantage that the correlated four-factor model had in terms of model-fit was outweighed by the negative consequences of increased test length.

A comparison of the oral and written factor model with the receptive and productive factor model revealed mixed results. While the oral and written factor model had a better fit at Grades K–5, the empirical data supported the receptive and productive factor model for Grades 6–12. Since the empirical data did not lead to a clear choice between these two factor models, further practical considerations were made. It is important to note that all receptive language skill items were multiple choice (objectively scored) items, and all productive language skill items were constructed response (scored by human raters) items. The results of the receptive and productive factor model could be interpreted as simple distinctions between two item types instead of latent language skills. One practical issue regarding scoring weights for kindergarten made the oral and written language model more viable than the receptive and productive factor model.

While one purpose of the ELPAC is to provide information about whether a student should be designated an EL, it is difficult to collect such information using assessments of reading and writing at kindergarten when native speakers of English are still developing those skills. As a result, educators in California wanted to place less weight on reading and writing scores than listening and speaking scores in producing overall proficiency scores at kindergarten. In this case, the oral and written language model was suitable because different weights could easily be applied to kindergarten reading and writing scores while maintaining the continuous scales between kindergarten and Grade 1. Since written language skill represented the combined score of reading and writing items, applying the weights on kindergarten students' scores was simpler using the oral and written factor model than the receptive and productive factor model.

The dimensionality analysis yielded empirical evidence regarding the model fit of four different factor models. Given both statistical analyses and practical considerations, the oral and written factor model was finally selected to represent the internal structure of the Summative ELPAC. The outcome of statistical evaluation across grades/grade spans based on the oral and written language model was considered as a whole to facilitate the anticipated development of continuous scales across the grades/grade spans.

Study Two: Vertical Scaling Analysis

Once the two dimensions of oral and written language skills were selected, further psychometric analyses were conducted in order to establish the continuous oral and written language score scales. In doing so, three key psychometric considerations were evaluated: (1) dimensionality assumption in IRT models, (2) linking approaches, and (3) proficiency estimations (see Briggs & Weeks, 2009 for more details on each consideration in vertical scaling).

First, two IRT models were evaluated for potential use in the creation of oral and written language scores on continuous scales across all grades/grade spans.

One possible approach was to establish two unidimensional IRT models (i.e., each item belongs to one dimension) that represent a unidimensional structure of each language skill (oral or written). Another potential approach was to establish a multidimensional IRT model (i.e., each item belongs to more than one dimension). This model would assume that items for the oral language score require not only oral language skill but also written language skill, and the same assumption would apply to items for the written language score.

The unidimensional IRT model was chosen instead of multidimensional IRT model for three practical reasons. First, the multidimensional score interpretation might be difficult since each item would contribute to both oral and written language scores. Second, the multidimensional item parameter estimates would make the process of developing parallel forms complicated since the target test information function would consider vectors of both oral and written item parameter estimates. Third, building the multidimensional continuous scales would be difficult because the multidimensional relationship between oral and written language skills is likely to vary across grades/grades spans. Some integrated task types in different grades/grade spans may show different relationships with the oral and written dimensions.

Second, two IRT linking approaches (i.e., separate and concurrent calibration linking) were evaluated for potential use in the development of the continuous oral and written language score scales across grades/grade spans. In the separate calibration approach, the first step would be to estimate item parameters and student proficiencies (i.e., oral and written language skills) in separate runs for each grade/grade span. Then a set of linear transformations between adjacent grades/grade spans would be applied sequentially to place the oral and written language scores from kindergarten through Grade 12 onto a continuous common scale. In the concurrent calibration approach, students from each grade/grade span would be treated as multiple groups and the item parameters and student proficiencies of all multiple groups would be calibrated simultaneously.

In this study, the separate linking approach was preferred over the concurrent linking approach because it could be used to detect the behavior of items across grades/grade spans, diagnose any convergence problems in estimation, and mitigate the effect of any potential unidimensionality violations (see Kolen & Brennan, 2004 for discussions on the separate linking approach). Unlike the concurrent linking approach, the separate linking approach could be used to resolve any issues regarding unreliable linking items by comparing the linking item parameter estimates that were generated for the adjacent grades/grade spans.

Finally, two IRT proficiency estimation approaches (i.e., maximum likelihood [ML] and expected a posteriori [EAP] estimations) were evaluated for potential use in estimating student proficiencies in the context of vertical scaling (Tong & Kolen, 2007). The ML approach would maximize the joint probability of a student's response pattern to estimate the most probable proficiency level. The

EAP approach would allocate weights to the joint probability distribution using a set of quadrature points to estimate student proficiency.

The ML estimation approach was chosen for this study because the EAP estimation approach tends to regress toward the population mean. The EAP estimates were likely to be biased because limited prior proficiency information was available for the California EL students in the field test. However, proficiency estimates for students with perfect scores or scores below the level expected by guessing cannot be calculated by ML estimation. In the ML estimation approach, additional steps (i.e., setting highest and lowest obtainable scale score) must be applied to develop proficiency estimates for these types of scores.

Analysis

Items on each grade/grade span were initially scaled separately so that estimated item parameters of oral or written language skill in a single grade/grade span could be put on the same scale. After all items for oral and written language scores in each grade/grade span were independently scaled, the vertical scaling analysis was conducted using commonly administered linking items between adjacent grades/grade spans. For example, some linking items were administered at kindergarten and Grade 1 and others were administered at Grade 1 and Grade 2 and so on. During the vertical linking analysis, linking items were placed on the same continuous scale from kindergarten through Grade 12.

To the extent possible, commonly administered linking items were selected for all task types that were administered at adjacent grades/grade spans. Overall, more than 20% of items from all four language domains were selected to link adjacent grades/grade spans. Using Grades 3–5 as the baseline, each grade/grade span was successively linked onto the continuous scale separately for oral and written language scores. As with the dimensionality analysis, the 2PLM and GPCM were chosen and implemented using the FlexMIRT program (Cai, 2013) with the ML estimation approach. Vertical scaling was undertaken using test characteristic curve (TCC) transformation methods (Stocking & Lord, 1983) in STUIRT (Kim & Kolen, 2004).

Using the Stocking-Lord transformation, slope and intercept terms were estimated and then applied to the targeted item parameter estimates to place them onto the continuous scale. The Stocking-Lord procedure minimizes the sum of the squared differences over students between the target and reference TCCs based on common items. Linking takes place by applying the resulting slope and intercept to the targeted item parameter estimates as well as to the student proficiency estimates and associated standard error of measurement estimates. The weights and quadrature points of the latent proficiency distribution output from FlexMIRT were used to implement the Stocking-Lord transformation.

In the process of constructing the vertical scale, several criteria were applied to evaluate the vertical scaling, including (a) correlation and item difficulty plots for the commonly administered items across grades/grade spans, (b) progression in test difficulty across grades/grade spans, (c) comparison of mean theta scores across grades/grade spans, and (d) comparison of overlap/separation of student proficiency distributions across grades/grade spans.

Results

Due to space constraints, limited results are presented here. This section provides the p-values of vertical scaling items averaged by grade/grade span, the item difficulty parameter estimates, the student proficiency estimates, and the TCCs.

Table 8.9 shows mean p-values of the vertical scaling items. Overall, the vertical scaling items performed consistently with the intuitive expectation that the mean p-values were lower when items were administered to on-grade students than when they were administered to grade-above students. This indicates that kindergarten items were more difficult when administered to kindergarten students than when they were administered to Grade 1 students, and so on across the grades/grade spans. However, the mean p-values in higher grade spans show that the students in high school grades (Grades 9 through 12) might have similar language oral proficiency.

Tables 8.10 provides the descriptive statistics of vertically scaled item difficulty parameter estimates and student proficiency estimates from all field test items for oral and written language skills. Overall, the mean item difficulty for items that contributed to the oral language score ranged from -3.1 to -1.4 from easiest to hardest. The mean item difficulty for items that contributed to the written language score showed a wider range of -4.4 to 0.7, indicating that the reading and writing items showed larger mean difficulty difference across lower grades than the speaking and listening items. Average difficulty increased as the grade/grade span level increased. Similar to test difficulty, the mean proficiency scores increased as the grade/grade span level increased. The effect size was also provided by standardizing the grade-to-grade difference in the means by the square root of the average of the within-grade variances. The results indicated that there was a strong grade-to-grade difference in the mean scores between lower grades/grade spans but weak or no mean student proficiency score difference between higher grades/grade spans.

Figures 8.4 and 8.5 show the item bank (Test) characteristic curves (TCCs) for oral and written language scores that are the sum of item characteristic curves across all oral and written items in the item bank.

Because the number of items was different across different grade/grade span levels, the item bank characteristic curve is expressed in a percentage metric. The percentage metric item bank characteristic curve is on the 0–100 scale,

TABLE 8.9 Item p-values of Vertical Scaling (VS) Items (Averaged by Grade/Grade Span).

Language Skill	Domain	Item Responses	Grade/Grade Span						
			K	1	2	3–5	6–8	9–10	11–12
Oral	Listening	All items	.76	.85	.83	.81	.70	.67	.67
		VS items from on grade		.89	.83	.88	.74	.64	.65
		VS items from grade below		.80	.76	.82	.70	.64	.63
	Speaking	All items	.74	.84	.85	.89	.86	.82	.82
		VS items from on grade		.85	.88	.90	.88	.84	.78
		VS items from grade below		.73	.84	.85	.87	.84	.78
Written	Reading	All items	.73	.78	.79	.60	.51	.49	.53
		VS items from on grade		.86	.84	.83	.64	.45	.56
		VS items from grade below		.70	.72	.70	.52	.40	.52
	Writing	All items	.76	.87	.80	.72	.72	.72	.74
		VS items from on grade		.95	.83	.86	.73	.73	.74
		VS items from grade below		.74	.78	.73	.67	.70	.71

Note. If the vertical scaling items performed consistently with expectations, they should have appeared to be easier and have a higher average item score on the responses from on-grade students compared to the responses from grade-below students.

making it more comparable across grade/grade span levels. Except for the TCCs from grade spans 9–10 and 11–12, each TCC was suitably aligned sequentially as grade/grade span level increased. The gaps across TCCs of oral language scores were smaller than the gaps in written language scores.

The vertical scaling analysis results demonstrated that the IRT-based oral and written language scores could represent student progress in ELP from kindergarten through Grade 12. Based on the results, the reporting score scales for both oral language and written language were built to have a mean of 500 and a standard deviation of 70 with the range of 000 to 999. Then, the reporting scores were placed on a scale from 1000 to 1999 along with the thousands place as a prefix (See Figure 8.2).

Discussion

In order to generate technically sound scores with consideration of the intended uses of the scores, two major types of psychometric analyses were performed (dimensionality and vertical scaling analyses). These analyses, which were conducted during test development, also offered empirical evidence to strengthen

TABLE 8.10 Descriptive Statistics of Vertically Scaled Difficulty Parameter Estimates and Student Proficiency Estimates.

Language Skill	Grade/Grade Span	Number of Items	Number of Students	Item Difficulty Estimate				Student Proficiency Estimate				Effect Size
				Min.	Max.	Mean	SD	Min.	Max.	Mean	SD	
Oral	K	78	5,360	-5.46	1.73	-3.08	1.12	-7.31	2.45	-1.76	0.97	
	1	99	6,376	-5.87	-1.02	-3.04	0.97	-6.49	2.29	-1.06	0.92	0.69
	2	105	6,353	-5.11	1.30	-2.67	0.99	-4.86	3.80	-0.59	1.04	0.41
	3–5	111	6,040	-5.87	2.56	-2.42	1.23	-4.47	4.97	0.04	1.15	0.51
	6–8	114	5,675	-4.67	6.06	-1.74	1.60	-6.93	9.70	0.43	1.54	0.23
	9–10	118	6,090	-5.54	5.64	-1.67	1.71	-7.88	12.05	0.58	2.07	0.07
	11–12	118	5,181	-4.33	8.96	-1.39	1.72	-7.75	13.76	0.72	2.04	0.07
Written	K	61	5,339	-9.84	-1.86	-4.35	1.22	-8.68	1.82	-2.88	1.18	
	1	109	6,374	-5.97	-0.28	-3.12	0.97	-6.09	1.58	-1.51	1.03	1.00
	2	116	6,369	-3.67	0.72	-2.26	0.73	-5.41	3.54	-0.83	1.13	0.48
	3–5	121	6,077	-5.48	6.78	-0.73	1.49	-4.09	7.78	0.03	1.10	0.62
	6–8	124	5,762	-2.62	7.20	0.40	1.71	-4.09	7.74	0.60	1.15	0.51
	9–10	124	6,163	-2.98	8.91	0.55	1.70	-5.99	9.00	0.86	1.42	0.21
	11–12	124	5,199	-2.83	8.94	0.69	2.27	-4.66	11.00	1.18	1.30	0.24

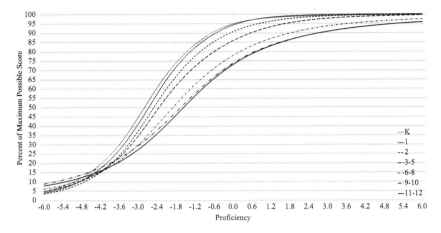

FIGURE 8.4   Percentage metric TCCs of oral language proficiency scores.

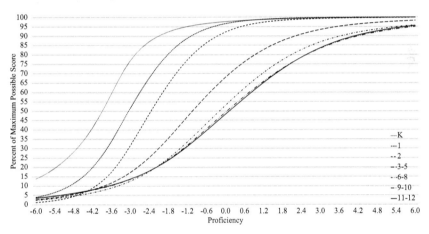

FIGURE 8.5   Percentage metric TCCs of written language proficiency scores.

a validity argument for the Summative ELPAC. That is, the results of these analyses support the claim that ELPAC scores can be used to monitor EL students' development of oral and written language proficiency across grades.

It is worth noting that both psychometric and practical issues were considered in determining the best-fitting dimensionality model for the Summative ELPAC. Key psychometric considerations were the number of dimensions, the relationship between dimensions, and the meaning of dimensions. Three of the four factor models included in the study were acceptable based on the model fit indices. Even though two of the factor models had slightly better statistical results for model fit, the oral and written factor model was selected because of three practical considerations: it allowed for shorter test length and testing time, it allowed for lower reading and writing score weights for kindergarten students, and it provided structural consistency across all grades/grade spans.

Additionally, the results from the dimensionality analysis yielded essential validity evidence regarding the internal structure of the Summative ELPAC. It is critical to evaluate the internal structure of the test to ensure that the structure is consistent with the defined constructs so as to facilitate appropriate test use and score interpretation (AERA, APA, & NCME, 2014). The dimensionality analysis results empirically evaluated the hierarchical structure of Summative ELPAC scores, supporting the conceptual framework suggested by the *CA ELD Standards.*

The dimensionality analysis was necessary but not sufficient to establish the intended use and interpretation of the test scores that satisfy the needs of the Summative ELPAC program. Both federal and California laws require that the state track the progress of student ELP from year to year. To satisfy this requirement, Summative ELPAC score reports need to provide information about ELP across grades/grade spans on a common scale that leads to valid interpretations of student progress. Thus, the vertical scale analysis was crucial to place Summative ELPAC scores from different levels of ELP on a single scale from kindergarten through Grade 12 to facilitate inferences about student growth.

In this study, the vertical scale analysis showed expected patterns of student performance across grades/grade spans, indicating that ELP was measured properly over time for a valid interpretation of student growth. Although there was a weak grade-to-grade difference in mean proficiency scores between higher grades (Grades 9–10 and Grades 11–12), overall both average item difficulty and mean proficiency estimates increased as the grade/grade span increased. As a result, appropriate information was provided in Summative ELPAC score reports for monitoring annual student progress in ELP, making instructional plans, and contributing to decisions about whether a student should be reclassified as fluent English proficient.

It is important to mention the limitations of our study, which are in turn worthwhile psychometric considerations for future study. In our study, four parallel field test forms were constructed to minimize the item pool exposure. A minimal student sample was selected for each form and each student completed only one form to limit the student fatigue and impact on instruction (1,250 to 1,500 students per form). The sparseness of data for each form and the complicated item sharing design limited the types of statistical analyses that were performed during the dimensionality analysis. For example, two different types of goodness of model fit indices (incremental and absolute measures of fit [Tucker-Lewis Index and Root Mean Square Error of Approximation]) were not performed during the field test analysis. It will be valuable to conduct a post-hoc dimensionality analysis using operational test data to determine whether additional analyses confirm the internal test structure established during the field test analyses. Collecting additional validity evidence in support of the measurement invariance of the oral and written language skills for subgroups (e.g., gender, ethnicity, native language, and test delivery mode) will be another interesting topic for future research since the measurement invariance study supports a valid score interpretation across subgroups.

References

American Educational Research Association, American Psychological Association, & National Council on Measurement in Education. (2014). *Standards for educational and psychological testing.* Washington, DC: American Educational Research Association.

Bachman, L. F., & Palmer, A. S. (1982). The construct validation of some components of communicative proficiency. *TESOL Quarterly, 16,* 449–465.

Bagozzi, R. P., & Yi, Y. (1988). On the evaluation of structural equation models. *Journal of the Academy of Marketing Science, 16,* 74–94.

Bailey, A., & Wolf, M. K. (2020). The construct of English language proficiency in consideration of college and career readiness standards. In M. K. Wolf (Ed.), *Assessing English language proficiency in U.S. K–12 schools.* New York, NY: Routledge.

Briggs, D. C., & Weeks, J. P. (2009). The impact of vertical scaling decisions on growth interpretations. *Educational Measurement: Issues and Practice, 28*(4), 3–14.

Cai, L. (2013). *FlexMIRT® 3.0: Flexible multilevel multidimensional item analysis and test scoring [computer software].* Chapel Hill, NC: Vector Psychometric Group, LLC.

California Department of Education. (2014). *California English language development standards, Kindergarten through grade 12.* Sacramento, CA: Author. Retrieved from www.cde.ca.gov/sp/el/er/documents/eldstndspublication14.pdf

California Department of Education. (2017). *Summative assessment test blueprints for the ELPAC.* Sacramento, CA: Author. Retrieved from www.cde.ca.gov/ta/tg/ep/documents/elpacadoptedblueprints.pdf

Educational Testing Service. (2009). *Guidelines for the assessment of English language learners.* Princeton, NJ: Author.

Every Student Succeeds Act. (2015). Every Student Succeeds Act of 2015, Pub. L. No. 114-95 § 114 Stat. 1177.

Faulkner-Bond, M., Wolf, M. K., Wells, C., & Sireci, S. (2018). Exploring the factor structure of a K–12 English language proficiency assessment. *Language Assessment Quarterly, 15*(2), 130–149.

Goodman, D. P., & Hambleton, R. K. (2004). Student test score reports and interpretive guides: Review of current practices and suggestions for future research. *Applied Measurement in Education, 17*(2), 145–220.

Hunsaker, R. A. (1990). *Understanding and developing the skills of oral communication: Speaking and listening* (2nd ed.). Englewood, CO: J. Morton Press.

Kenyon, D. M., MacGregor, D., Li, D., & Cook, H. G. (2011). Issues in vertical scaling of a K–12 English language proficiency test. *Language Testing, 28*(3), 383–400.

Kim, S. H., & Kolen, M. J. (2004). *STUIRT: A computer program for scale transformation under unidimensional item response theory models [computer software].* Iowa City, IA: University of Iowa.

Kolen, M. J., & Brennan, R. L. (2004). *Test equating, scaling and linking* (2nd ed.). New York, NY: Springer-Verlag.

Kunnan, A. J. (1995). *Test taker characteristics and test performance: A structural equation modeling approach.* Cambridge, England: Cambridge University Press.

Llosa, L. (2012). Assessing English learners' progress: Longitudinal invariance of a standards-based classroom assessment of English proficiency. *Language Assessment Quarterly, 9*(4), 331–347.

Sawaki, Y., Stricker, L., & Oranje, A. (2008). *Factor structure of the TOEFL internet-based test (iBT): Exploration in a field trial sample* (Research Report No. TOEFLiBT–04). Princeton, NJ: Educational Testing Service.

Stocking, M. L., & Lord, F. M. (1983). Developing a common metric in item response theory. *Applied Psychological Measurement, 7*(2), 201–210.

Tong, Y., & Kolen, J. M. (2007). Comparisons of methodologies and results in vertical scaling for educational achievement tests. *Applied Measurement in Education, 20*(2), 227–253.

Wolf, M. K., Guzman-Orth, D., & Hauck, M. C. (2016). *Next-generation summative English language proficiency assessments for English learners: Priorities for policy and research.* (Research Report No. RR–16–08). Princeton, NJ: Educational Testing Service.

Wolf, M. K., Kao, J., Griffin, N., Herman, J. L., Bachman, P., Chang, S. M., & Farnsworth, T. (2008). *Issues in assessing English language learners: English language proficiency measures and accommodation uses—Practice review* (CRESST Technical Report No. 732). Los Angeles, CA: University of California.

Yen, W. M. (2009). *Measuring student growth with large-scale assessments in an education accountability system.* A paper presented at the exploratory seminar: Measurement challenges within the Race to the Top agenda. Center for K–12 Assessment and Performance Management. Princeton, NJ: Educational Testing Service. Retrieved from www.ets.org/Media/Research/pdf/YenReactorSession1.pdf

Zenisky, A. L., & Hambleton, R. K. (2012). Developing test score reports that work: The process and best practices for effective communication. *Educational Measurement: Issues and Practice, 31*(2), 21–26.

9

VALIDATING THRESHOLD SCORES FOR ENGLISH LANGUAGE PROFICIENCY ASSESSMENT USES

Patricia Baron, Robert Linquanti, and Min Huang

In the United States, English Language Proficiency (ELP) assessments and standards are tools applied to measure and meet the long-term goal of successful academic achievement of English learner (EL) students in K–12 public schools (Bailey & Carroll, 2015). ELP assessment systems have been developed, both by consortia (e.g., the WIDA consortium and the English Language Proficiency Assessment for the 21st Century [ELPA21] consortium) and by individual states (e.g., California, Texas), to help EL students acquire the academic English language needed to engage with academic content and practices so they are prepared for college and careers.

Given EL students' need for English language support as part of preparation for college and careers, ELP assessment scores serve as criteria for determining which EL students need English language support, for monitoring EL students' English language development (ELD) progress over time, and as one source of evidence used for making reclassification decisions (i.e., exiting EL students from the EL designation). EL placement and reclassification decisions involve high-stakes uses of ELP assessments. Once students are classified as EL students, they are entitled to receive appropriate language support. Yet this support often takes time from academic subject learning. Furthermore, EL students must take a statewide ELP assessment annually until they meet the English-proficient level set using the ELP assessment. Therefore, during test design and development, decisions about measurement, scoring models and reporting of results must follow a rigorous process to determine adequate performance levels for EL students' ELP as well as their readiness to exit EL status. They must also maintain a focus on alignment to the ELD standards (Sireci & Faulkner-Bond, 2015).

This chapter describes such processes applied as part of the design, scoring and reporting decisions for one state's summative ELP assessment, the English Language Proficiency Assessments for California (ELPAC). Specifically, it describes empirical studies to validate the threshold scores determined from the initial standard-setting process during the development of the ELPAC. The threshold scores determined the four performance levels (PLs) that the ELPAC was intended to provide. A series of analyses was conducted, including consideration of the PLs from standard setting as a starting point for the state's English Proficient (i.e., reclassification from EL to former-EL) criterion. The validation studies described in this chapter provided triangulation across multiple sources of evidence, including expert judgment and empirical data, thus providing a model for using multiple sources in policy decision-making such as reclassification criteria for EL students. The multistep process undertaken to collect various sources of evidence increases confidence in decisions based on the threshold scores from the ELPAC. As noted earlier, the classification of EL students' ELP levels informs high-stakes decisions regarding students' ELD instruction, academic pathways, and school program funding. Thus, it is crucial to use multiple sources of evidence to triangulate the threshold scores for each ELP level.

Contexts of the Present Study: Timing for Setting and Validating Performance Levels

The ELPAC was designed to assess EL students in kindergarten through Grade 12 in California. The adoption and implementation in 2012 of new ELD standards in the state (California Department of Education, 2014) and development of a new ELP assessment (ELPAC) aligned to these standards necessitated a standard-setting process to evaluate EL students' ELP associated with the expectations of the CA 2012 ELD standards. This process included making decisions about PLs to measure ELD progress and determining an English-proficient performance standard to be used in EL reclassification decisions.

Since students' PLs should be reported soon after the first operational testing, setting the threshold scores and PLs was part of the ELPAC development process. Thus, once data were available from the ELPAC field test administration in summer 2017, a standard-setting workshop was conducted, and the resulting threshold scores were approved by California policymakers in November 2017 and used to report PLs for the spring 2018 Summative ELPAC administration. Considering that the initial standard setting utilized field-test data, not operational test data, additional studies were conducted both to validate the PLs and to determine the ELPAC score to be used for reclassification.

This chapter describes a strategy of conducting additional studies after the initial standard-setting workshop, once the first year of operational data became available. These subsequent steps used multiple data sources to triangulate across three methods, providing strong validity evidence of the appropriateness of the performance standard, allowing test developers, technical assistance providers, and state Department of Education (DOE) administrators to validate threshold scores and set policy for reclassification.

The two studies subsequent to the initial standard-setting workshop were (1) a study employing a student-focused standard-setting method known as Contrasting Groups (Livingston & Zieky, 1982) in which teacher judgments of student's ELP based on classroom performance are contrasted with the student's ELPAC assessment results and (2) a study that examined the performance of EL students on the ELP assessment (ELPAC) in relation to their performance on the state's English language arts (ELA) content assessment. The second study used the threshold scores determined by the state to set the English Proficient criterion for reclassification. We posit that taking into account the results from these two studies improved the alignment of threshold scores to educator expectations of EL students and their English-proficient peers, supported informed policy decision-making in setting an English-proficient standard aligned with ELA performance expectations, and increased the credibility and acceptance of the ELPAC and performance standards among educators in the nation's largest EL-enrolling state.

In this chapter we describe a sequence of activities, analyses, and decisions implemented, resulting in a first set of threshold scores for the Summative ELPAC utilized to report four PLs (i.e., Levels 1 through 4) in the first year of the Summative ELPAC, spring 2018 administration (hereafter called 2018 Summative) and a final set of threshold scores for the Summative ELPAC PLs and English-proficient criterion for use in the second year (2019 Summative). Figure 9.1 shows the multistep process undertaken over two years. First, ELPAC threshold scores and PLs were derived based on the standard-setting workshop (i.e., teachers' review of ELPAC items and spring 2017 field-test data). The recommended threshold scores and PLs were used to report four PLs for the 2018 Summative. Next, two studies (Contrasting Groups and data analyses of ELP and ELA content test scores) were conducted using 2018 Summative data. Revised threshold scores were proposed and approved based on findings from these two studies. A second round of data analyses was conducted by applying these revised threshold scores to the 2018 Summative ELPAC dataset. This second round of analyses was intended to facilitate an informed policy decision on an English-proficient criterion for EL reclassification. This reclassification criterion was applied and used beginning with the 2019 Summative assessment.

In the following sections, we delineate the design and results of the standard-setting workshop and the subsequent validation studies undertaken to determine evidence-based threshold scores for the ELPAC and to set policy for reclassification.

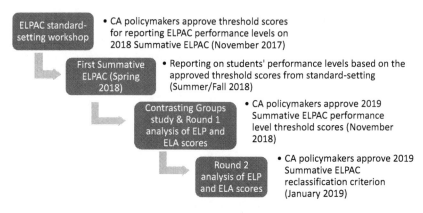

FIGURE 9.1 Sequence of standard-setting workshop, validity studies, and policy decisions.

ELPAC Standard-Setting

As described above, the purpose of the Summative ELPAC standard-setting workshop was to provide recommended threshold scores, to California policymakers and educators, that were to be used to classify EL students in kindergarten through Grade 12 into four PLs (i.e., Levels 1 through 4 with Level 4 being considered English-proficient). During the ELPAC development, the Summative ELPAC standard-setting workshop was convened, utilizing best-practice guidelines from the standard-setting literature (e.g., Hambleton, Pitoniak, & Copella, 2012) including the following:

- Careful selection of panel members
- Sufficient number of panel members to represent varying perspectives and provide for replication
- Sufficient time devoted to develop a common understanding of the assessment domain
- Adequate training of panel members
- Development of a description of the examinees at the threshold of each performance level
- Multiple rounds of judgments
- The inclusion of data, where appropriate, to inform judgments

The panels for the ELPAC standard setting included a diverse, representative group of California educators familiar with the CA 2012 ELD Standards and experienced in educating ELPAC examinees. Additionally, subject-area teachers working with EL students in Grades 6 and above were recruited to provide perspective on content-specific learning goals, which in California influence the classification of students as EL versus Reclassified Fluent English

Proficient (RFEP) students. Educator selection criteria thus included (a) having worked with EL students in the grade level(s) assigned to the panel, (b) familiarity with the CA 2012 ELD Standards, (c) having expertise in ELD, or having taught the subject areas of mathematics, science, and/or social studies. (For a thorough description of the standard setting workshop, see the Information Memorandum provided to the California State Board of Education in October 2017, available at www.cde.ca.gov/be/pn/im/documents/memo-pptb-adad-oct17item01.doc.).

Design of the Standard-Setting Workshop

The standard-setting workshop took place over four days. The process included a review and discussion of test items, the ELD standards, and performance level descriptors (PLDs) called General PLDs and Range PLDs. General PLDs describe overall performance expectations in each of four levels across all grades. The expectations defined the knowledge and skills measured by the ELPAC that differentiate students' PLs. Range PLDs more specifically define these expectations for each grade level. Educators worked in grade/grade-span standard-setting panels. They considered the assessment by domain and articulated the skills expected in reading, writing, listening, and speaking, as well as consideration of integrated scores (i.e., Written and Oral composite scores). Note that the ELPAC score report was designed to provide Written and Oral language scores rather than scores for each domain (listening, reading, speaking, and writing). Panelists evaluated students' Written composite scores (consisting of reading and writing items) and Oral composite scores (consisting of listening and speaking items) and made final threshold score recommendations by considering the interdependence of these skills.

Three standard-setting methods were utilized in the standard-setting workshop. For the Written composite score, the Bookmark standard-setting method (Lee & Lewis, 2008) was employed and for the Oral Composite score, the Performance Profile method (Morgan, 2003) was implemented. For the final judgments on the overall score, a holistic method developed for the ELPAC standard-setting process was employed, explicitly asking educators to consider information across domains as well as the integrated intention of the ELD standards (i.e., integrated language skills). By design, the Summative ELPAC and standard-setting methodology explicitly supported a treatment of skills *in combination* (e.g., Oral composite scores based on speaking and listening) rather than as isolated skills. In addition, panelists were advised that Overall Level 4 was the expected performance for students to be considered English-proficient and were reminded that the test score was only one of multiple criteria considered for reclassification.

In the final round of judgments, a panel of educators with representatives from all panels considered recommendations across the range of kindergarten through Grade 12. The result of the standard-setting workshop provided recommended threshold scores to allow four PLs to be reported for the two composite scores and the Overall Score in the ELPAC score report (for more details about the ELPAC score report, see Yoo, Wang, Anderson, & Zilbert, 2020, in this volume). The state DOE reviewed the threshold score recommendations, within and across panels, as well as the impact data reviewed by the panels. They also reviewed additional data (e.g., trends from the state's previous ELP assessment).

Standard-Setting Results and Recommendation for Validation Studies

The state Board of Education accepted the recommended threshold scores as preliminary for reporting scores on the first operational test, 2018 Summative ELPAC. Importantly, the state DOE requested that further analyses of the ELPAC be conducted when the first year of operational test data were available. It is a commonly recommended practice that statewide standardized assessments be used to determine performance level standards (see Geisinger & McCormick, 2010). As described earlier, the additional analyses included two types of validation studies: a Contrasting Groups analysis and two sets of analyses that examined the content-assessment performance (specifically in ELA) of EL students at the four ELPAC PLs determined by preliminary and subsequently revised threshold scores.

Study 1: Threshold Score Validation Study Using the Contrasting Groups Method

The Contrasting Groups study was designed to evaluate the degree to which the Summative ELPAC threshold scores and PLs were consistent with teachers' independent ratings about their students' ELP. That is, teacher judgments were contrasted with students' classifications based on Summative ELPAC scores. Teachers evaluated their students by classifying them on the basis of the ELPAC General and Range PLDs without knowledge of students' ELPAC scores. Teacher ratings of expected PLs were compared to those from the students' Summative ELPAC based on the preliminary threshold scores. Data were collected approximately six months into the 2017–2018 school year before the 2018 Summative ELPAC scores were available to teachers.

Note that the PLDs were the starting point for both the standard-setting workshop and the Contrasting Groups study, thereby maintaining the meaning of the PLDs for consistency and standardization. In both cases, Overall PL 4 was provided to the educators as the level that would be required on ELPAC for reclassification as English Proficient. The Contrasting Groups analysis compared students' Summative ELPAC scores to teachers' ratings. The degree of agreement between the preliminary threshold scores and the way teachers classified their students based on classroom observation is presented in the results.

Study Sample

The Contrasting Groups method (Livingston & Zieky, 1982) requires a large number of teacher ratings of students from a representative sample of local educational agencies (LEAs). It is also important to have ratings of students with a wide range of performance and to require a manageable number of student ratings from each teacher (i.e., 5–10) to not overburden teachers.

Sample recruitment was undertaken with the goal of obtaining a large, representative sample of EL students and the teachers working with those students. The recruitment effort aimed to obtain teacher ratings of students representing the full range across four ELPAC PLs. A key selection criterion was that teachers had *not* administered the operational ELPAC prior to providing their judgments. This was done to avoid biasing teacher judgments.

In the final sample, 1,521 teachers produced ratings for 11,128 EL students who later took the 2018 Summative ELPAC. Table 9.1 presents school size by total enrollment, for all California schools (state sample) and for the schools in the study (study sample). The study sample included a reasonable distribution of school sizes and school types.

The percentages of EL students by geographic region (North, Central, and South) and for the study sample are presented in Table 9.2. The study sample has the highest percentage of students in the southern region, as is the case for the state.

Student characteristics in the study sample were compared to the characteristics of all EL students who took the 2018 Summative (i.e., ELPAC test-taking population). In sampling students, efforts were made to ensure that the study sample was representative of the ELPAC test takers. For example, students' background characteristics were considered including gender, economic status, disability status, English Language Acquisition Status, and home language. Recruiting efforts for

TABLE 9.1 Number of Participating Schools by Total Enrollment.

School Size by Total Enrollment	Number and Percentage of Schools in Study	Number and Percentage of Schools in State
500 or less	136 (32%)	4700 (47%)
501–1000	194 (45%)	4046 (40%)
1001–2000	58 (14%)	903 (9%)
2001–3000	38 (9%)	339 (3%)
3001–4000	2 (0%)	39 (0%)
4001–5000	1 (0%)	6 (0%)

TABLE 9.2 Percent of California and Study Students by Geographic Region.

Region	EL students in California (%)	EL students in Study Sample (%)
North	8	9
Central	29	17
South	63	74

the study focused on students who were classified as EL students. The analysis of the percent of students in each PL based on ELPAC Overall Scores indicated that the sample was representative of the ELPAC test takers. The mean ELPAC overall scale scores for the two samples were comparable, and the standard deviation for the study sample was smaller. The performance of students in the study sample on ELPAC Overall Scores included a sample of greater than 100 students in each of four PLs for most grades, which is considered reasonable in a Contrasting Groups study (M. Zieky & P. Winter, personal communication, August 18, 2017).

To be consistent with the reference points used by the educators participating in the standard-setting workshop, teachers were provided the PLDs and asked to become familiar with these documents for their students' grade level. Participating teachers received an overview of the ELPAC, the types of scores provided on the ELPAC score report, and the manner in which Overall Score is calculated. Teachers were asked to provide the expected Overall PL for each student.

Study Findings

Table 9.3 displays cross-tabulations of the number of EL students classified in each ELPAC PL based on the teacher ratings versus the approved preliminary threshold scores from the ELPAC Overall Scores. The number of students classified as the same level by both methods is seen on the diagonal. For example, for kindergarten, 60 students were classified as Level 1 by both teacher rating and ELPAC scores. Table 9.4 provides a summary of the agreement by grade and shows the exact agreement and the sum of exact and adjacent agreement between teacher ratings and student PLs based on ELPAC Overall Scores. The results indicate a modest agreement between classifications on test performance and those based on teacher ratings.

Results from the rater-agreement analysis indicated a trend in PLs for most grades. Specifically, as illustrated in Table 9.3, the difference in PL classification between teacher ratings and the ELPAC using preliminary threshold scores

TABLE 9.3 Cross-Tabulation of Teacher Ratings by ELPAC Performance Levels.

Teacher Rating Level	ELPAC Level 1	ELPAC Level 2	ELPAC Level 3	ELPAC Level 4
Kindergarten				
Level 1	60	56	28	8
Level 2	33	85	76	78
Level 3	9	47	73	156
Level 4	2	8	28	96
Grade 1				
Level 1	55	37	34	4
Level 2	21	59	123	79
Level 3	2	17	80	187
Level 4	0	5	21	161
Grade 2				
Level 1	52	39	30	4
Level 2	14	67	159	80
Level 3	1	8	128	204
Level 4	0	0	23	165
Grades 3–5				
Level 1	203	117	39	5
Level 2	109	319	428	89
Level 3	29	138	544	271
Level 4	3	19	144	156
Grades 6–8				
Level 1	174	74	44	5
Level 2	85	187	263	121
Level 3	25	137	409	384
Level 4	3	22	148	287
Grades 9–10				
Level 1	158	29	10	2
Level 2	156	126	90	49
Level 3	38	130	198	168
Level 4	3	30	99	167
Grades 11–12				
Level 1	80	9	6	2
Level 2	99	86	82	23
Level 3	28	78	142	80
Level 4	8	24	58	91

TABLE 9.4 Percent Agreement between Teacher Ratings and ELPAC Performance Levels.

Grade(s)	Exact Agreement (%)	Exact or Adjacent Agreement (%)
K	37.2	84.2
1	40.1	86.0
2	42.3	88.2
3–5	46.8	93.0
6–8	44.6	90.7
9–10	44.7	90.9
11–12	44.5	89.8

shows that teachers placed their students at a *lower* level of performance than the ELPAC preliminary threshold score indicated, in particular for PL 4. The trend in ratings from the Contrasting Groups method suggested a higher threshold score for most grades. Acknowledging that different sources of evidence are sometimes inconsistent contributed to our recommendation that results across methods need to be considered together. The rater-agreement results contributed to the state reconsidering the threshold scores and, taken in concert with the first round of empirical analyses described next, provided sufficient evidence to warrant a change in policy.

Study 2: Analyses of the State ELP Assessment in Relation to the State ELA Assessment

In addition to the Contrasting Groups analyses described above, the state DOE requested additional analyses to examine the relationship between student performance on the state ELP assessment and the state ELA assessment. The goal of these analyses was to inform state policymakers in determining an English-proficient performance standard to be used in EL reclassification decisions for the 2019 Summative ELPAC administration and beyond. Such analyses are grounded in the conceptualization that ELP substantially influences performance on content assessments (e.g., ELA, mathematics, science) administered in English and that there is a discernible level of ELP beyond which ELP itself is no longer a substantial factor in EL students' performance on content assessments (Cook, Linquanti, Chinen, & Jung, 2012). Cook et al. suggest that this discernible level of ELP can be an indicator to determine the English-proficient performance standard.

The first round of ELP/ELA analyses examined the 2018 Summative ELPAC threshold scores developed from the standard-setting workshop. The state's ELA assessment reports four levels: Standards Not Met (Level 1), Standard Nearly Met (Level 2), Standard Met (Level 3), and Standard Exceeded (Level 4). The expectation is that EL students who attain a score on the ELP test that suggests they are English-proficient (i.e., Level 4 in the ELPAC assessment) will also demonstrate an equal likelihood (i.e., at least a 50% probability) of achieving a "Standard Met" score on the ELA assessment or have a comparable performance distribution to that of non-EL students. The combination of results from the Contrasting Groups and the first round of the ELP/ELA analyses described in this section were used by the state DOE and their state board to determine the threshold scores for reporting four PLs on 2019 Summative ELPAC and beyond. This round of analyses did not attempt to recommend an ELPAC performance standard for reclassification decisions.

The second round of ELP/ELA analyses served a somewhat different purpose; it was conducted after the state considered the results from the first round of analyses and the Contrasting Groups results. The sequence of analyses and policy decisions is depicted in Figure 9.1. Whereas the first round of ELP/ELA analyses focused on evaluating the threshold scores that determined the ELPAC performance levels, the second round of analyses, reported later in this section, informed the policy recommendation of the threshold score to be used in reclassification decisions for students taking the 2019 Summative and beyond. We provide here a description of the procedures and a brief summary of the results from the first of two rounds of analyses and then more detailed descriptions of the comparisons of ELP and ELA performance.

Data Sources

Our data set included a matched student-level data file containing (a) 2018 state ELA assessment data for all students in Grades 3–8 and 11, including overall scale score and PL results and (b) 2018 state ELP assessment data for all EL students in Grades 3–8 and 11, including scale score and PL results at the Overall, Oral (listening and speaking), and Written (reading and writing) composite levels as well as individual domain levels (listening, reading, speaking, and writing). Student data cases were required to have scores on both ELA and ELPAC to be included. Kindergarten to Grade 2 and Grades 9–10 and 12 were necessarily excluded from the analysis since state's ELA assessments were not administered in these grade levels.

Methods

Three analytical methods were employed, following the methods suggested by Cook et al. (2012):

1) **Descriptive box plot analysis** examines the distribution of overall scale scores on the state's ELA assessments for EL students by each PL on the ELP assessment. This analysis includes the distribution of overall scale scores on the state's ELA assessments for RFEP and non-EL students for comparison with current EL students. The purpose of the analysis was to identify an ELPAC PL where (a) EL students have an equal likelihood (i.e., 50% probability) of scoring at or above the ELA Level 3 (Standard Met) threshold or (b) EL students' score distribution on the ELA assessment is very similar to that of non-EL students statewide.

2) **Logistic regression analysis** estimates the probability of reaching Level 3 (Standard Met) on the state's ELA assessments for each ELP Overall Scale score. This approach helps to identify the ELP Overall Scale score range in which EL students have a 50% or greater probability of attaining that standard on the state's ELA assessment.

3) **Decision consistency analysis** analyzes ELP and ELA proficient-level categorizations and optimizes consistent categorization of EL students at or above the current ELA assessment threshold score for Level 3 (Standard Met). The analysis determines the ELP overall scale score range that maximizes the agreement between achieving ELP proficiency and ELA proficiency. The analysis takes the state's ELA Level 3 as given and determines the ELP Overall Score range that maximizes the percentage of agreement (i.e., proficient on state ELP assessment and "Standard Met" on ELA; not proficient on state ELP assessment and below "Standard Met" on ELA) and minimizes the percentage of non-agreement (i.e., proficient on ELP and below "Standard Met" on ELA; not proficient on ELP and "Standard Met" on ELA).

In what follows, we share two sets of analyses examining the distributions of EL students' overall PLs on the state ELP assessment and their relationship to EL students' test scores and PLs on the 2018 state ELA assessments—first using the 2018 Summative ELPAC threshold scores, then applying the 2019 Summative threshold scores to the 2018 Summative ELPAC. Both the ELP and ELA assessments were administered in 2018. In each round of analyses, findings from the three analytic methods largely converged. Given space limitations, only box plot analyses are discussed.[1]

Distribution of EL students by Overall Performance Level on ELPAC: Two Rounds of Analyses

The starting point for the first round of analyses was to examine ELP test results based on 2018 Summative ELPAC threshold scores; a total of 24% of ELPAC examinees across Grades 3–8 and 11 attained the 2018 ELP Overall PL 4, which was the ELPAC's intended threshold level for the English-proficient criterion. Figure 9.2 illustrates the distribution of EL students' ELP

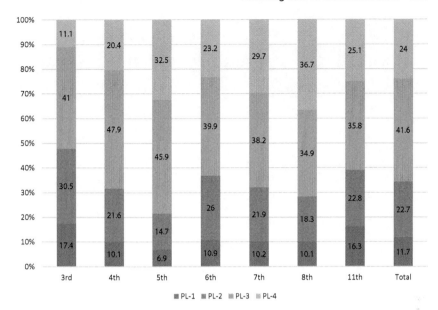

FIGURE 9.2 Distribution of EL students by ELPAC performance level (PL) and grade (2018 thresholds).

PLs by grade. As can be seen, EL students in Grade 3 had the lowest percentage of students at Overall PL 4 (11.1%), and the percentage increased from Grades 3 through 5. EL students' performance likewise increased from Grades 6 through 8, with higher percentages attaining Overall PL 4 compared to those tested in Grades 3 through 5. This performance pattern is not unusual in grade-span test forms where performance standards have been set by grade span. In the state's ELP assessment, the test forms were constructed by grade span (i.e., Grades 3–5, Grades 6–8).

In second-round analyses applying the 2019 summative ELPAC threshold scores, ELPAC examinees attaining Overall PL 4 on the 2018 ELPAC decreased to a total of 15.3% across all grades examined. While the proportion of examinees at Overall PLs 3 and 1 on ELPAC changed little in the examined grades (from 41.6% to 39.8%, and from 11.7% to 11.9%, respectively), the proportion of students at Overall PL 2 increased substantially (from 22.7% to 33.1%) under the 2019 threshold scores. Figure 9.3 illustrates the distribution of EL students' Overall PLs on ELPAC by grade. As can be seen, the new threshold scores, now set for each grade within grade-span test forms, yield more uniform proportions of EL students at each PL across grades, and effectively eliminate the "sawtooth" effect (i.e., performance outcomes rising across grades within a grade span, then dropping at the start of a new grade span) previously seen across grades within grade-span test forms where performance standards had been set by grade span.

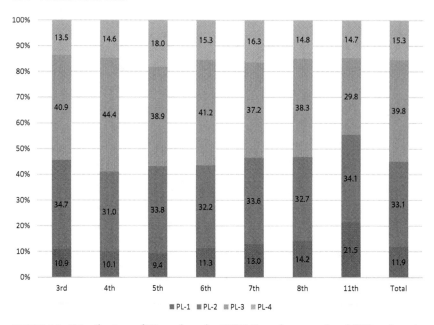

FIGURE 9.3 Distribution of EL students by ELPAC performance level (PL) and grade (2019 thresholds).

EL students' Performance on the State's ELA Assessment by Overall ELP Performance Level: Two Rounds of Analyses

First-round ELP/ELA analyses were conducted by grade level and largely converged across the three methods. Analyses suggested that, for Grades 4 through 8 and 11, after applying 2018 thresholds, EL students at Overall PL 4 on ELP assessments did not approximate an equal likelihood (i.e., 50% probability) of attaining Level 3 (Standard Met) on ELA assessment, nor did they approximate non-EL student performance. This is particularly so for EL students in Grades 7, 8, and 11. In Grade 3, EL students at ELP Overall PL 4 outperformed non-EL students and had a greater-than-equal likelihood of reaching Level 3 on the ELA assessment, suggesting that the ELP threshold scores for Grade 3 might be set too high.

Results from Descriptive Box Plots: Two Rounds of Analyses

Figure 9.4 displays box plots for Grades 4, 7, and 11, which examine the distribution of overall scale scores on the ELA assessment for EL students by each overall PL on ELPAC. The figure also displays the distribution of overall scale scores on the ELA assessment for comparison of non-EL students by language status: RFEP (former-EL students that have met multiple criteria to exit EL status); Initial Fluent English Proficient (IFEP, those language-minority students initially assessed as having sufficient English proficiency and never classified EL), and students initially identified based on the state home language survey as English-Only speaking students (EOs). As illustrated in Figure 9.4a, in Grade 4, the proportion of EL students at ELPAC Overall PL 4 attaining Level 3 on ELA drops below 50%, with median and mean scale score values that are slightly below those of their EO counterparts. Figures 9.4b and 9.4c illustrate that EL students at ELPAC Overall PL 4 in Grades 7 and 11, respectively, demonstrate substantially lower performance on ELA than their EO counterparts. This discrepancy is particularly so at Grade 11, where the proportion of EL students at Overall PL 4 attaining ELA Level 3 drops below 25%, with median and mean scale score values that are substantially below those of their EO counterparts. This result suggested that the ELPAC Overall PL 4 threshold scores at Grades 7 and 11 might have been set too low.

Second-round analyses also largely converged across methods. Analyses suggested that, across all grades tested on the state's ELA assessment, the performance of EL students at ELP Overall PL 4 improved under the 2019 Summative ELPAC threshold scores when compared to the 2018 threshold scores. That said, for Grades 5 through 8 and Grade 11, EL students at ELPAC Overall PL 4 still did not demonstrate an equal likelihood of attaining Level 3 on ELA, nor

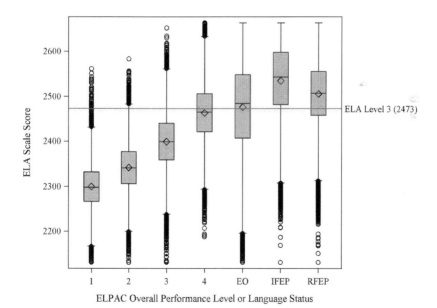

FIGURE 9.4a ELA performance by ELPAC overall performance level and EL status at Grade 4 (2018 thresholds).

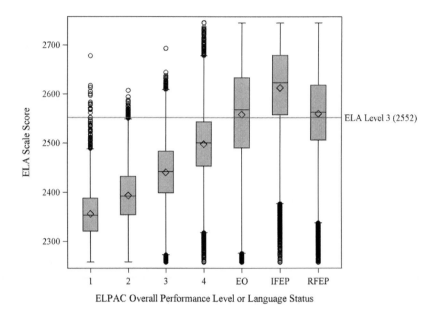

FIGURE 9.4b ELA performance by ELPAC overall performance level and EL status at Grade 7 (2018 thresholds).

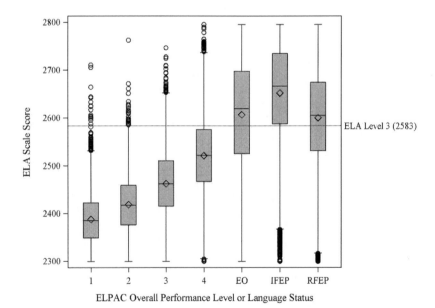

FIGURE 9.4c ELA performance by ELPAC overall performance level and EL status at Grade 11 (2018 thresholds).

did they approximate EO student performance, particularly EL students in Grades 7, 8, and 11. In Grades 3–4, EL students at ELP Overall PL 4 had an equal or greater likelihood of reaching Level 3 on ELA and of approximating or exceeding the performance of EO students on ELA.

Summary of Findings from Contrasting Groups and Two Rounds of ELP/ELA Analyses

The results from the Contrasting Groups study and the first round of ELP/ELA analyses conducted in fall 2018 suggested that raising the threshold scores, particularly the threshold demarcating ELPAC Overall PL 4, would allow the ELPAC PL 4 threshold to more closely approximate the PL estimations of EL students given by teachers and the achievement distribution of the monolingual EO students on the state ELA assessment. As a result, policymakers approved new threshold scores for the summative ELP assessment in November 2018. This decision triggered a second round of ELP/ELA analyses examining the achievement of EL students on the state's ELA assessment disaggregated by the Summative ELPAC performance levels using the newly adopted threshold scores (i.e., 2019 threshold). The results from the second round of analyses suggested that using these threshold scores would substantially reduce the percentage of EL students classified as ELPAC PL 4, which could result in fewer students exiting EL status. Subsequently, additional analyses were conducted to evaluate performance for subgroups of students on the state's ELA assessment; these are described below.

Comparing Performance on the State's ELA Assessment of EL students with ELPAC Overall PL 4 to Similarly Situated EO Students and New RFEP Students

Given that in several grades EL students meeting the higher ELPAC PL 4 performance threshold neither had an equal likelihood of scoring proficient on the ELA assessment nor approximated the performance of comparison groups (see Figures in 9.5 and 9.6, discussed below), we compared their performance to that of potentially more comparable subgroups within the EO and RFEP groups. Given that ELPAC PL 4 was considered a reclassification criterion, special attention was paid to this level for further analysis. Specifically, using the 2019 thresholds, we compared the performance of EL students scoring at ELPAC overall PL 4 to three subgroups of non-EL students on the state ELA assessment: (a) new RFEP students who were most recently reclassified (in school year 2016–2017) using locally determined district criteria in place across the state's LEAs; (b) EO students who are similarly situated to the EL student population with respect to economic disadvantage and disability status (that is,

EO students having both "economically disadvantaged" and "non-disability" status.); and (c) similarly situated new RFEP students (i.e., economically disadvantaged without disability status). Regarding similarly situated populations, the rationale for conducting these additional analyses was to consider factors (e.g., socioeconomic status, disability status) that are well documented to be negatively related to academic performance beyond ELP. Regarding new RFEP students, the aim was to consider those students who most recently exited EL status and are therefore most comparable to EL students that meet any proposed ELPAC exit criterion. For example, empirical research (e.g., Thompson, 2017; Umansky, 2016a, 2016b) in California and other states has shown that the longer students have been reclassified, the more likely they are to have received access to grade-level content instruction.

The results are illustrated in Figures 9.5a through 9.5c for the performance of EL students on the state's ELA assessments at ELPAC Overall PL 3 and PL 4 compared to (all) EO students and new RFEP students at Grades 4, 7, and 11, using the 2019 Summative ELPAC thresholds. Importantly, these figures depict the performance threshold for the state's ELA assessment Level 3 (with a solid line), as well as that for the midpoint of the scale score range for the state's ELA Level 2 (Standard Nearly Met) with a dashed line.

The results indicate that for all grades examined (except Grades 4 in Figure 9.5a and Grade 5 not shown), EL students at Overall PL 4 performed very similarly to new RFEP students on ELA. Specifically, they attained or exceeded an equal likelihood of scoring at ELA Level 3 in Grade 3 (not shown) and of scoring at the midpoint of ELA Level 2 in Grades 6 (not shown), 7 (Figure 9.5b), 8 (not shown), and 11 (Figure 9.5c). In Grade 5 (not shown), these EL students performed lower than EO and new RFEP students but still exceeded an equal likelihood of scoring at the midpoint of ELA Level 2. These results provided some support for the Overall PL 4 as the criterion for reclassification.

We repeated the above analysis using from each language group a subgroup of students that had both "economically disadvantaged" and "non-disability" status. The number and percent of each examined subgroup in Grades 3–8 and 11 matched data set satisfying these two "similarly situated" criteria are presented in Table 9.5.

When these similarly situated groups of EL, EO, and new RFEP students are compared, the performance gaps diminish between EL students at ELPAC PL 4 and new RFEP students, compared to EO students. Specifically, the performance of similarly situated EO students declines at all grade levels, while that of EL student and new RFEP students remains the same at Grades 3, 6, 8, and 11 and diminishes only slightly at Grades 4, 5, and 7. The results for students in Grades 4, 7, and 11 are illustrated in Figures 9.6a through 9.6c, respectively. These results provided additional support for using the Overall PL 4 as the threshold for reclassification.

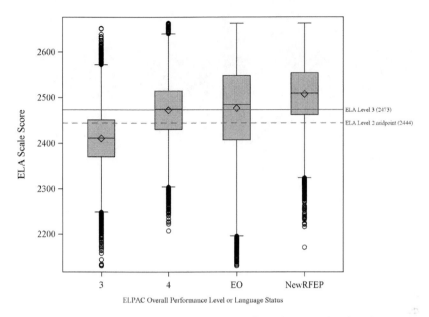

FIGURE 9.5a ELA performance by ELPAC overall performance level and EL status (EO and new RFEP) at Grade 4 (2019 thresholds).

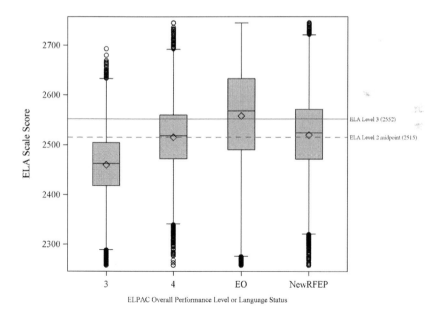

FIGURE 9.5b ELA performance by ELPAC overall performance level and EL status (EO and new RFEP) at Grade 7 (2019 thresholds).

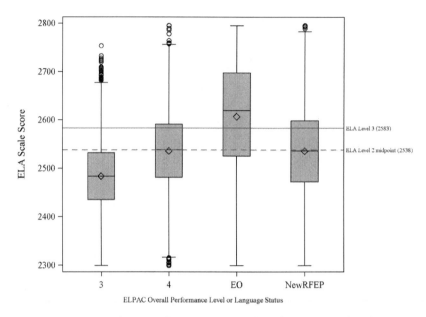

FIGURE 9.5c ELA performance by ELPAC overall performance level and EL status (EO and new RFEP) at Grade 11 (2019 thresholds).

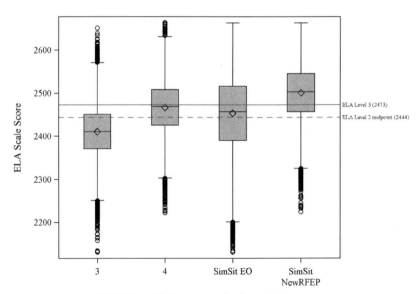

FIGURE 9.6a ELA performance by ELPAC overall performance level and EL status (similarly situated EO and similarly situated new RFEP) at Grade 4 (2019 thresholds).

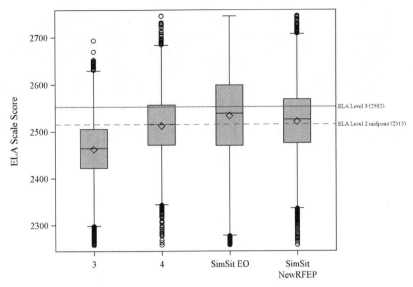

FIGURE 9.6b ELA performance by ELPAC overall performance level and EL status (similarly situated EO and similarly situated new RFEP) at Grade 7 (2019 thresholds).

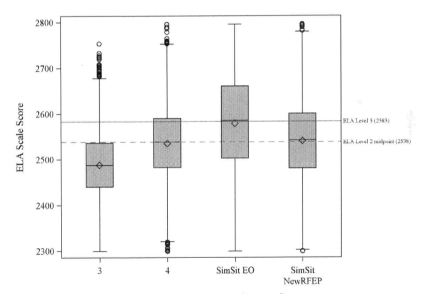

FIGURE 9.6c ELA performance by ELPAC overall performance level and EL status (similarly situated EO and similarly situated new RFEP) at Grade 11 (2019 thresholds).

TABLE 9.5 Number and Percentage of Economically Disadvantaged and Non-disabled Students among Each Subgroup, Grades 3–8 and 11 (2019 thresholds).

Subgroup	Total students	Economically disadvantaged and non-disabled students	Percent
EL students with ELPAC Overall PL=4	78,037	57,830	74.1%
English-only students (EOs)	1,785,409	716,985	40.2%
New RFEPs	136,605	106,282	77.8%

Summary and Discussion

Both the Contrasting Groups study and the ELP/ELA analyses summarized in this chapter were central to ensuring that threshold scores, used to measure ELD progress and to make EL reclassification decisions, were appropriately adjusted on the new ELP assessment of the nation's largest EL-enrolling state. By including both teacher judgments and additional student performance data, these analyses also ensured that the state's many stakeholder groups, including the state DOE and Board of Education, understood the implications of the ELPAC performance standard to be used for reclassification under changed threshold scores and through a transparent, public process, discussed and agreed on an English-proficient performance criterion that is rigorous and reasonable.

The results from the Contrasting Groups study and the first round of ELP-ELA analyses conducted in Fall 2018 suggested that increasing the threshold scores, particularly where ELPAC Overall PL 3 ends and PL 4 begins, would set the ELPAC PL 4 threshold to more closely approximate the PL estimations of EL students given by teachers and the achievement distribution of the EO students on the state ELA assessment. As a result, policymakers approved new threshold scores for the summative ELPAC. This decision triggered a second round of analyses examining the achievement of EL students on the state's ELA assessment disaggregated by the Summative ELPAC performance levels using the newly adopted threshold scores (2019 thresholds). The purpose of these analyses was to inform policymakers' decisions on the ELPAC English-proficient criterion to be used in EL reclassification beginning with the 2019 Summative ELPAC administration.

Initially, the goal of the ELP/ELA analyses was to identify a performance standard in which EL students at PL 4 showed an equal likelihood of performing at grade level on the state's ELA assessment and approximated EO student performance. However, analyses suggested that such a performance standard would greatly reduce the percentage of EL students deemed English proficient and, given the state's multiple criteria currently used for EL reclassification, would likely result in a substantial decline of students exiting EL status. This was due to the more rigorous 2019 thresholds adopted for the ELP assessment and to a more rigorous ELA assessment that the state of California adopted three years earlier, reflecting the increased academic and linguistic demands of the new college and career ready standards.

In additional analyses, we compared the performance on ELA of EL students scoring at overall PL 4 on the ELP assessment, using the 2019 thresholds to new RFEP students, as well as to similarly situated EO and new RFEP students. For all grades examined except Grade 5, EL students at Overall PL 4 performed very similarly to new RFEP students on ELA. When similarly situated groups of EL, EO, and new RFEP students are compared, the performance gaps further diminished between EL students at PL 4 and new RFEP students compared to EO students. These analyses also showed that EL students at Overall PL 4 attained or exceeded an equal likelihood of scoring at or above the midpoint of ELA Level 2. Such findings increased confidence in using Overall PL 4, the ELP criterion ultimately recommended and approved.

The findings from these supplemental analyses suggest that a balanced approach is merited in determining an English-proficient performance standard on the state's ELP assessment for EL reclassification. Using multiple measures, including classroom educator judgments and additional data analyses, provides alignment of threshold scores to educator expectations and allows an examination of convergence and divergence of evidence. Such an approach should examine the performance of EL students at the proposed standard in relation to ELA test performance with the following considerations: (a) the proportion that meet the standard, particularly when a state requires multiple criteria to exit EL status; (b) the performance of recently reclassified students as well as similarly situated students; and (c) the level of English proficiency necessary to ensure exited EL students can continue to progress both linguistically and academically on college and career readiness standards. Using this balanced approach, the evidence from these supplemental analyses supported policymakers in opting for a performance standard of Overall PL 4 on the state ELP assessment.

Setting performance standards for the state summative ELP assessment should include validity checks and consider the multiple uses of the performance levels. These assessments are used to measure and report on ELD progress for state and federal accountability as well as to determine which EL students should continue to receive ELD services. They are also used to set policy on the classification of students as EL students into ELP levels, which impacts school program funding as well as students' instruction. The validation studies reported in this chapter provide an example of a multistep process that might be used for continued validation research, which is important as the population of EL students in U.S. K–12 schools continues to grow.

Note

1 For the detailed findings of the ELA-ELP analyses, see www.cde.ca.gov/be/ag/ag/ yr18/documents/nov18item09.docx, for the round one analysis and www.cde.ca. gov/be/ag/ag/yr19/documents/jan19item09.docx, for the round two analysis.

References

Bailey, A. L., & Carroll, P. E. (2015). Assessment of English language learners in the era of new academic content standards. *Review of Research in Education, 39*(1), 253–294.

California Department of Education. (2014). *California English language development standards, Kindergarten through Grade 12.* Sacramento, CA: Author. Retrieved from www. cde.ca.gov/sp/el/er/documents/eldstndspublication14.pdf

Cook, H. G., Linquanti, R., Chinen, M., & Jung, H. (2012). *National evaluation of title III implementation supplemental report: Exploring approaches to setting English language proficiency performance criteria and monitoring English learner progress.* Washington, DC: US Department of Education, Office of Planning, Evaluation and Policy Development. Available from www2.ed.gov/rschstat/eval/title-iii/implementation-supplemental-report.pdf

Geisinger, K. F., & McCormick, C. M. (2010). Adopting cut scores: Post-standard-setting panel considerations for decision makers. *Educational Measurement: Issues and Practice, 29*(1), 38–44.

Hambleton, R. K., Pitoniak, M. J., & Copella, J. M. (2012). Essential steps in setting performance standards on educational tests and strategies for assessing the reliability of results. In G. J. Cizek (Eds.), *Setting performance standards: Foundations, methods, and innovations* (2nd ed., pp. 47–76). New York, NY: Routledge.

Lee, G., & Lewis, D. M. (2008). A generalizability theory approach to standard error estimates for Bookmark standard settings. *Educational and Psychological Measurement, 68*(4), 603–620.

Livingston, S. A., & Zieky, M. J. (1982). *Passing scores: A manual for setting standards of performance on educational and occupational tests.* Princeton, NJ: Educational Testing Service.

Morgan, D. L. (2003, November). *The performance profile method: A unique method as applied to a unique population.* Paper presented at the annual meeting of the California Educational Research Association, San Francisco, CA.

Sireci, S. G., & Faulkner-Bond, M. (2015). Promoting validity in the assessment of English learners. *Review of Research in Education, 39*(1), 215–252.

Thompson, K. D. (2017). What blocks the gate? Exploring current and former English learners' math course-taking in secondary school. *American Educational Research Journal, 54*(4), 757–798.

Umansky, I. M. (2016a). Leveled and exclusionary tracking: English learners' access to core content in middle school. *American Educational Research Journal, 53*(6), 1792–1833.

Umansky, I. M. (2016b). To be or not to be EL: An examination of the impact of classifying students as English learners. *Educational Evaluation and Policy Analysis, 38*(4), 714–737.

Yoo, H., Wang, J., Anderson, D., & Zilbert, E. (2020). Generating score reports: Psychometric issues to consider. In M. K. Wolf (Ed.), *Assessing English language proficiency in U.S. K–12 schools.* New York, NY: Routledge.

10

ACCESSIBILITY CONSIDERATIONS FOR ENGLISH LEARNERS WITH DISABILITIES IN ENGLISH LANGUAGE PROFICIENCY ASSESSMENTS

Danielle Guzman-Orth, Lorraine Sova, and Traci Albee

Inclusive and equitable assessments for all learners are necessary to ensure that students are meaningfully included and given comparable opportunities to demonstrate their language proficiency. Diversity and heterogeneity are well-known characteristics of English learner (EL) students in the United States. However, it is only recently that awareness has increased about other background characteristics like disability, which may impact how EL students acquire and demonstrate English language proficiency (ELP). English learners with disabilities (ELSWDs) range in prevalence across the nation (Guzman-Orth, Laitusis, Thurlow, & Christensen, 2016), but states' reporting of participation and performance of ELSWDs on their standardized content assessments (e.g., ELA and mathematics assessments) is still lagging behind that of non-ELSWDs. For instance, only two of 37 states reported participation and performance results for ELSWDs in the 2015–2016 school year (Albus, Liu, Lazarus, & Thurlow, 2018).

Including all students in statewide accountability systems can be challenging, and this is magnified with the need to produce valid and reliable assessments to measure ELP for all EL students, including ELSWDs and English learners with the most significant cognitive disabilities (ELSCDs; Every Student Succeeds Act, 34 CFR 299.17). The U.S. Department of Education has emphasized the need to ensure that ELSWDs and ELSCDs are appropriately included and accommodated on their ELP assessments (Rooney, 2017; U.S. Department of Education, 2014, 2015). An ELP assessment must be able to identify students as EL students, provide an indication of students' annual progress in their English language acquisition, and identify when students have demonstrated proficiency and may be considered for reclassification or removed from the EL designation (ESSA, 34 CFR § 200.14(b); Wolf, Guzman-Orth, & Hauck, 2016).

Despite growing emphasis on the importance of creating accessible ELP assessments for students, the practical need to balance standardization with individualization presents a test-design challenge. There is limited empirical research on standardized ELP assessments for ELSWDs, ELSCDs, and the educators who serve them (Guzman-Orth, Cavalie, & Blood, 2016). Efforts to ameliorate this practical and empirical knowledge gap are emerging, but more work is needed (Guzman-Orth, Cavalie, et al., 2016; Guzman-Orth, Laitusis, et al., 2016; Guzman-Orth & Sova, 2019; Shyyan et al., 2013; Thurlow, Liu, Ward, & Christensen, 2013; U.S. Department of Education, 2016).

The purpose of this chapter is to highlight key considerations and to provide guidance in designing accessible K–12 ELP assessments. We contextualize this guidance with findings from the literature and practice with examples from the California Department of Education (CDE) where this guidance was implemented in their ELP assessment development. Because this context focuses on ELSWDs taking the general ELP assessment (a statewide alternate ELP assessment is currently in development at the time of this writing), the ELSWD acronym will be used henceforth. In the following sections, we introduce the reader to a foundational background on ELSWDs. Next, we discuss accessibility issues in ELP assessment practice. Drawing from the literature and recent practices, we propose a set of recommendations to improve accessibility for ELP assessments and contextualize these recommendations with fairness and validity considerations. We close this chapter with implications for future research, policy, and practice.

English Learners with Disabilities

Adding complexity to the heterogeneity is the fact that disability characteristics vary widely and may be masked by students' language proficiency. Additionally, students' ongoing language development can result in delayed disability-identification due to the challenge in disentangling disability and language acquisition. Understanding the characteristics of ELSWDs is crucial to develop and use ELP assessments appropriately. Here, to orient the reader to important context on ELSWDs for the present chapter, we describe the ELP assessment context from California as a practical example of ELP assessment practice for ELSWDs and we articulate two critical, guiding beliefs about ELSWDs.

ELP Assessment Context for ELSWDs

Tensions exist between designing ELP assessments to meet multiple purposes while simultaneously meeting accessibility requirements. Adding to these tensions are the innovations in assessment design, such as using digital affordances to create more engaging task-based language tasks to simulate and elicit communication that is more authentic. Ultimately these competing tensions must work in concert and be balanced with the practical considerations for ELP assessment development (e.g., on time, on budget) and use in the field (e.g., time and cost to administer the assessment, administration training).

We use the English Language Proficiency Assessments for California (ELPAC) assessment development activities for the paper-pencil assessment as exemplars and use cases for accessibility steps for ELSWDs in the context of this chapter. Originally designed as a paper-pencil assessment in May 2019, the California State Board of Education approved the transition of the initial and summative ELPAC to a computer-based assessment (California Department of Education, 2019). Until this assessment is in operational use, however, the state continues to use the paper-pencil ELPAC. Borrowing heavily from the multi-tiered accessibility resources structure created for the state's content assessments, adaptations were made to ensure the accessibility resources on the ELPAC are appropriate for the students and the ELP construct. In addition, the State Board of Education approved the development of the Alternate ELPAC to measure ELP for students for whom the ELPAC, even with accommodations, does not provide enough access. Typically, these are ELSCDs, as determined by their individualized education program (IEP) (California Department of Education, 2019).

Assets-Based Perspective

ELSWDs can accomplish any academic or social goal by focusing on their assets and what they "can do," if they are provided with the necessary individualized support to do so (Trainor, Murray, & Kim, 2016). Expecting excellence and holding ELSWDs to the same high standards as their peers without disabilities is a critical mindset to help eliminate any deficit perspective. It is with these high expectations and standards in mind that we base our discussion on accessible ELP assessment practices for the remainder of this chapter.

Variability

Federal disability policy specifies 13 disability categories (Individuals with Disabilities Education Act, 2004) under which students are eligible to receive any protections or services identified in law. The disability categories are

- *Autism*
- *Deaf-Blindness*
- *Deafness*
- *Emotional Disturbance*
- *Hearing Impairment*
- *Intellectual Disability*
- *Multiple Disabilities*

- *Orthopedic Impairment*
- *Other Health Impairments*
- *Specific Learning Disability*
- *Speech or Language Impairment*
- *Traumatic Brain Injury*
- *Visual Impairment*

There is variability within each of these categories. Students will also present with different characteristics ranging in severity from mild presentations to significant presentations.[1] Additional disability labels are used in practice and taxonomies with which one can categorize disability-related information, but we focus our attention on the federally provided categories. Further, these categories are not discrete (i.e., students can have more than one disability), and students with the same disabilities do not equally benefit from specific accommodations (e.g., not all students with visual impairments read braille, not all students who are deaf/hard of hearing use manual communication systems). This variability is critical to attend to as it has the potential to significantly impact the accessibility and efficacy of accommodations on ELP assessments.

Designing Accessible Assessments

Numerous conceptual and theoretical frameworks exist to guide thinking and development processes for accessible assessment design and implementation. Underlying the commitment to accessibility are the foundational principles of fairness and equity (AERA, APA, & NCME, 2014; Educational Testing Service, 2015). Likewise, assessment validity is dependent on students' assessment scores reflecting their ability to access the content and demonstrate their knowledge, skills, and abilities with minimal confounding factors (e.g., Kane, 1992). With this overarching framework in mind, the following section outlines key considerations critical for ELSWDs.

Accessibility theory focuses on individual test taker characteristics and how they interact with individual items or the overall assessment (Beddow, 2012; Beddow, Kurz, & Frey, 2011; Ketterlin-Geller, 2008; Ketterlin-Geller & Crawford, 2011). These individual characteristics can be cognitive, linguistic, physical, sensory, or emotive. In concert, they can interact to introduce construct-irrelevant variance. Students' assessment scores may not be entirely reflective of their knowledge, skills, and abilities but rather of the extent to which students can access and interpret assessment content, with or without the use of an accommodation. Because this accessibility challenge is not something experienced equally by all students, any accessibility challenge could be considered unfair (Ketterlin-Geller, 2017).

One approach to promote fairness and accessibility in assessment is universal design through which multiple means of expression, representation, and engagement can be utilized (CAST, 2018). Universal design for assessment guidelines

(Thompson, Johnstone, & Thurlow, 2002) have been created to help minimize accessibility challenges in the development process by integrating accessibility from the initial stages rather than as a "fix" at the end of development. According to these guidelines (Thompson et al., 2002; pp. 6–20), assessment developers should

- acknowledge the target population of the assessment (including any special populations within the target population);
- design constructs so that each item measures what it is designed to measure (i.e., minimizing construct-irrelevant variance);
- ensure that items are accessible and non-biased;
- ensure that items can be accommodated without compromising the validity of the assessment scores;
- ensure that the instructions and general testing procedures are simple, clear, and intuitive;
- ensure that the language in the items is accessible and promotes maximum readability and comprehensibility (i.e., minimize construct-irrelevant variance for non-reading items); and
- ensure presentation details such as font, style, spacing, contrast, and white space do not become sources of construct-irrelevant variance.

Accessibility in ELP Assessment in Current Practice

Assessment Accommodations

Critically, students' needs are addressed through accommodations during the assessment administration to make content accessible *in addition to* attending to accessibility considerations at the design level (Liu & Anderson, 2008). Accommodations can help students access content and demonstrate their knowledge, skills, and abilities on the assessment. Historically, accommodations taxonomies included features that were categorized based on the types of support that was provided (e.g., linguistic support, equipment support; Thurlow, House, Scott, & Ysseldyke, 2000). In contrast, current accommodation structures in many large-scale state assessments in U.S. K–12 schools are designed as multi-tiered models for student access (PARCC, 2014; Smarter Balanced, 2014). In these multi-tiered models, access tiers are the distinguishing feature. Supports are available to students based on pre-identified need; common access tiers are similar to those three modeled in Figure 10.1. In Figure 10.1, the bottom tier illustrates *all* students have access to a range of supports (e.g., universal tools). On the middle tier, *some* students have access to more supports (e.g., designated supports). On the top tier of Figure 10.1, *few* students have access to a specific set of supports (e.g., accommodations, allowable through an IEP or Section 504 plan).

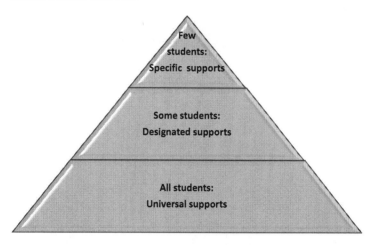

FIGURE 10.1 Illustration showing three access tiers of supports.

California is an example of a state that uses a multi-tiered access model to organize the accessibility resources on their statewide assessments. For the ELPAC paper-pencil assessment, this model outlines allowable resources available for all students (universal tools), some students identified by school personnel (designated supports), or few students including those with an IEP or Section 504 plan who are entitled to receive testing accommodations by law (accommodations; see California Department of Education, 2018). Since the ELPAC includes four different domain tests (listening, speaking, reading, writing), considerations specific to each domain are included such as whether read-aloud supports are allowed on the reading domain. Additionally, local education agencies (LEAs) could request unique accommodations for students with very specific needs beyond the comprehensive multi-tiered access structure. These multi-tiered access models are seen across many states and ELP assessment consortia such as English Language Proficiency Assessments for the 21st Century (ELPA21; ELPA21, 2018) and WIDA (2018).

Complex Interactions between Construct, Disability, and Accommodations

Despite the similarity in the structure of the accommodation guidelines across states and multi-state consortia, other decisions or design features may be challenging given that not all content can be appropriately accommodated to meet the diverse accommodation needs of ELSWDs. Particularly in the case of ELP content (generally measured in domains of listening, speaking, reading, and writing) certain cognitive or sensory disabilities present unique challenges to identifying and implementing appropriate, permissible accommodations for an ELP assessment.

Accommodations are numerous, and common examples like read aloud (digital or human reader) for students with mild cognitive disabilities (i.e., reading disabilities) as well as other commonly used resources (e.g., breaks, line readers) are now categorized as universal tools or designated supports, not accommodations. Although it is possible for an ELSWD with any disability to have difficulty on the assessment in any domain due to factors other than just the target construct (e.g., amount of directions, type of task, desired response format; see Guzman-Orth, Laitusis, et al., 2016 for more about EL students with cognitive disabilities), we focus on particular disabilities that may present more of a challenge to accommodate given the presentation of the ELP content.

One such example involves students with visual impairments taking ELP assessments. Visual impairment designations can include both low vision or blindness. Requiring students to interact with traditional ELP instructional and assessment content utilizing visuals and graphics poses significant challenges. Likewise, accommodating these visuals and graphics without cueing the construct adds further complexity to creating a universally designed ELP assessment. The visuals help to provide another means of input to support and, at times, minimize the language and/or cognitive load of any given task, particularly for very young students who are emergent readers (e.g., kindergarten, first grade, second grade). Options for ameliorating the accessibility challenges include removing the graphics completely, simplifying the graphics, and adding a text-based description (e.g., alternative text), to name a few. However, removing the graphics may reduce the authenticity of the assessment for sighted students. Instances like this demonstrate the need for *equitable* ELP assessment so that accessibility considerations are *balanced* for *all* students taking the assessment.

Validity and Fairness of ELP Assessments for EL students with Disabilities: An Example from One State

With the advent of the summative paper-pencil ELPAC administration, ETS, in collaboration with the CDE, conducted a research study using the cognitive laboratories (lab) methodology to investigate the accessibility of the ELPAC for ELSWDs. In this section, we use examples from this investigation to discuss key validity and fairness issues related to ELP assessments. For ELSWDs in particular, the validity of the assessment inferences is inextricably linked with fairness (AERA et al., 2014; Kunnan, 2004; Xi, 2010). Specifically, we present a select component of the cognitive lab study through the lens of the interpretive validity argument (Kane, 1992). While six inferences are commonly part of an interpretive argument, our discussion focuses on evaluation of the complexities in ELP assessment design and interactions with ELSWD test taker characteristics. This discussion also points to complex validity and fairness issues for assessment use. We close this section by highlighting a critical step taken to improve the ELP assessment experience for ELSWDs.

An ELPAC Cognitive Lab Study

The purpose of the empirical study was to gather evidence of the extent to which content was accessible and the accommodations were appropriate. The study findings yielded a number of suggestions and implications to improve ELSWDs' access to the ELPAC particularly regarding accommodations and directions for administration (Guzman-Orth & Sova, 2019).

Forty-two students from select high-incidence disability groups (speech language impairment, specific learning disability) and low-incidence disability groups (visual impairment, deaf/hard of hearing) participated in the study. Students demonstrated varying degrees of their disabilities and familiarity with their accommodations. A variety of data were collected including student background (detailing information about accommodations and teacher judgment), observers' ratings across key variables of interest, observers' field notes, interview responses from students and test examiners, and student responses from the test administration (e.g., writing samples, both print and embossed braille). The next subsection discusses the challenges and validity issues that emerged from the study.

Validity and Fairness Issues

Designed with the purpose of investigating the paper-pencil ELPAC for ELSWDs to provide recommendations for improvement, the ELPAC cognitive labs collected student feedback from a range of grade levels and disabilities. Interpreting observational measures from the data collected through the cognitive lab led to key inferences about student performance that are necessary steps for any fairness and validity argument (Chapelle, Enright, & Jamieson, 2010; Xi, 2010). In these arguments, claims that the observed performance or scores obtained during the ELP assessment administration reflect the students' language proficiency are further critiqued by key assumptions that are underlying the claim. Assumptions can include statements indicating that the ELP assessment tasks demonstrate construct representation for ELSWDs; the assessment administration procedures are appropriate for ELSWDs; and ELP assessment accommodations are appropriate for the construct and ELSWDs.

Fairness issues emerged from the cognitive lab evidence and impacted the validity of the claim (i.e., student performance is a measurement of language proficiency). Those issues also challenged underlying assumptions compared to the following observations:

- For students with visual impairments or are deaf/hard of hearing, the ELP construct may not be appropriately defined to be inclusive of ELSWDs who require use of language-based accommodations to function in English-based contexts. In other words, their language proficiency is measured through accommodations that are functioning as a moderating factor in the ELP assessment. At certain times, accommodation policies prohibited students from accessing the content. For example, test examiners noted that their students had not yet learned certain stylistic features in braille that are commonly used on a print version of a test (e.g., bold, underline, italics used to emphasize or denote special meaning in text) or that their students were in the process of learning more contracted braille, so they were more inclined to read the transcribed braille in an unintended fashion (e.g., instead of reading "Washington D.C." in a reading passage, a student got confused when reading it as "Washington do can"; or when reading answer options (A, B, C, D) students read them as "A. ... ., but ... ., can ... ., do ... ." since the abbreviated letters have alternative meaning in contracted braille). As a result, students were not always able to engage in a meaningful or authentic demonstration of their proficiency for English speaking contexts.

- Assessment administration procedures for ELSWDs, particularly for students who were deaf/hard of hearing, were generally unclear for both students and test examiners (both overall and task level) due to the minimal direction provided to interpreters to sign for the student.
- Accommodation efficacy was questioned for EL students with visual impairments when some students demonstrated significant difficulties reading their academic grade-level assigned braille codes (i.e., Unified English Braille uncontracted and contracted versions) as opposed to being allowed to select the braille code transcription they use in the classroom. Additionally, EL students who were deaf/hard of hearing experienced pervasive challenges with the selective allowance of the American Sign Language (ASL) accommodation, and instead reported the need for ASL support throughout the assessment.

Taken together, this evidence suggests that while the validity claim and assumptions may be supported for some target groups participating in this small-scale study (e.g., for EL students with speech/language impairments) the observations and inferences suggest emerging opportunities to improve assessment fairness and validity for EL students with visual impairments or who are deaf/hard of hearing.

Enhancing Validity and Fairness of ELP Assessments for ELSWDs

Evidence from this cognitive lab was used by the CDE to make numerous enhancements to the accessibility of the ELPAC. Key examples demonstrating this change were the actions taken to establish ongoing partnerships with stakeholders (e.g., advocacy groups, teachers, and parents of EL students with disabilities) so they are consulted on the accessibility decisions made for the assessment content before operational test administrations and to change state testing regulations to allow ASL on the ELPAC through the listening, speaking, and writing domains for both presentation of content and responses (California Code of Regulations, 2019). These examples are indicative of how California is implementing a continuous model of improvement and how other states might be better able to meet the needs of their students.

Recommendations to Improve Accessibility of ELP Assessments

Drawing from the evidence in the field, we present general recommendations for improvements to ensure maximal accessibility to the target range of students eligible to take general ELP assessments and not alternate ELP assessments (those specifically designed to meet the needs of ELSCDs).

Recommendations for accessible assessment development practices include the previously mentioned universal design considerations. However, because of the unique challenges in developing an ELP assessment for ELSWDs (as discussed previously) that is more universally accessible for all students, we discuss additional recommendations to consider in improving the accessibility of ELP assessments. Understanding that states and multi-state consortia may produce computer-based as well as paper-based assessments (such as those available for students needing specific accommodations), we view the recommendations presented in the next sections as applicable for both computer-based and paper-based contexts.

Clearly Define the Constructs to Be Measured in an Inclusive and Universally Accessible Manner

In addition to identifying the target population, it is necessary to provide an accurate, explicit definition of the construct(s) (AERA et al., 2014; ETS, 2015) to consider accessibility implications from design and onward. As federal legislation requires that ELP assessments measure the four language domains of listening, speaking, reading, and writing, many state ELP assessments are designed according to these four domains to meet accountability purposes. However, ELSWDs may access one or more of these language domains in non-traditional ways. For instance, students who are deaf/hard of hearing often experience challenges with ELP assessments because of the nature of the construct and the target skills to measure the construct. These students participate in mainstream settings through accommodations such as manual communication systems (e.g., sign language) or other assistive devices. In these instances, students may listen with their eyes and voice with their hands. This is in contrast to the typical sensory-oriented skills of listening with one's ears and voicing with one's mouth. Building on the previous recommendations, documenting the knowledge, skills, and abilities associated with the construct is necessary so that assessment developers can then design task types and develop items to fit with the allowed accommodations that precisely reflect the intended construct in a valid and reliable manner. When the construct is clearly defined, "all construct irrelevant cognitive, sensory, emotional, and physical barriers can be removed" (Thompson, Thurlow, & Malouf, 2004, p. 6).

Identify the Range of Test Taker Characteristics from Disabilities to Accommodations in Need

Critical issues related to accessible assessment development are assumptions that disabilities are static, well-defined categories and that accommodations are universally beneficial when assigned to students. To design an optimally accessible assessment for all students, it is critical to clearly identify and understand the target population of test takers (AERA et al., 2014; ETS, 2015). Sample questions to ask are *What is the likely range of disabilities of the target participants taking the assessment? What sensory or cognitive characteristics do these students use to listen, speak, read, and write in English-speaking contexts? What are their commonly used accommodations? What are the ages, language, cultural and educational backgrounds and how might these characteristics impact their accommodations? What are the characteristics of the test examiners who might serve these students and conduct the administrations of the accommodated ELP assessments?* Having these demographic and other characteristics of the test taking population detailed and documented at the onset allows for the design and development of appropriate and accessible items targeted to specific yet diverse groups of test takers.

Returning to our example of students with visual impairments, one possible path forward to enhance the accessibility of the assessment is to go beyond identifying the disability by acknowledging how the disability can manifest differently across students (e.g., low vision, blindness, congenital, early onset, late onset, etc.). These details may impact the range of accommodations that students have access to and are familiar with using. Taking this information into account, developing task types that are more universally accessible and avoid or minimize the use of graphics and avoid references to experiences that require visual acuity could be achieved sooner in the development process. Where graphics are determined to be necessary, art guidelines could be developed with this population in mind so that any graphics created could more easily be adapted into tactile graphics and/or picture descriptions could be written that are appropriate in terms of length, content, and the population, following standard braille and tactile graphic guidelines and for computer-based assessments, Web Content Accessibility Guidelines conformance (WCAG; see Web Content Accessibility Guidelines 2.0, 2019).

Include a Multidisciplinary Design Team

From the creation of assessment specifications through item development, assessment assembly, administration, and scoring, a multidisciplinary panel of experts should be engaged to evaluate the design and materials (inclusive of supporting documents, such as assessment blueprints and score reports) and advise on accessibility for the target population of test takers. This advisory panel should include accessibility, EL, and special education researchers and practitioners as well as additional experts (e.g., content-area specialists, educators of young learners) based on the construct(s) measured and the grade level(s) of the assessment. Working closely and collaboratively with item writers (i.e., educators, contractors, or other qualified professionals who author items) and assessment developers (i.e., qualified professionals who create assessments), the expert panel will help to ensure that the construct of the assessment, task types, items, and response options are designed to be maximally accessible to all test takers to the extent possible. The expert panel will recommend revisions to the design and items to enhance accessibility, and, where item adaptations are required, will help to ensure the adapted items parallel the original items to preserve construct and rigor.

Consider Appropriateness, Efficacy, and Opportunity to Learn in Accommodation Assignment

In some cases, the process of assigning accessibility resources to individual students is a challenging practice given the reality that accommodations are not uniformly appropriate and thus may pose a threat to the validity of the interpretation of test scores. In the context of next generation computer-based assessments, there may be some interactions with students' opportunity to learn assessment devices or digital versions of their accommodations (Guzman-Orth, Laitusis et al., 2016; Guzman-Orth, Supalo, & King, 2019). Additionally, changing standards and policies can have a lag-time for implementation in practice, evidenced in the recent shift in standard braille codes used in the U.S. Traditionally, English Braille, American Edition (EBAE) was the norm and used in instruction and assessment. Since 2015, the standard braille code changed from EBAE to UEB. This shift resulted in some students experiencing new difficulties taking assessments due to the change in braille standards and subsequent testing regulations (Guzman-Orth, Supalo, & King, 2019). As a result, the act of assigning a braille accommodation to a student who reads braille may have face validity, but the accommodation assignment lacks efficacy because the *implementation* may not be in the manner familiar to the student.

Determine Whether Domain Exemptions Will Be Needed

Born-accessible assessments are the goal, especially since accommodations may not provide enough support for ELSWDs. When the assessment is not sufficiently accessible and accommodations do not provide enough support, domain exemptions, or *selective participation* in ELP assessments (i.e., where a student may take some assessment sections but not others; see Christensen et al., 2014) may also be needed for some ELSWDs. For example, states who receive federal funding for ELP assessments may grant domain-level exemption(s) for which appropriate accommodations are not available to the student following ESSA requirements. One example of this is when EL students who are deaf/hard of hearing are exempted from the listening domain. This exemption is common when the construct definition is more traditional by constraining listening to an auditory act, in contrast with a more universally designed, inclusive definition that recognizes the practical act of students who are deaf/hard of hearing *listening with their eyes* (i.e., with the assistance of signed communication or printed text). In some cases (e.g., where federal or state regulations do not apply), assessment developers, along with the multidisciplinary advisory panel and other stakeholders, must determine whether selective participation should be allowed or those domains should be provided as a special version and/or following an alternative administration approach. Further questions to consider include *Should the listening domain of an ELP assessment be administered to students who are deaf or hard of hearing? How would listening be defined for this subgroup of test takers? What task type, item level, and/or administration adaptations might be necessary?*

Develop Guidance for Which Students May Need an Alternate Assessment

In some instances, designing an accessible assessment and pairing numerous accessibility features with that assessment will not be sufficient. Some of these students are ELSCDs, who "… may participate in a state's Alternate English language proficiency assessment if they cannot participate in the regular ELP assessment with accommodations" (U.S. Department of Education, 2018, p. 6).

Alternate ELP assessments are new to the field. Although one is currently in operational use (WIDA's Alternate ACCESS), limited empirical evidence exists about alternate ELP assessments or even background characteristics for those ELSCDs who qualify to participate in their state's alternate content assessments (Guzman-Orth, Cavalie, et al., 2016). In light of the federal mandates to ensure that ELSCDs are included in standards-based accountability assessments, the field is now coming together in response to these requirements. Advances in defining who these students are (Christensen, Gholson, & Shyyan, 2018; Thurlow, Christensen, & Shyyan, 2016), measuring background characteristics (Shyyan, Gholson, Mitchell, & Ceylan, 2018), designing standards (Michaels, Gholson, & Scheinker, 2018), and conceptualizing theories of action for alternate ELP systems (Gholson & Guzman-Orth, 2019) are emerging as states strive to design these alternate ELP assessments based on the latest information addressing the needs of ELSCDs.

Attend to Accessibility at Every Stage of the Assessment Design and Development Process

Accessibility should be considered during each stage of development, from the initial design work to the administration of the items. Assessments designed for maximum accessibility from the onset can "reduce the need for individualized accommodations, thereby reducing potential threats to validity across the test-taker population" (Elliott, Beddow, Kurz, & Kettler, 2011, p. 10). Key considerations for an iterative process of accessibility reviews during the design phase could include the following:

- Involve disability experts at the onset of the design work to articulate an inclusive target construct and comprehensive accessibility solutions, minimizing likelihood for ELSWDs to be unintentionally excluded and assessments needing retrofitting to allow access.
- Intentionally design tasks in concert with administrative considerations and allowable accommodations to promote maximum accessibility for the target population without compromising the construct, technical quality, or test taker engagement.
- Invite groups of disability experts and stakeholders for review and feedback of the assessment materials (e.g., teachers of the visually impaired; teachers of the deaf; teachers of students with multiple disabilities such as visually impaired and deaf/hard of hearing).
- Conduct systematic reviews for accessibility and usability with students, such as piloting and field-testing activities targeting all disability groups, accommodations users, and test examiners who administer these accommodated assessments.
- Continue collecting updated accessibility and usability evidence on the iterative changes made and revise assessment specifications as needed; repeat these steps for all content, and expand findings to accessible ancillary materials (directions for administration, practice tests, training tests, etc.) to ensure that students with disabilities have opportunities to access accommodated content and ancillary materials that are equitable to those of their non-disabled peers.

These key considerations for an iterative approach to enhancing the validity and efficacy of an accessible ELP assessment are imperative. Further, inclusion of diverse groups of stakeholders during the duration of the assessment development process can ultimately minimize the likelihood that content will introduce accessibility challenges for students during the operational assessment administration. Examples of publicly available instruments that enable the systematic review of items for accessibility are the *Test Accessibility and Modification Inventory* (TAMI; Beddow, Kettler, & Elliott, 2008) and the *TAMI Accessibility Rating Matrix* (ARM; Beddow, Elliott, &

Kettler, 2009). Documenting the attention and effort toward improving accessibility supports claims about technical quality and appropriateness for ELSWDs, an area under much scrutiny and evaluation by federal requirements.

While universal design is the gold standard, it is possible that even when adhering to these considerations, content may not be fully accessible to each test taker. Task type and item adaptations or special versions may still be needed. Our previous example of EL students with visual impairments taking graphics-heavy ELP assessments is one such instance where, despite all the attention to accessibility in the initial design phases, additional equitable versions may be needed to ensure meaningful presentation of the content for each student group (Guzman-Orth, Supalo, Pooler, & Sova, 2019).

Implications for Future Research, Policy, and Practice

Ongoing collaboration of policy makers, researchers, and practitioners from special education (including high-incidence and low-incidence experts with backgrounds such as teachers of students with visual impairments, teachers of students who are deaf/hard of hearing, teachers of ELSCDs), language development, and assessment fields is a critical next step to better serve ELSWDs and ELSCDs taking ELP assessments. Because of considerable heterogeneity in this student group, opportunities to increase and improve practices to better meet the needs of ELSWDs, ELSCDs, and the teachers who serve them.

Throughout this chapter, we have argued that creating accessible ELP assessments is critical for states to remain compliant with federal mandates. This act of creating accessible assessments is a complex process, and we have identified key challenges and considerations in this chapter. Further impacting this work is the need to specify *who* ELSWDs and ELSCDs are, ensure they are receiving access to high quality education, and ensure they are college-and-career ready to achieve post-secondary education or competitive employment.

In this section, we articulate directions for future exploration so that states may better meet the needs of their ELSWDs and ELSCDs. We recognize that some states are already beginning to examine the intersection of policy and practice, providing guidance to assist LEAs in serving their ELSWDs. One such approach to support LEAs is with ELSWD resource documents. The CDE has provided a resource document for voluntary use to support instruction for dually identified students, based on Assembly Bill 2785 and motivated by educators' needs (California Department of Education, 2019). Intentionally framing the supporting document as suggestions enables educators to exercise autonomy to pick and choose resources as they see fit, depending on their students' needs.

Additionally, we have stressed the importance of this work being a collaborative effort across multidisciplinary teams to create assessments, including supporting assessment policies and procedures and recommendations for score uses that are inclusive and equitable in nature. Complementing these efforts is the need to establish evidence for validity and fairness of the assessment for its intended uses with ELSWDs and ELSCDs. For instance, with our earlier example of challenges experienced by EL students with visual impairments taking ELP assessments, there are similar challenges associated with ensuring their assessment scores are a valid reflection of their English proficiency. One common approach to accommodate students is through twinning, one process for creating accessible items that are authentic to the experiences of the test taker (Guzman-Orth, Supalo, Pooler et al., 2019).

As noted earlier in the chapter, including visuals and graphics in ELP assessments is an authentic representation of language instruction, but the visuals and graphics are not authentic to the experience of students with visual impairments who are learning English. Embracing this variation and validating the student experience through twinning—creating comparable versions of the items that measure the same language construct and rigor through a means that is authentic and valid for the target test taker—is one such approach that is gaining awareness and traction in ELP assessment and other content areas (ELPA21, 2016; Guzman-Orth, Supalo, Pooler et al., 2019; Guzman-Orth & Sova, 2019). Similarly, efforts are being complemented with new strategies to attend to psychometric challenges of low-incidence disability n-counts that impact the range of traditional psychometric investigations needed for assessment development purposes (Ho, 2018; Winter, Hansen, & McCoy, 2019).

Spurred by the need to ensure that state accountability systems serve all students, we recognize that, at the time of this writing, the field has devoted unprecedented attention to accessibility and inclusion. This zeitgeist is the time for the field to come together to continue advancing the agenda to ensure equity for all EL students with disabilities.

Note

1 For the federal definitions of each disability category, go to https://sites.ed.gov/idea/regs/b/a/300.8.

References

Albus, D. A., Liu, K. K., Lazarus, S. S., & Thurlow, M. L. (2018). *2015–2016 publicly reported assessment results for students with disabilities and ELs with disabilities*. (NCEO Report 407). Minneapolis, MN: University of Minnesota, National Center on Educational Outcomes. Retrieved from https://nceo.umn.edu/docs/OnlinePubs/NCEOReport407.pdf

American Educational Research Association, American Psychological Association, & National Council on Measurement in Education. (2014). *Standards for educational and psychological testing*. Washington, DC: Author.

Beddow, P. A. (2012). Accessibility theory for enhancing the validity of test results for students with special needs. *International Journal of Disability, Development and Education, 59*(1), 97–111.

Beddow, P. A., Elliott, S. N., & Kettler, R. J. (2009). *TAMI accessibility rating matrix*. Nashville, TN: Vanderbilt University.

Beddow, P. A., Kettler, R. J., & Elliott, S. N. (2008). *Test accessibility and modification inventory*. Nashville, TN: Vanderbilt University.

Beddow, P. A., Kurz, A., & Frey, J. R. (2011). Accessibility theory: Guiding the science and practice of test item design and test-taker in mind. In S. N. Elliott, R. J. Kettler, P. A. Beddow, & A. Kurz (Eds.), *Handbook of accessible achievement tests for all students* (pp. 163–182). New York: Springer.

California Code of Regulations. (2019). 5 CCR § 11518.35 (e) (1). Westlaw.

California Department of Education. (2018). *Matrix four: Universal tools, designated supports, and accommodations for the English language proficiency assessments for California*. Sacramento, CA: Author. Retrieved from www.cde.ca.gov/ta/tg/ep/documents/elpacmatrix4.docx

California Department of Education. (2019). *California practitioners' guide for educating English learners with disabilities*. Sacramento, CA: Author.

CAST. (2018). Universal design for learning guidelines version 2.2. Retrieved from http://udlguidelines.cast.org

Chapelle, C. A., Enright, M. K., & Jamieson, J. (2010). Does an argument-based approach to validity make a difference? *Educational Measurement: Issues and Practice, 29*(1), 3–13.

Christensen, L. L., Albus, D. A., Kincaid, A., Christian, E., Liu, K. K., & Thurlow, M. (2014). *Including students who are blind or visually impaired in English language proficiency assessments: A review of state policies*. Minneapolis, MN: University of Minnesota, Improving the Validity of Assessment Results for English Language Learners with Disabilities (IVARED).

Christensen, L. L., Gholson, M. L., & Shyyan, V. V. (2018). Establishing a definition of English learners with significant cognitive disabilities (ALTELLA Brief No. 1). Retrieved from the Alternate English Language Learning Assessment website https://altella.wceruw.org/pubs/ALTELLA_Brief-01_Definition_070218.pdf

Educational Testing Service. (2015). *ETS standards for quality and fairness*. Princeton, NJ: Author.

Elliott, S. N., Beddow, P. A., Kurz, A., & Kettler, R. J. (2011). Creating access to instruction and tests of achievement: Challenges and solutions. In S. N. Elliott, R. J. Kettler, P. A. Beddow, & A. Kurz (Eds.), *Handbook of accessible achievement tests for all students: Bridging the gaps between research, practice, and policy* (pp. 1–16). New York, NY: Springer Science & Business Media.

English Language Proficiency Assessment for the 21st Century (ELPA21). (2016). *ELPA21 Blind and low vision information sheet*. Washington, DC: Author. Retrieved from https://elpa21.org/wp-content/uploads/2019/02/Blind-and-Low-Vision-Information-Sheet.pdf

English Language Proficiency Assessment for the 21st Century (ELPA21). (2018). *ELPA21 Accessibility and accommodations manual, 2018–2019 school year*. Washington, DC: Author. Retrieved from http://elpa21.org/wp-content/uploads/2019/02/18-19-AA-Manual.pdf

Gholson, M. L., & Guzman-Orth, D. (2019). *Developing an alternate English language proficiency assessment system: A theory of action* (Research Report No. RR-19-25). Princeton, NJ: Educational Testing Service.

Guzman-Orth, D., Cavalie, C., & Blood, I. (2016, April). *English learners with disabilities: Representation in the empirical literature for alternate assessments designed to measure alternate achievement standards (AA-AAS).* Poster presented at the Council for Exceptional Children Conference, St. Louis, MO.

Guzman-Orth, D., Laitusis, C., Thurlow, M., & Christensen, L. (2016). *Conceptualizing accessibility for English language proficiency assessments.* (Research Report No. RR-16-07). Princeton, NJ: Educational Testing Service.

Guzman-Orth, D., & Sova, L. (2019). *English Language Proficiency Assessments for California (ELPAC): English learner students with disabilities cognitive lab study* (Unpublished manuscript). Educational Testing Service, Princeton, NJ.

Guzman-Orth, D., Supalo, C., & King, T. (2019). *California science test cognitive lab study for students with visual impairments* (Unpublished manuscript). Educational Testing Service, Princeton, NJ.

Guzman-Orth, D., Supalo, C., Pooler, E., & Sova, L. (2019). *Adapting items for students with visual impairments: A conceptual approach to item twinning* (Unpublished manuscript). Educational Testing Service, Princeton, NJ.

Ho, M. (2018, June). ELPA21 accessibility and English language proficiency: Where are we now and what's next? In C. Laitusis, (Chair) (Ed.), *Accessibility and English language proficiency assessments: Where are we new and what's next?* Symposium conducted at the meeting of National Conference on Student Assessment, San Diego, CA.

Individuals with Disabilities Education Act of 2004. (2004). 20 U.S.C. § 1400 *et seq.*

Kane, M. T. (1992). An argument-based approach to validity. *Psychological Bulletin, 112*(3), 527.

Ketterlin-Geller, L. M. (2017). Understanding and improving accessibility for special populations. In A. A. Rupp & J. P. Leighton (Eds.), *The handbook of cognition and assessment: Frameworks, methodologies, and application* (pp. 198–225). Hoboken, NJ: John Wiley & Sons.

Ketterlin-Geller, L. R. (2008). Testing students with special needs: A model for understanding the interaction between assessment and student characteristics in a universally designed environment. *Educational Measurement: Issues and Practice, 27*(3), 3–16.

Ketterlin-Geller, L. R., & Crawford, L. (2011). Improving accommodations assignment: Reconceptualizing professional development to support accommodations decision making. In M. Russell & M. Kavanaugh (Eds.), *Assessing students in the margin: Challenges, strategies, and techniques* (pp. 105–126). Charlotte, NC: Information Age Publishing.

Kunnan, A. J. (2004). Test fairness. In M. Milanovic & C. J. Weir (Eds.), *European language testing in a global context* (pp. 27–48). Cambridge: Cambridge University Press.

Liu, K. K., & Anderson, M. (2008). Universal design considerations for improving student achievement on English language proficiency tests. *Assessment for Effective Intervention, 33*, 167–176.

Michaels, H. R., Gholson, M. L., & Scheinker, J. (2018, September). *ALTELLA standards prioritization process evaluation.* Retrieved from https://altella.wceruw.org/pubs/Standards-Prioritization-Evaluation.pdf

Partnership for Assessment of Readiness for College and Careers (PARCC). (2014). PARCC accessibility features and accommodations manual: Guidance for districts and decision-making teams to ensure that PARCC summative assessments produce valid results for all students. Retrieved from https://files.eric.ed.gov/fulltext/ED582054.pdf

Rooney, P. (2017). *U.S. Department of Education update on English language proficiency assessments.* Washington, DC: ESEA Network. Retrieved from www.eseanetwork.org/news-and-resources/blogs/others/u-s-department-of-education-update-on-english-language-proficiency-assessments

Shyyan, V., Christensen, L., Touchette, B., Lightborne, L., Gholson, M., & Burton, K. (2013). *Accommodations manual: How to select, administer, and evaluate use of accommodations for instruction and assessment of English language learners with disabilities.* Minneapolis, MN: University of Minnesota, National Center on Educational Outcomes. Available from www.cehd.umn.edu/NCEO/OnlinePubs/ELLSWDAccommodationsManual.pdf

Shyyan, V. V., Gholson, M. L., Mitchell, J. D., & Ceylan, I. E. (2018). *ALTELLA individual characteristics questionnaire.* Retrieved from http://altella.wceruw.org/pubs/ALTELLA-Individual-Characteristics_Tool.pdf

Smarter Balanced Assessment Consortium. (2014). Accessibility and accommodations framework. Retrieved from https://portal.smarterbalanced.org/library/en/accessibility-and-accommodations-framework.pdf

Thompson, S., Thurlow, M., & Malouf, D. B. (2004). Creating better tests for everyone through universally designed assessments. *Journal of Applied Testing Technology, 6*(1), 1–15.

Thompson, S. J., Johnstone, C. J., & Thurlow, M. L. (2002). *Universal design applied to large scale assessments* (NCEO Synthesis Report No. 44). Minneapolis, MN: University of Minnesota, National Center on Educational Outcomes.

Thurlow, M. L., Christensen, L. L., & Shyyan, V. V. (2016). *White paper on English language learners with significant cognitive disabilities.* Minneapolis, MN: University of Minnesota, National Center on Educational Outcomes, English Language Proficiency Assessment for the 21st Century. Retrieved from https://nceo.umn.edu/docs/OnlinePubs/AAATMTWhite%20Paper.pdf

Thurlow, M. L., House, A. L., Scott, D. L., & Ysseldyke, J. E. (2000). Students with disabilities in large-scale assessments: State participation and accommodation policies. *The Journal of Special Education, 34*(3), 154–163.

Thurlow, M. L., Liu, K. K., Ward, J. M., & Christensen, L. L. (2013). *Assessment principles and guidelines for ELLs with disabilities.* Minneapolis, MN: University of Minnesota, Improving the Validity of Assessment Results for English Language Learners with Disabilities (IVARED).

Trainor, A., Murray, A., & Kim, H.-J. (2016). English learners with disabilities in high school: Population characteristics, transition programs, and postschool outcomes. *Remedial and Special Education, 37*(3), 146–158.

U.S. Department of Education. (2014, July). Questions and answers regarding inclusion of English learners with disabilities in English language proficiency assessments and title III annual measurable achievement objectives. Retrieved from www2.ed.gov/policy/speced/guid/idea/memosdcltrs/q-and-a-on-elp-swd.pdf

U.S. Department of Education. (2015, January). Dear colleague letter, English learner students and limited English proficient parents. Retrieved from www2.ed.gov/about/offices/list/ocr/letters/colleague-el-201501.pdf

U.S. Department of Education. (2016). Tools and resources for monitoring and exiting English learners from EL programs and services (English learner toolkit). Retrieved from www2.ed.gov/about/offices/list/oela/english-learner-toolkit/chap6.pdf

U.S. Department of Education. (2018). *A state's guide to the U.S. Department of Education's assessment peer review process.* Retrieved from www2.ed.gov/admins/lead/account/saa/assessmentpeerreview.pdf

Web Content Accessibility Guidelines 2.0. (2019). *W3C World Wide Web consortium recommendation.* Retrieved from http://www.w3.org/TR/WCAG20/

WIDA. (2018). *2018–2019 accessibility and accommodations supplement.* Madison, WI: Board of Regents of the University of Wisconsin System. Retrieved from https://wida.wisc.edu/sites/default/files/resource/ACCESS-Accessibility-Accommodations-Supplement.pdf

Winter, P. C., Hansen, M., & McCoy, M. (2019). *Ensuring the comparability of modified tests administered to special populations* (CRESST Report 864). Los Angeles, CA: University of California, Los Angeles, National Center for Research on Evaluation, Standards, and Student Testing (CRESST).

Wolf, M. K., Guzman-Orth, D., & Hauck, M. C. (2016). *Next-generation summative English language proficiency assessments for English learners: Priorities for policy and research* (Research Report No. RR-16-08). Princeton, NJ: Educational Testing Service.

Xi, X. (2010). How do we go about investigating test fairness? *Language Testing, 27*(2), 147–170.

SECTION III

Some Future Considerations in K–12 ELP Assessment

11

USING AUTOMATED SCORING IN K–12 ENGLISH LANGUAGE PROFICIENCY ASSESSMENTS

Keelan Evanini, Yoko Futagi, and Maurice Cogan Hauck

There has been increasing interest in the use of automated scoring technology in K–12 English language proficiency (ELP) assessments in recent years. This rise in interest is due to a combination of an increased demand for these assessments, which stems from state requirements and growing populations of English learner (EL) students, and continued pressure to reduce scoring costs for state assessments. In addition, recent technological advances have led to dramatic improvements in automated scoring system performance, which has made it feasible to consider using the technology in new areas. As U.S. states and school districts begin to adopt automated scoring technology for K–12 ELP assessments, there is a need to ensure that applications of automated scoring adhere to best practices for reliability, validity, and fairness and that they meet the practical needs of students, teachers, and administrators. This can be a challenge because there are few resources that non-specialists can use to learn about the complex and rapidly evolving technology behind automated scoring systems. Also, since automated scoring is a relatively new field, shared standards for appropriate use of automated scoring have yet to be developed within the community. This chapter aims to address these gaps by describing the current state-of-the-art capabilities for automated scoring as applied in K–12 ELP assessments and by making recommendations to stakeholders to ensure a responsible and effective operational use of the technology.

In this chapter, we are using the term "automated scoring" to refer to a procedure for scoring constructed responses using statistical models that are "trained" using natural language processing (NLP), speech processing, and machine learning technology (the "training" process refers to estimating the parameters of the statistical models based on previously collected responses in order to optimize the model's performance on responses that weren't seen during the training process). This process is also commonly referred to as "Artificial Intelligence scoring" or "AI scoring," but those terms will be avoided in this chapter since they are often misinterpreted, especially by writers in the popular media, who tend to ascribe a higher level of "intelligence" to machine learning-based systems than is warranted. While automated scoring technology can be used for a wide range of constructed responses, this chapter focuses on automated scoring for extended written responses and monologic spoken responses. In this chapter, we will first briefly describe some of the main benefits and challenges associated with using automated scoring technology. Then, we will present the key technical components of automated scoring systems in a manner suitable for non-specialists and discuss the current state-of-the-art with regard to the application of automated scoring to ELP assessments. Finally, we will provide some recommendations about decisions that stakeholders need to make when considering the use of automated scoring for large-scale ELP assessments for K–12 EL students.

Benefits and Challenges of Automated Scoring

Several potential benefits can be realized through the use of automated scoring. The main considerations are typically a reduction in the expenses associated with the operational administration of the assessment and faster score reporting times. In addition, automated scoring systems can have a positive impact on the quality of scores; for example, automated scores can be combined with human ratings to produce a more reliable score (Breyer, Rupp, & Bridgeman, 2017).

However, despite recent advances in NLP and speech processing technology, automated scoring systems are still somewhat limited in their ability to evaluate the full range of writing or speaking proficiency characteristics that may be part of the targeted construct for an assessment. This shortcoming could reduce the validity of the automated scores. In addition, while the operational expenses of using automated scoring are typically quite low compared to human scoring for large-scale assessments, there may be substantial up-front costs associated with the development of automated scoring systems, such as collecting pilot data for training the scoring model, which would also need to be taken into account in a cost-benefit analysis. Furthermore, automated scoring systems can have specific infrastructure requirements for capturing and processing the constructed responses, such as ensuring that students' spoken responses are recorded digitally with high-quality audio and minimal background noise. Finally, there are some specific challenges associated with capturing, processing, and scoring constructed responses provided by young EL students that make automated scoring especially difficult for this population. For example, young EL students may not yet have sufficient keyboarding skills to type a written constructed response in a computer-delivered assessment. In addition, the characteristics of spoken language produced by young EL students differ substantially from those of adult speech due to physiological differences (e.g., shorter vocal tract lengths) and maturational differences (e.g., young learners' pronunciations in a second language may be influenced by their trajectory in the first language acquisition process); these differences can make automated speech scoring more challenging, since it can be hard to obtain a sufficient amount of training data to represent these differences from adult speech in the models. Furthermore, behavioral characteristics of young EL students can also lead to additional challenges for automated scoring in comparison to adults, including higher incidences of whispered speech, non-English responses, and very short or empty responses. These challenges have a real impact on the overall feasibility of an automated scoring approach since young EL students often make up a disproportionately large part of the K–12 EL population.

Automated Scoring System Components

This section provides an introduction to the main components that are used in automated scoring systems for both extended written responses and monologic spoken responses. This information is an important foundation for discussing the benefits and limitations of employing automated scoring systems specifically for K–12 ELP assessments. Figure 11.1 illustrates the four main components of a typical automated scoring system that will be discussed in this section: pre-processing, feature extraction, the scoring model, and the filtering model. These will be described in more detail in each of the following subsections.

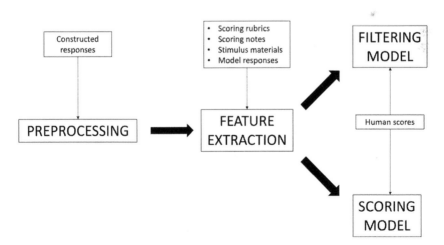

FIGURE 11.1 Schematic diagram of the main components of an automated scoring system.

Preprocessing

The first main component of an automated scoring system is the preprocessing step. This step may be used to transform the test taker's constructed response as captured in the test administration interface into a form that can be more easily processed by the automated scoring system. For example, an extended written response may be captured in a web-based interface and stored as an HTML document. Since most automated text scoring systems require the input to be in plain-text format, a preprocessing step of stripping out the HTML markup would be necessary. Additionally, if the assessment is delivered on paper, handwritten responses would first need to be converted to a digital representation using human transcription or optical character recognition technology; since these processes can be costly and error-prone, it is typically not recommended to use automated scoring for paper-based writing assessments. Similarly, for spoken responses, the digital audio capture component of the test administration interface may capture the audio file in a format that cannot be processed by the automated speech scoring system. In this case, a preprocessing step such as audio file format conversion (e.g., MP3 to WAV) or downsampling (e.g., 44,100 Hz to 16,000 Hz) may be required.

In addition, converting the spoken response to a text transcription using automatic speech recognition (ASR) is a necessary preprocessing step for most applications of automated spoken response scoring, and it is one that makes automated scoring overall somewhat more challenging for spoken responses than for written ones. The ASR system is based on a complex statistical model that takes into account the acoustic characteristics of phoneme pronunciations from EL students and word co-occurrence frequencies; ideally, this ASR model would be trained using a large data set of spoken responses produced by test takers who represent a population that is similar to the test takers whose responses will be scored by the system and who responded to similar test questions. Due to the wide range of variation exhibited in spoken language produced by EL students, state-of-the-art ASR systems still typically make more errors for this population than they do for native English speakers. In one study, Qian, Evanini, Wang, Lee, and Mulholland (2017) report ASR word error rate (WER) values of 21.0% for a picture-based narration task and 23.2% for a summarization task on a large sample of adolescent EL students from diverse L1 backgrounds who participated in a pilot data collection for the *TOEFL Junior®* Comprehensive speaking assessment. In another study, Cheng, Chen, and Metallinou (2015) report a WER value of 33.0% for open-ended spoken responses produced by K–12 EL students who took the K–12 ELP assessment in the state of Arizona.

In addition to these preprocessing steps, additional preprocessing can be conducted to extract further information about the spoken or written response that can be useful for evaluating speaking and writing proficiency. For a spoken response, this could include additional information about the speech signal, such as the pitch and intensity values. For a written response, this could involve steps such as automated part-of-speech tagging (to obtain part-of-speech labels, such as noun, verb, and adjective, for each word in the response) and syntactic parsing (to obtain a hierarchical tree representing the grammatical relationships between the words and phrases in the response). These preprocessing steps can also be applied to the output of an ASR system, although the resulting output may contain errors due to erroneous ASR output in the transcriptions.

Feature Extraction

After the necessary preprocessing steps have been completed, the feature extraction component of the automated scoring system analyzes the response to extract evidence that relates to the construct targeted by the task. As shown in Figure 11.1, this process typically takes into account the information that is used by human raters when scoring responses to the task, such as scoring rubrics, scoring notes, and information contained in the prompt and stimulus materials (e.g., reading and listening passages) as well as sample test taker responses. Then, NLP techniques are used to extract quantitative measures, referred to as "features," that relate to different aspects of the scoring rubrics and aim to approximate the human scoring process.

For evaluating writing quality in extended written responses, some of the most common features evaluate the writer's degree of control over writing conventions by detecting errors in grammar, usage, and mechanics as well as stylistic aspects of writing, such as excessive repetition of specific words. Burstein, Chodorow, and Leacock (2003) provide a description of some specific NLP-based features that are commonly used to evaluate writing conventions. In addition to evaluating writing conventions, NLP features can also be extracted to evaluate additional aspects of writing quality, such as discourse structure, for example, whether the test taker's response includes an introductory paragraph with a thesis statement (Burstein, Marcu, & Knight, 2003) and vocabulary usage, for example, the proportion of lower frequency and higher frequency words in the response (Attali & Burstein, 2006).

In addition to these basic types of features that address fundamental traits of writing quality, additional task-dependent features can also be extracted to assess aspects of writing quality that are relevant to specific tasks. For example, features that evaluate whether a test taker uses information from the source materials appropriately in the written responses have been shown to be effective for source-based writing tasks (Beigman Klebanov, Madnani, Burstein, & Somasundaran, 2014). Additionally, NLP features have been developed to assess a test taker's ability to produce effective written responses for specific genres of writing, such as argumentative (Nguyen & Litman, 2018) and narrative (Somasundaran et al., 2018) writing tasks.

For evaluating speaking quality in monologic spoken responses, features relating to speech delivery, such as fluency, rhythm, and pace, can be calculated by using information obtained from the time stamps of the words and phonemes in the response that are produced by the ASR system. In addition, measurements of pitch and intensity can be used to extract features relating to intonation, stress, and other prosodic characteristics that can influence a speaker's intelligibility and naturalness. Zechner, Higgins, and Williamson (2009) provide an overview of many specific features that have been developed to assess these aspects of delivery in spoken English produced by EL students. In addition to evaluating delivery, features relating to language use and meaning can also be extracted for spoken responses using NLP approaches similar to the ones used for extracting analogous features from extended written responses. The presence of errors introduced in the ASR preprocessing step can make it more challenging to extract features relating to language use and meaning for spoken responses produced by young EL students to open-ended speaking tasks, since the content of the ASR transcription may not correspond exactly to what the test taker said. However, substantial progress has been made in recent years to develop features to measure these aspects of speaking that are robust to potential ASR errors; some examples include features to evaluate vocabulary sophistication (Yoon, Bhat, & Zechner, 2012), grammatical errors (Lu et al., 2019), discourse coherence (Wang, Evanini, Zechner, & Mulholland, 2017), and content appropriateness (Xie, Evanini, & Zechner, 2012).

Scoring Model

After the features that measure different aspects of an EL's writing or speaking proficiency have been extracted from the response using NLP techniques, they can be combined to produce a single final score designed to match the score that a human rater would most likely give to the same response. The statistical approach that is used to weight and combine the individual features to produce a single score is referred to as the "scoring model," and its parameters are trained using a collection of responses scored by human raters.

Human raters typically provide scores on a numerical range with a small number of discrete score points, such as a 1–5 scale. When a discrete scale is used, scoring models can be trained either to output the same set of discrete scores as human raters (these models are referred to as *classification* models) or to output continuous numerical values such as 2.375 and 4.119 (these models are referred to as *regression* models). Most researchers and system developers use regression-based models and then round the continuous scores to the nearest integer if required for evaluation or score reporting purposes. For example, Loukina, Zechner, Chen, and Heilman (2015) describe an approach to building scoring models for an automated speech scoring system for spontaneous speech that uses a combination of linear regression and expert judgment that aims to maximize model performance while keeping the model simple and transparent.

Filtering Model

In any given operational deployment of automated scoring technology there will invariably be at least a small number of responses that have atypical characteristics that may impact the ability of automated scoring systems to provide accurate scores. To handle such responses, automated scoring systems may include another model, commonly referred to as a "filtering model," which flags atypical responses and filters them out of the standard automated scoring pipeline. These responses may be routed to human raters for review or undergo some other special processing.

Responses can have atypical characteristics for two types of reasons: ones related to test taker behavior and ones that are beyond the control of the test taker. Atypical responses that are due to test taker behavior include responses in which the test taker does not make a good faith attempt to respond to the question, for example, by providing an incomplete or irrelevant response, or by attempting to inflate the score through a gaming strategy. In addition, test taker responses may contain indications of psychological distress such as threats of self-harm. An automated scoring system would ideally be able to identify cases of potential crisis like this and route them immediately for special attention. Atypical responses that are caused by circumstances beyond the test taker's control may be the result of processing issues in the test administration interface (such as an incorrect text encoding for a written response or a microphone failure for a spoken response) or contextual factors (such as loud background noise that is recorded along with a spoken response).

Some specific types of atypical written responses for which filtering models have been developed include off-topic responses, responses that consist of random characters ("keyboard banging"), responses in languages other than English, responses in which the test taker has only copied the text of the prompt, responses that consist of plagiarized material, and responses in which the test taker uses complex vocabulary in a nonsensical or incoherent manner (Cahill, Chodorow, & Flor, 2018). Filtering models have also been developed for automated speech scoring systems for off-topic responses (Malinin, Van Dalen, Knill, Wang, & Gales, 2016), plagiarized responses (Wang, Evanini, Bruno, & Mulholland, 2016), non-English responses (Yoon & Higgins, 2011), responses for which the automated scoring model has a low confidence value (van Dalen, Knill, & Gales, 2015), and responses that have severe audio quality issues that could cause problems for the extraction of features related to speaking proficiency (Jeon & Yoon, 2012).

Automated Scoring Use Cases

While most K–12 ELP assessments are still scored exclusively by human raters, some pilot studies and operational assessments have implemented automated scoring approaches. In this section, we present case studies of a few of these applications of automated constructed response scoring systems for extended written responses and spoken responses in the K–12 ELP domain. For each case study, we briefly review the population that was targeted in the assessment, the task types included in the assessment, and the empirical results that were reported in publications describing the case studies. These publications, however, typically do not provide sufficient information to fully demonstrate of the reliability, validity, and fairness of the automated scoring systems, especially if they are being considered for operational use as a sole rater in K–12 ELP assessments. These limitations and considerations are discussed more thoroughly in the final section of this chapter after the case studies are presented.

Extended Written Response Scoring

The Test of English Language Learning (TELL) developed by Pearson Education was the first ELP assessment to use automated writing evaluation technology to score all of its written constructed responses tasks. It is a tablet-based assessment and consists of screener, diagnostic, and progress monitoring tests when purchased as a complete package. A white paper describing scoring procedures for the TELL assessment (Bonk, 2016) lists two types of extended written constructed response items: the "Write about the picture" item type for the grade band 1–2, and "Read and summarize" for the grade bands 3–5, 6–8, and 9–12. In the first item type, the student is asked to "write a description for the picture shown on screen." Items of this type are scored for the content of the responses. In the second item type, the student is asked to "read a text passage and then summarize it in writing, followed by a comprehension question." These items are scored for the content and language use characteristics such as grammatical complexity and vocabulary. Bonk (2016) reports that the human-machine correlations based on aggregating scores for all of the extended written response items in the Writing section are high (0.96–0.97) for all of the grade bands except kindergarten (0.38); however, human-machine agreement statistics for each individual extended written response item are not reported. As a comparison, the item-level human-human correlations for the "Read and summarize" item were 0.70 for the content trait and 0.59 for the language use trait, respectively.

Looking outside of the domain of operational uses of automated scoring, the William and Flora Hewlett Foundation sponsored the Automated Student Assessment Prize in 2012, which compared results from scoring engines from eight commercial vendors and one academic institution using the same eight essay prompts covering standard writing tasks from Grades 7, 8, and 10 (i.e., narrative, descriptive, persuasive, and source-based writing tasks). In terms of reliability, the summary of results by Shermis and Hamner (2013) shows that the scores produced by the engines that participated in the study generally correlated with human ratings at around the same level as human-human agreement (correlations ranged between 0.70–0.80 for most data sets). Demographic information was not available for the data set, so there was no EL-specific analysis. However, the study is still valuable, since controlled evaluations of multiple commercial automated systems on a standardized data set are rare.

In the domain of English as a foreign language (EFL) learners, Evanini, Heilman, Wang, and Blanchard (2015) examined an automated writing scoring system that was applied to responses from the *TOEFL Junior Comprehensive* assessment from ETS. This assessment was designed for adolescent EL students in EFL contexts and contains the following three writing task types that elicit extended written responses: (1) Email: the test taker reads an email message and writes a response; (2) Opinion: the test taker writes a paragraph presenting an opinion on the topic in the prompt; and (3) Listen-write: the test taker listens to a presentation about an academic topic and then writes an answer to a question about the content of the presentation. Evanini et al. (2015) applied *e-rater*®, an automated writing scoring system developed at ETS, to extract 10 features evaluating different aspects of writing proficiency, including grammar, word usage, and mechanics, among others (Burstein, Tetreault, & Madnani, 2013) in test takers' responses. The data were collected from test takers with an average age of 13.1 years representing 14 different L1 backgrounds. The automated scores produced using these features for the three TOEFL Junior extended writing tasks resulted in human-machine correlations of 0.67 (Email), 0.65 (Opinion), and 0.66 (Listen-write). In comparison, human-human correlations for the three tasks were 0.76, 0.72, and 0.79, respectively. When the scores for all five writing items on the assessment (including the three extended written responses and two constrained writing items) were aggregated for each test taker, the resulting human-machine correlation on the 1,244 test takers in the evaluation set was 0.83, compared to a human-human correlation of 0.90.

Spoken Response Scoring

One of the first applications of automated speech scoring in an operational K–12 ELP assessment is the system provided by Pearson Education for scoring the Arizona English Language Learner Assessment (AZELLA), the statewide K–12 ELP assessment used in Arizona. The speaking component of the AZELLA assessment is delivered over the telephone and consists of several different types of speaking tasks ranging from heavily constrained tasks (e.g., reading individual words out loud or repeating a sentence), moderately constrained tasks (e.g., providing instructions or giving directions from a map), to more unconstrained tasks (e.g., answering open-ended questions on a given topic). A technical report submitted to the Arizona Department of Education (Pearson Education, Inc., 2017) provides some details about how the automated speech scoring system was used in practice to score spoken responses to these tasks. The ASR component of the automated scoring system consisted of a model that was trained on 360 hours of children's speech. The automated scoring model included features that evaluated the appropriateness of the test taker's response as well as features that measured aspects of the test taker's speech delivery, including fluency and pronunciation. An evaluation was conducted on a set of 850 test takers (170 test takers for each of the five stages of the AZELLA assessment). After aggregating the scores from all speaking responses in the form at the candidate-level, human-machine correlations ranged from 0.85 to 0.95, with an average value of 0.92. These agreement results can be compared to human-human candidate-level correlations ranging from 0.92 to 0.99, with an average value of 0.97. No item-level agreement results are presented in the report, and it is not clear how many items were aggregated for each test taker to produce the candidate-level scores. Further details of the technical underpinnings of the automated scoring system used in the AZELLA assessment are provided in Cheng et al. (2015).

The TELL assessment from Pearson Education also employs automated scoring for spoken responses. Similar to the AZELLA assessment, the TELL assessment includes a variety of speaking tasks ranging from highly constrained to more open-ended, and different versions of the test are available for 5 different grade bands: K, 1–2, 3–5, 6–8, and 9–12. The only publication available that describes the technical components of the automated scoring system used in the TELL assessment appears to be the white paper that was described in the previous section (Bonk, 2016). TELL's automated speech scoring system includes features for assessing content appropriateness, delivery (pronunciation, fluency, and expressiveness), and reading accuracy (for read-aloud speaking tasks). On an evaluation set of 750 test takers (150 test takers for each of the five grade bands), the observed human-machine correlations for aggregated candidate-level scores were as follows: 0.70 (K), 0.79 (Grades 1–2), 0.85 (Grades 3–5), 0.77 (Grades 6–8), and 0.59 (Grades 9–12). The white paper also indicates that a filtering model based on the ASR model's confidence score was used to filter out problematic responses (such as ones with high levels of background noise or ones in which the test takers do not speak intelligibly) and that the human-machine correlations improved after these responses were excluded. However, this report also does not include item-level human-machine agreement scores or information about how many item-level scores were aggregated to produce the candidate-level scores.

Evanini et al. (2015) report on the performance of an automated speech scoring system that was developed based on a pilot administration of the speaking section of the *TOEFL Junior Comprehensive* assessment from ETS. The speaking section in this pilot administration consisted of the following four task types: (1) Read aloud: the test taker reads a paragraph out loud; (2) Picture narration: the test taker narrates a story based on a sequence of six pictures; (3) Listen-speak nonacademic: the test taker listens to a conversation about a school-related topic and provides a spoken response to answer a question about the content of the conversation; and (4) Listen-speak academic: the test taker listens to a presentation about an academic topic and provides a spoken response to answer a question about the content of the presentation.

The study used ASR models that were trained on 137 hours of spoken responses provided by 1,625 test takers in the pilot administration. These ASR models achieved WER results of 9.7% (Read aloud), 26.5% (Picture narration), and 29.4% (Listen-speak). The study employed SpeechRater®, an automated speech scoring engine developed at ETS, to extract 13 features that addressed the following aspects of the speaking proficiency construct: fluency, pronunciation, prosody, grammar, reading accuracy, and content appropriateness (Zechner et al., 2009). These features were combined using a linear regression scoring model, which resulted in the following item-level human-machine correlations: 0.70 (Read aloud), 0.62 (Picture narration), and 0.66 (Listen-speak); the corresponding human-human correlations were 0.70, 0.70, and 0.72, respectively. Each test taker responded to a total of five items for the four task types (the Listen-speak academic task had two items). When the scores for the five responses per candidate were aggregated to produce candidate-level scores for a subset of 374 test takers, the human-machine correlation was 0.81, compared to a human-human correlation of 0.89.

As demonstrated by this review of case studies of automated scoring for both written and spoken responses, the automated scoring systems can typically achieve levels of agreement that are near or equal to human-human agreement levels, especially when item-level scores are aggregated across many responses in a test section. On the surface, these empirical results seem to demonstrate the promise of automated scoring for operational use. However, the results presented in some of the studies may not paint a complete picture of the automated scoring system's reliability, validity, and fairness, especially if analyses of empirical performance are only conducted based on aggregated scores at the section-level; this is especially the case if the number of items included in the section is not reported. There are many challenges associated with automated scoring, in particular for K–12 ELP assessments, which typically are not discussed in much detail (or at all) in the case studies. Some examples of these are construct underrepresentation due to the inability of state-of-the-art automated scoring systems to adequately measure aspects of proficiency, such as discourse coherence and content appropriateness, that are important for common writing and speaking tasks, potential biases in the automated scores related to differential performance across population subgroups, and the ability of the system to handle atypical responses (such as responses in the test taker's L1 or whispered responses). The final section of this chapter will take a closer look at some of these considerations and how they relate to the empirical results that were presented in the case studies reviewed above.

Practical Considerations and Recommendations[1]

Thus far, we have described state-of-the-art automated scoring capabilities and several case studies that are relevant to K–12 ELP assessment. Due to the potential benefits of the technology, it is clear that the field is moving forward with exploring the use of automated scoring for large-scale, K–12 ELP assessments. In this section, we discuss key considerations and recommendations for stakeholders who are considering the use of automated scoring in this context (see Madnani & Cahill, 2018, for a more in-depth discussion of the priorities of different stakeholders and how they relate to automated scoring system development). We also argue that an automated scoring system for a K–12 ELP assessment should meet the following three criteria:

- It should support assessment of the construct in a reliable, valid, and fair manner;
- It should work practically and meet the needs of students, administrators, and score users; and
- It should make efficient use of available human, technological, and financial resources.

If a system meets these criteria for all of the tasks types included in an assessment, it can be labeled as "mature" and ready to be considered for operational use.

This section addresses a range of factors that contribute to these three criteria by discussing (1) assessment construct and task design considerations that affect the reliability, validity, and fairness of scores based on automated speech scoring; (2) scoring and score reporting considerations that influence how students, administrators, and score users interpret and use assessment results; and (3) automated scoring model development and test delivery considerations that have a practical impact on the use of available resources.

Assessment Construct and Task Design Considerations

The most important decisions are those about the aspects of the speaking or writing construct—that is, the test taker's knowledge, skills, and abilities—for which the assessment should elicit evidence. For K–12 ELP assessments, these decisions are based on the applicable standards for ELP for EL students. If an automated scoring system is used for the assessment, the system should be able to extract evidence that is related to the construct targeted by the task. Automated scoring tends to be most effective on tasks that are more constrained in nature, in which the content of the student's response is predictable from the content of the prompt. For open-ended tasks, automated scoring systems may not be able to extract features that cover the full range of the construct, such as whether a test taker has provided relevant details in a narrative writing task or whether a test taker has used appropriate argumentation strategies in support of a position in an argumentative writing task.

In the domain of automated speech scoring, mature automated scoring systems exist for task types that elicit constrained speech. One such task type is a read-aloud task, in which a test taker reads aloud a selection of printed text (word list, sentence, paragraph, etc.). Since the content is fixed, the main aspects of the speaking construct assessed by this task are pronunciation, fluency, and intonation. Mature systems can provide broad coverage of these aspects of the speaking construct and typically produce scores that correlate with human scores at or above human-human agreement rates. Automated scoring systems can therefore be used for tasks of this nature with a high degree of confidence in their reliability and validity. On the other hand, state-of-the-art automated speech scoring systems are not yet fully mature for most task types that elicit spontaneous speech, since the features they can extract related to vocabulary, grammar, content, and discourse do not typically assess all aspects of the targeted speaking construct.

Automated writing evaluation systems can also be considered on a similar continuum. Mature systems exist for evaluating writing quality, such as grammatical correctness and complexity, vocabulary use, discourse, and organization. Systems for automated evaluation of written content have been maturing rapidly in the recent decade as well, for item types in which the correct content can be pre-defined (e.g., science, math, reading comprehension). An example of a developing capability in automated writing evaluation is argumentation. ELP standards typically emphasize the importance of argumentative writing, in other words, the ability to persuade in written English. Research on argumentative features for automated writing evaluation systems has produced many features in recent years, and these features have been shown to improve the performance of automated scoring of argumentative writing (Nguyen & Litman, 2018). However, the rate of agreement with human raters and the coverage of the construct are not quite mature yet.

The strengths and limitations of automated scoring systems across the continuum create some interesting challenges for the design of speaking and writing tasks and the assessment of the related constructs. In order to increase the likelihood of success of an automated scoring system, it is advantageous to constrain the content of the student's response in some way. However, any ELP assessment must appropriately sample the applicable domain as defined in ELP curriculum standards that the assessment is designed to assess. Current ELP standards often emphasize the aspects of language proficiency that are required to express higher-order skills involving critical thinking, and these aspects of language proficiency are best assessed via assessment tasks that elicit spontaneous speech or extended writing and that match the target language use of the classroom. However, if an automated assessment system is not able to score responses to these tasks based on features that fully cover the targeted construct, then the scores that it produces will not be fully valid. Therefore, it is crucial to find a balance between these constraints when designing tasks to be included in an ELP assessment that employs automated scoring. The overall goal must be to ensure that scores on the speaking or writing domain, on the whole, support the claims that the assessment wishes to make regarding the ability of students.

Scoring and Score Reporting Considerations

Automated scoring technology can be used in a wide variety of ways to enhance English language learning and assessment for K–12 EL students, and there are several aspects of scoring and score reporting that need to be taken into account depending on how automated scoring is applied. One decision that needs to be made is whether automated scoring will be used as the sole scoring mechanism for an assessment (a *fully automated* approach) or in conjunction with human rating (a *hybrid* approach). A fully automated approach has great appeal, as it assumes that, once the scoring models have been built and appropriately tested, scores can be reported very rapidly (either instantly or within a small number of hours) and that incremental costs associated with scoring additional test takers are modest. However, unless the construct can be assessed appropriately by task types for which automated scoring is fully mature and/or the decisions to be made based on constructed responses scores are low-stakes in nature, it is very likely that some degree of human involvement will be necessary to ensure the validity of scores.

In addition to deciding whether to take a *fully automated* approach or a *hybrid* approach, further decisions need to be made about how the automated scoring system will be used in the process of producing the scores that are reported for the assessment. For example, the automated scoring system could report only *holistic* scores in which a single number is used to represent the overall success of the response, or also report *analytic* scores corresponding to different aspects of the speaking construct (such as pronunciation, fluency, and grammar) or the writing construct (such as writing conventions, organization, and elaboration). Furthermore, the scores can be reported at the *item-level* or at the *section-level*; item-level scores can provide more descriptive feedback about students' abilities, whereas a high-stakes summative assessment that uses a hybrid scoring approach would typically report only a single section-level speaking or writing proficiency score based on both item-level automated and human scores.

Automated Scoring Model Development and Test Delivery Considerations

Practical considerations related to automated scoring model development and test delivery also play an important role in deploying automated scoring capabilities in K–12 ELP assessments. First of all, it is crucial to ensure that high-quality data are available for training the automated scoring models. Aspects of data quality that are important for automated scoring model development include adequate human scoring agreement, appropriate score distribution, and demographics that closely match those of the overall test taker population. The quantity of data is important, too. Roughly speaking, a minimum of 1,000 responses per item is needed for training, and another 500 or more per item for evaluation, depending on the number of subpopulations of interest. In addition, at least 500 of the responses for evaluation should be double-scored by independent human raters (so that automated scoring performance can be compared to human–human agreement). Finally, a sufficient amount of time needs to be built into the schedule for deploying the automated scoring system operationally to account for model training and evaluation (which can take substantially longer if new features need to be added to the model to expand the construct coverage) and for system integration and testing.

While automated scoring has the potential to substantially reduce the cost of scoring by reducing or eliminating human scoring, there are several additional expenses associated with automated scoring that need to be considered. Some of the up-front costs of implementing an automated scoring system (i.e., those that would be incurred only once prior to the initial launch of an automated scoring capability) are as follows: test delivery hardware, data collection (pilot and field tests), obtaining human scores for training scoring models, and development and evaluation of the automated scoring system. In addition to these up-front costs, there also may be recurring operational expenses, such as IT infrastructure and ongoing monitoring of the automated scoring system's performance, which should be included in the annual budget for the assessment. Since the financial benefit of implementing an automated scoring system is realized when the up-front expenses are offset by the savings of not using human raters for operational scoring, automated scoring systems are most cost-effective for assessments that have high volumes of test takers.

Conclusion

Given the increasing numbers of EL students who are entering K–12 schools in the United States, a continued focus on cost savings in school budgets, and the recent improvements in speech and NLP technology, it is likely that many more states and school districts will consider the use of automated scoring technology in their K–12 ELP assessments in the near future. In preparation for this eventuality, we have attempted to provide technical as well as practical information to consider. Specifically, we have described (1) technical underpinnings of automated scoring systems, (2) automated scoring systems that have been developed for specific assessments, and (3) practical considerations that should help inform decisions about whether using automated scoring is appropriate for a given assessment.

Going forward, it is incumbent upon the research community to continue to conduct research to ensure that automated scoring systems produce reliable, valid, and fair results when applied to K–12 ELP assessments and to disseminate the results of these research studies in a transparent and comprehensive manner. First and foremost, it is important for researchers to continue to improve the speech and NLP technology components that make automated scoring possible. One main area that needs further attention is improving ASR models for spoken language produced by young EL students. While ASR systems have become quite accurate for spoken English produced by adult native speakers, generally they are still significantly less accurate for young EL students, especially if the speech is captured in an environment that contains background noise (a common characteristic of ELP speaking assessments administered in school settings). One reason for the lower performance of ASR systems for young EL students is the relative lack of data available for training ASR models for this population. Since it is difficult and costly to record speech produced by a large number of young EL students and since there are more privacy concerns about recording speech from children than from adults, it is likely that acquiring data for ASR model training will continue to be a challenge in the future. In addition to improving the ASR component in automated speech scoring systems, a substantial amount of research is still needed to improve the construct coverage of automated scoring systems for both speech and text. Many aspects of the construct, such as the appropriate use of argumentation strategies in persuasive writing tasks or the appropriate use of different formality registers for different interlocutors in speaking tasks, are currently not covered well (if at all) by the features that state-of-the-art automated scoring systems can extract. In order to increase the validity of automated scoring systems that are applied to constructed response tasks, it will be necessary to develop additional features that enable a more complete coverage of the construct targeted by the task.

In addition to improving the technological components of automated scoring systems, researchers also need to conduct additional studies about the fairness of automated scoring systems to ensure that they do not produce biased or inaccurate scores for any identified subset of the test taker population. Such studies, however, typically require a large number of test takers in order to support conclusions about the subgroup populations of interest, and it is only feasible to obtain large data sets of this nature through a large-scale operational administration of the assessment, not through a smaller pilot test. In order to address these potential concerns about fairness, as well as questions about reliability and validity due to construct underrepresentation, a responsible approach is needed. One such approach to implementing automated scoring for a K–12 ELP assessment would be to first implement a hybrid approach that uses the automated score as either a confirmatory score or a contributory score along with a score from a human rater. Then, only after sufficient evidence about the fairness, reliability, and validity of the automated scores is available, should there be a discussion about the possibility of using the automated scoring system as the sole rater.

Note

1 The section of Practical Considerations and Recommendations was largely adapted from Evanini, Hauck, and Hakuta (2017).

References

Attali, Y., & Burstein, J. (2006). Automated essay scoring with e-rater® V.2. *The Journal of Technology, Learning, and Assessment, 4*(3), 3–30.

Beigman Klebanov, B., Madnani, N., Burstein, J., & Somasundaran, S. (2014). Content importance models for scoring writing from sources. *Proceedings of the 52nd Annual Meeting of the Association for Computational Linguistics*, v. 2 (pp. 247–252). Baltimore, MD: Association for Computational Linguistics.

Bonk, W. J. (2016). Scoring TELL (Test of English Language Learning). Retrieved from www.pearsonassessments.com/content/dam/school/global/clinical/us/assets/TELL-WhitePaper-Scoring.pdf

Breyer, F. J., Rupp, A. A., & Bridgeman, B. (2017). *Implementing a contributory scoring approach for the graduate record examination analytical writing section: A comprehensive empirical investigation* (Research Report No. RR-17-14). Princeton, NJ: Educational Testing Service.

Burstein, J., Chodorow, M., & Leacock, C. (2003). Criterion^{SM} online essay evaluation: An application for automated evaluation of student essays. *Proceedings of the 15th Annual Conference on Innovative Applications of Artificial Intelligence* (pp. 3–10). Acapulco, Mexico: Association for the Advancement of Artificial Intelligence.

Burstein, J., Marcu, D., & Knight, K. (2003). Finding the WRITE stuff: Automatic identification of discourse structure in student essays. In Harabagiu S. & Ciravegna F. (Eds.), Special Issue on Advances in Natural Language Processing. *IEEE Intelligent Systems, 18* (1), 32–39.

Burstein, J., Tetreault, J., & Madnani, N. (2013). The e-rater automated essay scoring system. In M. D. Shermis & J. Burstein (Eds.), *Handbook for automated essay scoring* (pp. 55–67). New York, NY: Taylor and Francis.

Cahill, A., Chodorow, M., & Flor, M. (2018). Developing an e-rater advisory to detect Babel-generated essays. *Journal of Writing Analytics, 2*, 203–224.

Cheng, J., Chen, X., & Metallinou, A. (2015). Deep neural network acoustic models for spoken assessment applications. *Speech Communication, 73*, 14–27.

Evanini, K., Hauck, M. C., & Hakuta, K. (2017). *Approaches to automated scoring of speaking for K–12 English language proficiency assessments* (Research Report No. RR-17-18). Princeton, NJ: Educational Testing Service.

Evanini, K., Heilman, M., Wang, X., & Blanchard, D. (2015). *Automated scoring for the TOEFL Junior® Comprehensive writing and speaking test* (Research Report No. RR-15-09). Princeton, NJ: Educational Testing Service.

Jeon, J. H., & Yoon, S.-Y. (2012). Acoustic feature-based non-scorable response detection for an automated speaking proficiency assessment. *Proceedings of Interspeech 2012* (pp. 1275–1278). Portland, OR: International Speech Communication Association.

Loukina, A., Zechner, K., Chen, L., & Heilman, M. (2015). Feature selection for automated speech scoring. *Proceedings of the 10th Workshop on Innovative Use of NLP for Building Educational Applications* (pp. 12–19). Denver, CO: Association for Computational Linguistics.

Lu, Y., Gales, M. J. F., Knill, K. M., Manakul, P., Wang, L., & Wang, Y. (2019). Impact of ASR performance on spoken grammatical error detection. *Proceedings of Interspeech 2019* (pp. 1876–1880). Graz, Austria: International Speech Communication Association.

Madnani, N., & Cahill, A. (2018). Automated scoring: Beyond natural language processing. *Proceedings of the 27th International Conference on Computational Linguistics (COLING 2018)* (pp. 1099–1109). Santa Fe, NM: International Committee on Computational Linguistics.

Malinin, A., Van Dalen, R., Knill, K., Wang, Y., & Gales, M. (2016). Off-topic response detection for spontaneous spoken English assessment. *Proceedings of the 54th Annual Meeting of the Association for Computational Linguistics* (pp. 1075–1084). Berlin, Germany: Association for Computational Linguistics.

Nguyen, H. V., & Litman, D. J. (2018). Argument mining for improving the automated scoring of persuasive essays. *Proceedings of the Thirty-Second Association for the Advancement of Artificial Intelligence Conference* (pp. 5892–5899). New Orleans, LA: Association for the Advancement of Artificial Intelligence.

Pearson Education, Inc. (2017). *AZELLA: Arizona English language learner assessment* (2017 Technical Report). Retrieved from https://cms.azed.gov/home/GetDocument File?id=5c3c983d1dcb25108ca0dda6

Qian, Y., Evanini, K., Wang, X., Lee, C. M., & Mulholland, M. (2017). Bidirectional LSTM-RNN for improving automated assessment of non-native children's speech. *Proceedings of Interspeech 2017* (pp. 1417–1421). Stockholm, Sweden: International Speech Communication Association.

Shermis, M. D., & Hamner, B. (2013). Contrasting state-of-the-art automated scoring of essays. In M. D. Shermis & J. Burstein (Eds.), *Handbook of automated essay evaluation: Current applications and new directions* (pp. 313–346). New York, NY: Routledge.

Somasundaran, S., Flor, M., Chodorow, M., Molloy, H., Gyawali, B., & McCulla, L. (2018). Towards evaluating narrative quality in student writing. *Transactions of the Association for Computational Linguistics, 6,* 91–106.

van Dalen, R. C., Knill, K. M., & Gales, M. J. F. (2015). Automatically grading learners' English using a Gaussian process. *Proceedings of the ISCA Workshop on Speech and Language Technology in Education (SLaTE 2017)* (pp. 7–12). Leipzig, Germany: International Speech Communication Association.

Wang, X., Evanini, K., Bruno, J., & Mulholland, M. (2016). Automatic plagiarism detection for spoken responses in an assessment of English language proficiency. *Proceedings of the IEEE Workshop on Spoken Language Technology* (pp. 121–128). San Diego, CA: IEEE.

Wang, X., Evanini, K., Zechner, K., & Mulholland, M. (2017). Modeling discourse coherence for the automated scoring of spontaneous spoken responses. *Proceedings of the 7th ISCA Workshop on Speech and Language Technology in Education (SLaTE 2017)* (pp. 140–145). Stockholm, Sweden: International Speech Communication Association.

Xie, S., Evanini, K., & Zechner, K. (2012). Exploring content features for automated speech scoring. *Proceedings of the 2012 Meeting of the North American Association for Computational Linguistics: Human Language Technologies (NAACL-HLT)* (pp. 103–111). Montréal, Canada: Association for Computational Linguistics.

Yoon, S.-Y., Bhat, S., & Zechner, K. (2012). Vocabulary profile as a measure of vocabulary sophistication. *Proceedings of the Seventh Workshop on Building Educational Applications* (pp. 180–189). Montréal, Canada: Association for Computational Linguistics.

Yoon, S.-Y., & Higgins, D. (2011). Non-English response detection method for automated proficiency scoring system. *Proceedings of the Sixth Workshop on Innovative Use of NLP for Building Educational Applications* (pp. 161–169). Portland, OR: Association for Computational Linguistics.

Zechner, K., Higgins, D., & Williamson, D. (2009). Automated scoring of non-native spontaneous speech in tests of spoken English. *Speech Communication, 51*, 883–895.

12

TEACHERS' PERSPECTIVES ON THE USE OF SUMMATIVE ENGLISH LANGUAGE PROFICIENCY ASSESSMENTS FOR INSTRUCTIONAL PURPOSES

Alexis A. Lopez and Georgia Earnest García

The Every Student Succeeds Act (2015) requires states to develop an English language proficiency (ELP) assessment that focuses on state English language development (ELD) standards in English speaking, listening, reading, and writing and to administer it annually to English learner (EL) students. The ELP assessment should address several English proficiency levels, and it should correspond with the state college and career readiness standards in reading/language arts, mathematics, science, and social studies (ESSA, 2015; Wolf, Guzman-Orth, & Hauck, 2016). The ELP assessment is not supposed to overlap with content area assessments but instead reflect the English language demands necessary for EL students to attain the college and career standards in the specific academic domains. The state summative ELP assessments are primarily accountability measures (i.e., to measure students' progress in ELD, to inform appropriate educational placements, or to facilitate student reclassification). However, the ELD standards that underlie them are supposed to "assist teachers in moving EL students towards both proficiency in the English language and proficiency on a State's academic content standards" (U.S. Department of Education, 2016, p. 16).

Wolf and her colleagues (2016) predicted that the emphasis on college and career standards would result in increased academic and language expectations for EL students because the college and career standards require advanced and complex levels of language and academic tasks. Several researchers have argued that the instruction of EL students would also improve when summative ELP assessments were based on ELD standards and explicitly linked to the academic language demands involved in the state content-area assessments (Evanini, Hauck, & Hakuta, 2017). However, very few researchers have investigated the extent to which teachers of EL students have employed information from summative ELP assessments to inform their instruction.

While there is tension regarding the use of summative assessments for accountability and instruction purposes (Herman, 2007; Koretz, 2017; Wilson, 2018), current statewide summative assessments have also been designed to provide useful information for instruction. For example, guidelines for one of the summative ELP assessments that is currently used in the United States recommend that stakeholders use the assessment to provide information that enhances instruction and learning in programs for EL students (Center for Applied Linguistics, 2018). In this chapter, we present teachers' perspectives on using such summative ELP assessments for their instruction. In doing so, we discuss challenges and opportunities of utilizing summative ELP assessments not only for meeting accountability requirements but also for informing instruction. The chapter begins by briefly describing the current landscape of summative ELP assessments across states and prior research on how educators have viewed and employed summative ELP assessments. Then, we present an empirical study that we recently conducted to find out more about teachers' views and use of summative ELP assessments. The chapter concludes with a discussion of the findings and their implications for practice and future research.

Current Summative ELP Assessments

Due to the time and effort involved in developing ELD standards and summative ELP assessments that meet large-scale assessment requirements, 44 states have joined consortia to administer summative ELP assessments. At the time of writing this chapter, 37 states plus the District of Columbia had joined the WIDA consortium, while an additional seven states had joined the English Language Proficiency Assessment for the 21st Century (ELPA21) consortium. According to their states' Department of Education official websites, four other states have developed their own standards and summative ELP assessments (Arizona, California, Texas, and New York), while Mississippi and Connecticut are implementing the LAS Links exam.

We briefly describe the summative assessment delivery modes for two consortia and the scores that are provided. We focus on these two consortia as their summative ELP assessments are predominant in the nation. The information about the delivery modes and score reports provides an important context for readers to understand teachers' use of summative ELP assessments, which are described in the subsequent sections.

The ELD standards-based assessment developed by the WIDA consortium was named "Assessing Comprehension and Communication in English State-to-State for English Language Learners" (ACCESS for ELLs). ACCESS 2.0, delivered online, is the version that addresses the language demands in the college and career readiness standards. It evaluates EL students' social, instructional,

228 Alexis A. Lopez and Georgia Earnest García

and academic ELP according to their English listening, speaking, reading, and writing performance. ACCESS 2.0 reports EL students' scores according to six proficiency levels: Entering, Emerging, Developing, Expanding, Bridging, and Reaching (WIDA, 2017). ACCESS 2.0 also reports combined scores in oral language (listening and speaking), literacy (reading and writing), comprehension (listening and reading), and an overall composite score (which combines the listening, speaking, reading, and writing scores). Scores are also provided in the content domains of language arts, mathematics, science, and social studies.

The other consortium, ELPA21, has produced an online summative ELP assessment that measures EL students' English knowledge and skills in reading, writing, listening, and speaking (Washington State Office of Superintendent of Public Instruction, 2019). ELPA21 reports scale scores for each of the four domains, overall performance, and comprehension (listening and reading), which are classified into five levels of performance (Beginning, Early Intermediate, Intermediate, Early Advance and Advanced).

Educators' Views and Uses of Summative ELP Assessments

In this section, we review studies that have explored how educators view and use summative ELP assessments, and we discuss some of the challenges they face in using these assessments to make instructional decisions. The review begins by discussing the timing of the summative ELP assessments. Next, we discuss classroom practitioners' views and employment of summative ELP scores.

Assessment Timing

One of the major challenges involved in classroom practitioners' use of summative ELP assessment scores is the timing of the assessment (Hauck, Wolf, & Mislevy, 2016). For example, in Illinois, ACCESS 2.0 is administered every spring, usually during late January to early February. EL students in California annually take the California ELP assessment between February and May (Wolf et al., 2016). However, the score reports are usually delivered to schools months after their students take the summative ELP assessment, either late in the summer or in the following school year (Kim, Chapman, Kondo, & Wilmes, 2020). The significant time gap between test administration and score reporting makes it difficult for classroom practitioners to utilize the scores to inform their instruction because the scores might not reflect their students' current ELP levels (Kim et al., 2020).

Classroom Practitioners' Use of the Summative ELP Scores

Very few researchers have investigated how classroom practitioners interpret and employ the summative ELP scores of EL students. Kim et al. (2020) surveyed

1,437 educators to examine their perceptions of the meaningfulness and useful-ness of summative ELP assessment score reports. The researchers also inter-viewed 18 educators (12 EL teachers and 6 EL coordinators) from 13 different states about (a) how they interpreted the information in the score reports and (b) how they thought score reports could be improved. Although the educators reported that they had problems comprehending some of the technical termin-ology employed in the score reports (e.g., scale score, confidence band), they could comprehend and employ other types of information in the score reports (e.g., proficiency levels). However, they thought that some general education teachers might have difficulty interpreting scores because they did not under-stand the WIDA proficiency levels. Several of the educators suggested including additional information about students' past performance so they could assess how much the students had grown in their ELD over time.

Because students' performance on the summative ELP assessment and content-area assessments were not combined or linked, schools and teachers had to com-pile this information themselves. School personnel did not receive information that indicated how EL students at different proficiency levels performed on the content area assessments (Hauck et al., 2016). As a result, they did not know if the low performance of EL students was due to their lack of content knowledge and skills or to their low levels of English (Abedi, 2006).

Purpose of the Study and Research Questions

It is critical for teachers to provide adequate instruction to support the develop-ment of EL students' English language skills to give these students a better opportunity to succeed in U.S. schools. A report of the WIDA states' employ-ment of ACCESS 2.0 indicated that the increased language demands on the assessment resulted in more EL students being retained in English as a second language (ESL) or bilingual education services than in the past (Mitchell, 2017). For this reason, it is important to understand how classroom practitioners use the new summative ELP assessments to improve their instruction of EL students. The purpose of this research study was to report how classroom practitioners who taught EL students employed and viewed their summative ELP assessment. This study could shed light on how summative ELP assessments can shape teachers' instructional practices and on the types of instructional decisions they can make based on their students' scores on the summative ELP assessments. This study could also provide information about the types of difficulties teachers face in making use of the scores from summative ELP assessment for instruc-tional purposes. The following research questions guided the inquiry:

1. How did the content and delivery mode of a summative ELP assessment influence teachers' classroom practices?

2. What types of instructional decisions did teachers make based on their EL students' scores on the summative ELP assessment?
3. What factors affected teachers' use of student scores on the summative ELP assessments for instructional purposes?

Methods

We used a qualitative research design in our study because our focus was to understand how teachers use summative ELP assessments to inform their instruction. This exploratory qualitative research design allowed us to have a rich understanding of the teachers' viewpoints using in-depth semi-structured interviews. Below we describe the participants, the interview procedure, and data analysis.

Participants

For this study, we used a convenience sample technique to recruit participants. This means that we did not randomly sample a population for our participants. Instead, we invited all the ESL teachers that had previously participated in other studies that we conducted. We also asked some of our partners or consultants to suggest names of ESL teachers. These teachers also suggested other potential participants. We targeted language teachers with ESL endorsements in grades K–12 who taught in ESL or bilingual programs. We recruited both primary and secondary teachers from different grades, with a few teaching at both levels. Eighteen ESL teachers from three states (New Jersey, Illinois, and North Carolina) participated in the study. Table 12.1 shows background information on the participating teachers. As shown in Table 12.1, most of the teachers worked in different types of ESL programs (self-contained, sheltered, push-in, and pull-out; see note in Table 12.1); only one of the teachers worked in a bilingual program. Their teaching experiences ranged from one to 30 years ($M = 15.2$). Fifteen of the teachers taught students at different levels of English proficiency; the other three taught more homogenous groups of EL students who had low or advanced proficiency levels. The teachers also varied in terms of the home languages of their students. Eight teachers worked with students who mostly spoke Spanish, while one of them worked with students who mostly spoke Chinese. The other nine teachers worked with students from diverse home language backgrounds. All of the teachers in this study used the same summative ELP assessment, the ACCESS for ELLs, developed by the WIDA Consortium.

Procedures

We employed semi-structured interviews through a web-based video conferencing platform to collect data to address the three research questions. We developed an interview protocol, which helped to guide each interview and allowed

TABLE 12.1 Background Information about the Participant Teachers.

Teacher	State	Grade(s)	Language support program type★	Years of experience teaching EL students
1	New Jersey	K-1	Pull-out	10
2	New Jersey	K-3	Push-in	29
3	New Jersey	K-5	ESL class	20
4	New Jersey	3–8	ESL class	1
5	New Jersey	3–8	Pull-out	15
6	New Jersey	5–6	ESL class	4
7	New Jersey	6	Pull-out	15
8	New Jersey	6–8	ESL class	18
9	New Jersey	7	ESL class	10
10	New Jersey	7	ESL class	15
11	New Jersey	7–8	ESL class	16
12	New Jersey	7–10	Pull-out	22
13	New Jersey	8	ESL class	13
14	Illinois	PreK-12	Bilingual	19
15	Illinois	K-1	ESL class	30
16	Illinois	1–3	ESL class	10
17	Illinois	3 & 5	Sheltered	12
18	North Carolina	K-5	Pull-out	14

★ Self-contained ESL class with only EL students; in pull-out ESL, the teacher pulls students out of the general education classroom to provide language support; in push-in ESL, the teacher comes into the general education classroom; in sheltered English instruction the teacher integrates language and content instruction.

us to ask follow-up questions as needed (Kvale, 1996). The main aims of the interviews were to understand how the summative ELP assessment used in the teachers' schools influenced their classroom practices and how they used the scores on this assessment to make instructional decisions to support their teaching and students' ELD. All of the interviewees were asked questions about the implementation of the summative ELP assessment, about how their teaching and assessment practices were influenced by the summative ELP assessment, how they used the scores, what types of decisions they made, what they needed to employ the assessment to guide their instruction, and what perceptions they had towards the assessment. Each interview lasted approximately one hour. All interviews were audio recorded and transcribed.

Analysis

Each interview transcript was manually coded independently by a pair of researchers. We first used structural coding (Saldaña, 2009) to identify categories that indicated how the teachers used the summative ELP assessment and the types of instructional decisions they made. By using structural coding, we were able to use content-based phrases to identify three topics of inquiry. The structural codes were closely aligned to the research questions: impact of the summative ELP assessment on instructional practices, types of instructional decisions made, and challenges that the teachers identified related to their use of the assessment. Then for each of structural codes, we used descriptive coding (Saldaña, 2009) to help identify recurring themes. Descriptive coding refers to assigning descriptive labels to data to provide an inventory of important issues within each of the structural codes. After completing all the coding, the two researchers met to compare their ideas and codes to determine if they arrived at similar data interpretations. All of the disagreements in the coding were resolved through discussion to reach consensus as suggested by Strauss & Corbin (1990). An overview of the codes is provided in Table 12.2.

Findings

We present the study's findings according to each of the three research questions. We discuss how the summative ELP assessments shaped the teachers' instructional practices, the types of instructional decisions they made based on their students' scores on the summative ELP assessments, and some of the challenges they faced when they employed or wanted to employ the scores for instructional purposes.

TABLE 12.2 Overview of the Coding Scheme.

Structural Codes	Descriptive Codes	Number of Participants
Impact of the summative ELP assessment on instruction	Impact of the content of ELP assessments	14
	Impact of the delivery mode	18
Types of instructional decisions	To inform assessment practices	18
	To make placement and grouping decisions	18
	To measure EL students' progress over time	10
	To inform other teachers about how to support their EL students	5
Challenges in using ELP assessments to inform instruction	Timing of the score report	18
	Lack of detail in the score reports	18
	Score reports not meaningful to students	16
	Validity concern about the speak score	8

Research Question 1: How Did the Content and Delivery Mode of a Summative ELP Assessment Influence Teachers' Classroom Practices?

Content of the ELP Assessment

All of the teachers stated that the summative ELP assessment was not the main factor guiding their teaching practices. The state's ELD standards helped the teachers to think about what they were going to teach. Because the summative ELP assessment was aligned to the ELD standards, the teachers did not feel that they had to modify their instruction significantly to align it to the content of the assessment. One of the teachers explained that the students are "given tasks that are aligned to the standards and ... that they ... have to do academically, so I don't feel like there's anything different that needs to be taught or addressed in terms of ACCESS" (Grades 3 & 5 ESL teacher in Illinois).

Whether the summative ELP assessment influenced the teachers' instruction appeared to depend on how much the teachers already emphasized the ELD standards in their EL instruction. A K–3 pull-out ESL teacher in New Jersey explained that she added content from the summative ELP assessment to her instruction because she needed to make sure that her students could do all of the tasks on the summative assessment. She stated,

> It [ACCESS] does influence what I do in the classroom. The kids really need to know how to compare and contrast, which is apparent on the WIDA test. It influences my teaching and what I'm going to be doing with the kids.

Eight teachers reported that they tried to incorporate some of the summative ELP assessment design features into their complementary materials. These included using similar item types, prompts, stimulus materials, types of supports, and response expectations. Their goal was to simulate what students would encounter on the summative ELP assessment. A K-5 ESL teacher in North Carolina explained:

> I don't use many of the same tasks as the WIDA, but ... try to give them some tasks that are comparable .... With writing, I will try to set it up where it has the word bank like the WIDA writing prompt would .... If the WIDA writing has an illustration that they're having to talk about, I would try to pull some things like that, so they know how to do the writing when they get to the task on WIDA.

Delivery Mode of the ELP Assessment

The delivery mode of the test influenced some of the teachers' instructional practices. Given that the summative ELP assessment was administered on a computer, some of the teachers felt a need to help their students become familiar with the computerized testing process. Six teachers commented that not all of their students knew how to use a computer, and even those who did were generally inexperienced with taking tests on a computer.

Some teachers, across all grades, mentioned that most of their students had difficulty with the computer-based speaking or listening subtests. Thirteen teachers explained that the speaking subtest was particularly difficult for many students because they were required to speak into a microphone to record their responses. Thus, teachers provided opportunities in their classes for students to practice recording their oral responses online. A K-3 pull-out teacher in New Jersey commented:

> I noticed that when my students were taking the ACCESS that they were very unsure when it came to talking on the microphone and doing the speaking portion of the test. I have added more activities ... where they're recording themselves talking about a subject and things like that to make them feel more comfortable.

Eleven teachers commented that the listening subtest was difficult for some students because they could only listen to the stimulus once. Therefore, teachers tried to incorporate more listening activities into their lessons to help their students become more accustomed to the pace of the speakers. A Grade 8 ESL teacher in New Jersey explained how she prepared her students for the listening subtest:

> I also give them activities where [they] have to listen to the text on audio ... to train their ears to listening. Because all of their exams are mainly on computer now .... They have to train their ears to listen at that pace, so I try to introduce them to that, too.

Seven teachers commented that they used practice tests to help their students prepare for the summative ELP assessment. Test preparation activities were usually conducted a few weeks before the test was administered to help students become familiar with the content of the test and to provide opportunities for them to practice taking tests online. For some teachers, preparing their students for the summative ELP assessment was the only type of impact it had on their teaching practices. An ESL teacher in New Jersey who taught Grades 5–6 explained how little the summative ELP assessment affected her teaching: "I don't really think about the ACCESS much throughout the year. My assessments are not modeled after the WIDA .... The week before WIDA, we'll do the WIDA practice [test] just so that they're familiar with the format."

Research Question 2: What Types of Instructional Decisions Did Teachers Make Based on Their EL students' Scores on the Summative ELP Assessment?

To Inform Assessment Practices

All of the teachers stated that they used the scoring and interpretive rubrics from the summative ELP assessment to help them understand the expectations at various levels of ELP and to know where their students were in terms of their ELP levels. Eleven teachers reported that they also used these rubrics to score their students' classroom oral and written responses. The teachers liked using these scoring rubrics because they could determine their students' levels of ELP in speaking and writing and track their progress throughout the year. A middle-school ESL teacher in New Jersey explained how she used the summative ELP assessment rubrics:

> I do use the WIDA writing rubric and the WIDA speaking rubric as an additional assessment when they are doing something for me. It's usually not the primary one, but it's just to kind of get an idea of where they would fall.

In a school district in Illinois, the summative ELP assessment influenced how the teachers periodically assessed their EL students. A K–12 ESL teacher mentioned that her district had developed quarterly ELP assessments that mirrored the content and format of the summative ELP assessment used in their state. The motivation for designing these quarterly assessments was that the district wanted to have more updated and frequent information about their students' levels of ELP. The ESL teacher explained the rationale for designing and implementing quarterly district ELP assessments based on the summative ELP assessment:

> We've been frustrated for a long time with how ACCESS only happens once a year, and we really wanted a tool that would allow us to monitor their progress much more frequently. [For] the prompts that we use, just for speaking and writing, [we] looked very closely at WIDA .... We made sure [to] include the same supports, the same kind of checklist at the bottom where they check their writing, [so] that when it comes to ACCESS time, it's not something that's very out of the ordinary for them.

To Make Placement and Grouping Decisions

All of the teachers reported that they considered the scores on the summative ELP assessment when making program decisions for the following academic year, for example, to decide whether a student should stay in or exit the language support program. In addition to employing the summative ELP assessment scores, school personnel made placement decisions based on other criteria such as teacher recommendations, grades, and the amount of time that the students had been in the program. For students who stayed in the program, the summative ELP assessment scores were used to determine the types of support students needed and class placement. A pull-out ESL teacher (Grades 7–10) in New Jersey explained how her school employed the summative ELP assessment to make placement decisions: "So, for the placement of students for the next year, their [ACCESS] score would help us determine if they would go to intermediate level or advanced."

Eight teachers reported that they utilized the scores on the summative ELP assessment to group students and to differentiate instruction within their classes at the beginning of the school year. Five teachers commented that the scores were useful for grouping new students by proficiency levels or by the domains in which they needed to improve. Twelve teachers reported that they used this information to determine which skills the students needed to improve and which skills they needed to emphasize more in their instruction. An ESL teacher who taught Grades 3–8 in New Jersey explained how he used the scores on the summative ELP assessment to group students and to differentiate his instruction: "I use that data to dictate my small groups and what I focus on with each student. I would like to differentiate the instruction within those classes based on where their weakness is."

To Measure EL students' Progress over Time

When students took the summative ELP assessment more than once, teachers compared their scores over time to determine how much they had improved. Sometimes, the schools used this information for accountability purposes. Ten teachers stated that school administrators frequently asked them to create reports based on student scores on the summative ELP assessment to share with state and district personnel. A K–5 pull-out ESL teacher in North Carolina explained that every year she had to create a report showing her students' growth between tests "because that is what my administrator has me calculate to show her."

To Inform Other Teachers in the School about How to Support EL Students

The scores on the summative ELP assessment were also shared with other teachers in their schools. Five ESL teachers reported that they often used the scores on the summative ELP assessment and other information that WIDA provided related to the ELD standards (i.e., the Can Do descriptors) to create language profiles to inform other teachers about what they could expect the EL students to do in their classes and to create awareness of potential problems that the EL students might have in English listening, speaking, reading, and writing. One of the ESL teachers in New Jersey who taught Grades 3–8 explained:

> I share it with their other teachers because a lot of times ... they're in classes where they might be the only ESL student among 25 kids. So, based on how they do on that test, I'm able to ... share with their class-room teachers where they fall using the can do descriptors—what they can expect to be able to do.

Research Question 3: What Factors Affected Teachers' Use of Student Scores on the Summative ELP Assessments for Instructional Purposes?

Timing of the Score Reports

One of the biggest challenges that teachers faced in using the summative ELP assess-ments to inform their instruction was the late timing of the score reports: Schools usually received the score reports at the end of the current school year or at the beginning of the following year. All of the teachers stated that they could not use the scores when their students had moved to another class or school. Although teachers took into consideration the scores on the summative ELP assessment to help make placement decisions, they rarely employed them to guide their teaching and student learning because the scores were outdated and did not necessarily reflect the students' current ELP levels. A K–1 ESL teacher in Illinois explained:

> I do not use them [the scores] for almost [any] purpose. The scores I get don't really tell me ... where the kids were ... what their actual needs are. If I am sitting down and we are doing writing, I can see what your actual needs are. [With the scores,] you are just handed a piece of paper saying, there are one, two [students] at this level and three, four [students] at that level, and that doesn't tell me what I need to teach them next.

Three teachers commented that the summative ELP assessment was useful when they had the same students during the following academic year because they could track their progress and see where they had grown or where they still needed to grow. They could also use this information to determine the areas in which their students needed to improve and to decide if they needed to spend additional time working in a specific domain. A K–5 pull-out ESL teacher in North Carolina commented,

> It [the ELP assessment] does [have an impact] for me because I have the same kids. I do the entire elementary school. So, any student that doesn't exit, I have them again the next year. So, I always get a spreadsheet that will show what their growth is, and I'll look at what areas they're struggling more with .... I will try to work extra on that so they can exit whenever the next test comes around.

However, the other 15 teachers felt the summative ELP scores were not very useful even when they continued with the same students because they thought that they knew their students better than what was reported on the assessment. A K–5 ESL teacher in New Jersey explained that the scores on the summative ELP assessment were not very useful because by the time he got the scores, he already knew his students' current ELP development: "The information is out-dated .... I just got my scores at the end of ... last week [June]. It's not useful to me because I already know these students. I know where they are now."

Lack of Detail in the Score Reports

Another issue was the type of information provided on the score reports. Although the teachers had access to summary and individual student reports for their EL students, all of them thought this information was not detailed enough to guide their instruction. The teachers said that they could use the subscores to determine in which domains the students needed to improve, but that they did not receive information on students' specific language skills in each of the domains. In order to use the summative ELP assessment to guide their instruction, 10 teachers said that they would like to receive item-level data (i.e., which items the students answered correctly or incorrectly) and the students' actual responses on the speaking and writing subtests. An ESL teacher in New Jersey who taught Grades 7–10 described the type of information that she needed to guide her instruction:

> So we can see ... what students are scoring ... on the different language skills .... We can adjust our instruction individually ... towards the students who are lacking those skills. But it doesn't give us ... the idea of exactly what kind of a skill within reading comprehension or within writing, they were struggling with.

Score Reports Not Meaningful to Students

Although the teachers wanted to share the students' ACCESS scores with their students to inform them about their own learning and language development, they didn't think that the students would understand the information. Eight teachers complained that the reports were not written in a friendly language that EL students could understand. Sixteen teachers mentioned that there were no instructions provided on how to help EL students to understand and interpret the score reports. Nonetheless, 12 teachers reported that they did meet with their students to discuss their performance on the summative ELP assessment and to provide information about where they needed to improve. However, they could not pinpoint the specific skills that their students needed to work on.

Another limitation was the amount of time that elapsed between test administration and teacher-student meetings to discuss test scores. Many of the students did not remember what was on the test. A seventh-grade ESL teacher in Illinois pointed out, "It's like over a year ago for them; they have forgotten. They're like, 'What test did we take?' So, again, it's just not meaningful for them to go over those scores."

Validity Concerns about the Speaking Scores

Eight teachers expressed concerns about the speaking scores on the online summative ELP assessment. Currently, the online ELP assessment requires students to record their responses by speaking into a microphone. The teachers did not think that the student scores on this subtest were very accurate because they did not always reflect the students' true speaking skills. They attributed this to several factors, including the online administration of the test. They pointed out that it was difficult for many students to speak to a computer. The teachers also reported that the speaking tasks did not elicit long responses and, therefore, did not provide opportunities for students to demonstrate their speaking skills. An ESL teacher in New Jersey who taught Grades 3–8 explained:

> There is a lot of complaining statewide about the scores being … substantially inaccurate in the speaking [domain] …. The speaking [subtest] was by far the weakest section [for] almost all students, including students who … anecdotally [we] wouldn't have expected speaking to have been the problem. It just seems like that particular domain was scored lower than the other.

The teachers explained that it was better when they personally administered the speaking subtests because they could prompt their students to continue speaking or ask follow-up questions, which provided more meaningful information about the students' speaking strengths and weaknesses. In addition, when the teachers administered the speaking subtests, they did not have to wait until the following year to learn what types of speaking difficulties their students had. They could incorporate this information immediately into their lesson planning. An ESL teacher in New Jersey explained why she preferred administering the speaking part of the assessment herself:

Before the ACCESS was online, the instructor, the teacher, myself, would do the speaking part of the test .... you can prompt them to continue speaking or you can ask additional questions. I just feel it was better when it was in person, not online .... The information was more meaningful and useful whereas ... right now, [it's] just ... a computer ... asking them a question, and they're answering in a microphone. Previously, I could say, 'Is there anything else you'd like to add?' Like I can prompt them to speak more, which should be ... a more accurate assessment of their speaking skills.

Discussion

The purpose of this chapter was to understand the relationship between summative ELP assessments and teachers' instructional practices. We presented the results of an empirical study that examined how teachers viewed and used summative ELP assessments and students' assessment scores to make instructional decisions to guide their teaching and students' ELD. All of the teachers in the study used the same summative ELP assessment, ACCESS 2.0. In this section, we summarize the main findings related to each of our three research questions, provide implications for practice, describe the limitations of the study, and suggest areas for future research.

Our first research question sought to examine how the content and delivery mode of the summative ELP assessment shaped teachers' instructional practices. We found that the content and the delivery mode of the test did have some impact on the teachers' instructional practices. Although the content of the summative ELP assessment was not the main force that drove ESL teachers' classroom behaviors, some teachers did use tasks similar to those on the summative assessment. For example, some teachers used activities that allowed students to record their responses onto computers and to read texts similar to those on the summative assessment. We also found that the summative ELP assessments influenced some of their assessment practices. For example, some teachers used similar item or task types in their classroom assessments, and others used the summative ELP assessment rubrics to score their students' oral and written responses. Also, several weeks before students took the summative ELP assessment, some teachers administered practice tests and provided other test preparation materials so that students could become familiar with the content of the summative assessment. Consistent with Chapelle and Voss's (2017) finding, the teachers also had their students practice taking tests on computers in order to compensate for their lack of computer experience.

The second research question sought to investigate the types of instructional decisions that ESL teachers made based on their EL students' scores on the summative ELP assessment. We found that teachers used the scores to make various types of instructional decisions. For example, they used their students' scores to make placement or grouping decisions at the beginning of the school year, to measure their progress over time, and to gain a better understanding of what EL students could do and the type of additional support they needed.

For the last research question, we examined the challenges that the teachers faced related to their use of summative ELP assessment scores for instructional purposes. Some teachers explained that by the time they received their students' scores on the summative ELP assessment, some of their students had already moved to another grade or another school. Thus, to use the scores for instructional purposes, they would like to receive scores much sooner, hopefully within the same academic year. The teachers also complained that the scores were not detailed enough to determine exactly which English language skills their students needed to improve. They reported that they needed more detailed information (e.g., item-level data) about their students' performance on the summative ELP assessment to guide their instruction. The teachers also wanted to receive score reports that they could share with their EL students. They argued that the current score reports were not tailored to K–12 EL students in terms of the language used and the relevance of the information reported. Finally, a few teachers commented that they would prefer to administer the speaking part themselves because this would allow them to have a better sense of their students' speaking skills and the ways in which they could better support them.

Implications for Score Reporting

Technology could be leveraged to address some of the challenges that the teachers voiced about the summative ELP assessment and score reports. For example, Evanini et al. (2017) argue that automated scoring technology could be used to evaluate EL students' spoken and written responses, resulting in faster score turnaround time. The use of automated scoring technology might enable both teachers and students to access summative ELP assessment data sooner than is now possible. As suggested by Zapata-Rivera and Katz (2014), technology could also be utilized to design online "interactive" score reports to facilitate teachers' access to and management of assessment data. Interactive score reports are learning management systems that allow teachers to customize reports and access the type of information needed to support teaching and student learning. For example, such reports could pinpoint the specific language skills that students need to improve and, thereby, help their ESL teachers determine the type of instructional support that students need.

If scores can be provided sooner, teachers can strive to make students more actively involved in the assessment process in order to use the summative ELP assessments for instructional purposes. One way to accomplish this is by providing EL students with meaningful and relevant information about their performance on the summative ELP assessment: their strengths, weaknesses, and what they need to improve. Zapata-Rivera and Katz (2014) emphasize that the focus should be on "actively aiding students' comprehension and interpretation of their assessment results" (p. 456). Moreover, test publishers should strive to make scores more user friendly to help students and parents interpret and use the assessment results.

Limitations and Directions for Future Research

Limitations of the study included our sample size restriction: only 18 ESL teachers from three states participated in the study. Also, given that this was an exploratory study, we used a convenience sample to recruit all the participants. Another limitation was that although there are multiple summative ELP assessments in the United States, all of the participants in this study used the same assessment. Lastly, the study employed in-depth interviews with each participant but did not include observational data to document teachers' responses to and employment of the summative ELP assessment in real time. Because of the small sample size and non-random sampling, there is a possibility that the 18 teachers we selected under-represent the population of teachers using summative ELP assessments, and thus the study findings cannot be construed as reflecting the mandated assessments by class practitioners across U.S. K–12 public schools. However, the findings provide useful information about how the participants used summative ELP assessments to inform instruction and the challenges of using these assessments in EL classrooms.

Future research should be conducted to expand the sample to reflect a wider range of ESL programs, summative ELP assessments, and geographical diversity. Within this larger context, as Molle (2013) recommended, researchers need to examine how ESL teachers employ summative ELP assessments to improve their teaching and student learning. It also seems important to examine the relationship between teachers' classroom assessment practices and the summative ELP assessments as suggested by Tsagari and Banerjee (2014).

In addition, we agree with Zapata-Rivera and Katz's (2014) recommendation to conduct audience analyses to develop appropriate score reports for different types of stakeholders. Audience analysis helps assessment developers to understand the needs of different stakeholder groups (e.g., administrators, teachers, parents, and students) so that the stakeholders can better understand and use the assessment data. Given that most of the EL population is in the primary grades, it is important to examine to what extent EL students' scores on summative ELP assessments are shared with the students' parents. In particular, researchers need to know about the parents' awareness of the assessment, how they interpret the score report, how they use information in the report to support their children, and how the test impacts their children. Finally, score reporting could also be improved by leveraging technology. Future researchers need to explore the use of interactive score reports to examine the type of assessment data teachers need to inform their instructional practices and to improve teaching and learning.

References

Abedi, J. (2006). Language issues in item development. In S. M. Downing & T. M. Haladyna (Eds.), *Handbook of test development* (pp. 377–398). Mahwah, NJ: Erlbaum.

Center for Applied Linguistics. (2018). *Annual Technical Report for ACCESS for ELLs® 2.0 Online English Language Proficiency Test, Series 401, 2016–2017 Administration* (WIDA Consortium Annual Technical Report No. 13A). Retrieved from http://www.cde.state.co.us/assessment/accessforellsonlinetechreport

Chapelle, C. A., & Voss, E. (2017). Utilizing technology in language assessment. In E. Shohamy, I. G. Or, & S. May (Eds.), *Language testing and assessment, encyclopedia of language and education* (pp. 149–161). Gewerbestrasse, Switzerland: Springer International Publishing.

Evanini, K., Hauck, M. C., & Hakuta, K. (2017). *Approaches to automated scoring of speaking for K–12 English language proficiency assessments* (ETS Research Report No. RR-17-18). Princeton, NJ: ETS.

Every Student Succeeds Act of 2015. (2015). Pub. L. No. 114-95 § 114 Stat. 1177. Retrieved from https://legcounsel.house.gov/Comps/Elementary%20And%20Secondary%20Education%20Act%20Of%201965.pdf

Hauck, M. C., Wolf, M. K., & Mislevy, R. (2016). *Creating a next-generation system of K–12 English learner (EL) language proficiency assessments* (ETS Research Report No. RR-16-06). Princeton, NJ: Educational Testing Service.

Herman, J. L. (2007). *Accountability and assessment: Is public interest in K–12 education being served?* (CRESST Tech. Rep. No. 728). Los Angeles, CA: University of California, National Center for Research on Evaluation, Standards, and Student Testing (CRESST).

Kim, A. A., Chapman, M., Kondo, A., & Wilmes, C. (2020). Examining the assessment literacy required for interpreting score reports: A focus on educators of K–12 English learners. *Language Testing, 31*(1), 54–75.

Koretz, D. (2017). *The testing charade: Pretending to make schools better*. Chicago, IL: University of Chicago Press.

Kvale, S. (1996). *Interviews: An introduction to qualitative research interviewing*. Thousand Oaks, CA: Sage Publications.

Mitchell, C. (2017, July 17). Thousands of English-learners fall short on test of English language skills. *Education Week, 36*(37). Retrieved from www.edweek.org/ew/articles/2017/07/19/thousands-of-english-learners-fall-short-on-test.html

Molle, D. (2013). *Implementation of the language proficiency standards across the WIDA consortium*. Madison, WI: Wisconsin Center for Education Research. Retrieved from https://wida.wisc.edu/resources/implementation-english-language-proficiency-standards-across-wida-consortium

Saldaña, J. (2009). *The coding manual for qualitative researchers*. London: Sage Publications.

Strauss, A. L., & Corbin, J. (1990). *Basics of qualitative research*. Thousand Oaks, CA: Sage.

Tsagari, D., & Banerjee, J. (2014). Language assessment in the educational context. In M. Bigelow & J. Ensser-Kanenen (Eds.), *Handbook of educational linguistics* (pp. 339–352). New York, NY: Routledge/Taylor & Francis Group.

U. S. Department of Education. (2016). *Non-regulatory guidance: English learners and title III of the Elementary and Secondary Education Act (ESEA), as amended by the Every Student Succeeds Act (ESSA)*. Washington, DC: Author. Retrieved from www.ed.gov/

Washington State Office of Superintendent of Public Instruction, Washington. (2019). *English language proficiency assessments*. Retrieved from www.k12.wa.us/student-success/testing/state-testing-overview/english-language-proficiency-assessments

WIDA. (2017). *ACCESS for ELLS 2.0 interpretive guide for score reports ("Interpretive guide")*. Madison, WI: Board of Regents of the University of Wisconsin System. Retrieved from www.isbe.net/Documents/WIDA_interpretive_guide.pdf

Wilson, M. (2018). Making measurement important for education: The crucial role of classroom assessment. *Educational Measurement: Issues and Practice, 37*(1), 5–20.

Wolf, M. K., Guzman-Orth, D., & Hauck, M. C. (2016). *Next-generation summative English language proficiency assessments for English Learners: Priorities for policy and research* (ETS Research Report No. RR-16-08). Princeton, NJ: Educational Testing Service.

Zapata-Rivera, J. D., & Katz, I. R. (2014). Keeping your audience in mind: Applying audience analysis to the design of interactive score reports. *Assessment in Education: Principle, Policy & Practice, 21*(4), 442–463.

13

TOWARD A MODEL OF VALIDITY IN ACCOUNTABILITY TESTING

Micheline B. Chalhoub-Deville

A basic premise in this chapter is that accountability testing, which also includes K–12 English language proficiency (ELP) assessments, mandates a reconceptualization of prevailing validity models and operations. This chapter provides a critical examination of key validity models to discern the extent to which key accountability-related concepts are addressed. The focus is primarily on the joint *Standards for Educational and Psychological Testing* (hereafter Standards), authored by the American Educational Research Association (AERA), the American Psychological Association (APA), and the National Council on Measurement in Education (NCME) (2014), the Interpretation and Use Argument (IA/IUA) framework by Kane (2006, 2013, 2016), and the Assessment Use Argument (AUA) by Bachman and Palmer (2010). Accountability systems have particular goals, variables, and processes that compel reconsideration of established validity models and operations. The present chapter suggests an approach with key principles that need to be considered in validity models and operations. The chapter is intended to present an argument that accountability-related validity compels attention toward not only individual student scores but also aggregate scores and systems (e.g., educational, economic, and social) where key interpretations and decisions are made. I contend that in such systems, it is a grave error not to attend to issues of consequences as part of the technical documentation of a testing program. Communication and engagement with policy makers, education professionals, and other key stakeholder groups beyond the measurement community are also key. Moreover, anticipatory research is called for to help facilitate the design of more viable educational reform policies that can better utilize testing systems and to formulate validation plans that anchor test development and related processes in targeted deliverables and goals.

Reform Policies and Accountability Testing

Educational reform and accountability is a global phenomenon. This has been documented in countries such as Australia (Brindley, 2001), Canada (Klinger, DeLuca, & Miller, 2008), China (Jin, 2018), the United Kingdom (Broadfoot, 1996), Germany (Rupp & Vock, 2007), and the United States (Chalhoub-Deville, 2009b; Deville & Chalhoub-Deville, 2011; Wixson, Dutro, & Athan, 2003). This phenomenon has been the focus of international organizations and reports (OECD, 2011; UNESCO, 2017). The wide-reaching scope of educational reform and accountability has prompted labels such as *the Global Education Reform Movement* (Sahlberg, 2011, 2016) or the *Age of Accountability* (Hopmann, 2008). Governments are engaged in such educational reform efforts because they assert that education is central for a nation's economic advancement, international competitiveness, and social order (Haertel & Herman, 2005).

Over the nearly past 20 years in the United States, government policies have coupled educational reform with accountaility testing in the form of government policies: the No Child Left Behind Act (2002), the Race to the Top Act (U.S. Department of Education, 2009), and the Every Student Succeeds Act (U.S. Department of Education, 2016). Such policy systems have been characterized as "test-driven, top-down, remediating and penalizing" policies (Mathis & Trujillo, 2016, p. 7). The Standards (AERA et al., 2014) describe accountability as "a system that imposes student performance-based rewards or sanctions on institutions such as school systems or on individuals such as teachers ..." (p. 215). With educational reform, testing shifts its focus from students to teachers and schools. Deville and Chalhoub-Deville (2006) note that test scores are typically employed to hold students accountable for their performance. This changed in the 1980s where the federal government began to hold educators and schools accountable. This shift has been affirmed by Democrat and Republican Presidents—Clinton, W. Bush, Obama, and Trump. Both parties have upheld the banner of educational reform, accountability and testing.

Professionals in the language-testing field have also been embroiled in educational reform and accountability testing. This edited volume, for example, showcases the wide-ranging language testing projects and activities because of reform policies and accountability laws. Articles such as "Validity theory: Reform policies, accountability testing, and consequences," by Chalhoub-Deville (2016); symposia including one titled The Next Generation of Policy-driven Language Testing Systems: Accountability, Consequences, and Learning, jointly sponsored by the International Language Testing Association and the American Association of Applied Linguistics (AAAL) (Chalhoub-Deville, 2018), and one presented at the Language Testing Research Colloquium titled Language Proficiency Assessment and Social Justice in the US K–12 Educational Context (Gottlieb & Chapman, 2019) speak to the ubiquity of accountability language testing in the United

States. The realities of accountability language testing necessitate reconsideration of validation thinking and operations.

This accountability testing movement has significantly impacted English learner (EL) students in the schools, starting with the No Child Left Behind Act of 2001 (NCLB). NCLB signals an important shift in terms of how this EL group is treated. As detailed in other chapters of the present volume, NCLB and the subsequent accountability regulations have mandated that EL students be included and appropriately assessed. Since the enactment of NCLB, states are required to not only assess EL students but also show that they are meeting academic ELP goals and achieving mastery in academic content as their peers do (U.S. Department of Education, 2003). Accountability testing for EL students reflects the same features that have governed the assessment of the general population including non-EL students.

The more recent Every Student Succeeds Act (ESSA, 2015) continues to push for accountability testing, including for EL students. Anchored in a standards-based approach to education, ESSA continues to mandate setting and achieving proficiency expectations, to demand that assessments meet rigorous technical requirements, to hold educators (as opposed to students) accountable for achieving state goals, and to adopt a structure of rewards/punishment to drive reform. One notable change with ESSA is the more elevated importance accorded to EL students. With ESSA, accountability for ELP is no longer addressed in Title III (Language Instruction for English Learners and Immigrant Students), as observed with NCLB. ESSA targets ELP accountability in Title I (Improving the Academic Achievement of the Disadvantaged) where only academic content testing was previously addressed (U.S. Department of Education, 2016; see also Bailey & Wolf, 2020; Sato & Thompson, 2020 in this volume). This inclusion of ELP in Title I implies that validity challenges faced in ELP testing systems mirror those observed with the testing of academic content achievement.

Educational reform initiatives, with their reliance on high-stakes accountability testing systems to advance the quality of teaching, learning, and educational practice broadly, change the mechanisms by which we provide evidence to support the quality of testing instruments and outcomes. Accountability testing requires that we attend to not only individual student scores but also aggregate scores, the unit of accountability in educational reform systems where rewards and sanctions are enacted. Validity evidence in such systems cannot address traditional notions of accounting for the interpretation and use of individual student scores. Accountability testing compels us to consider aggregate and socio-educational consequences.

Validity in the Standards: Sources of Evidence

The current edition of the Standards (AERA et al., 2014) has reaffirmed that validity targets score interpretation and use as well as the notion that validity is not all or nothing; it is a nuanced line of reasoning. The Standards emphasize that validity encompasses different evidence types as opposed to different validities. The Standards list five sources of validity evidence: Test Content, Response Processes, Internal Structure, Relations to Other Variables, and Validity and Consequences of Testing. It is interesting that the 2014 Standards have moved away from an all-inclusive validity documentation that attends to all five sources of evidence. Test developers and researchers are encouraged to pursue the line of evidence they think is appropriate to make their intended argument. The Standards contend: "each type of evidence … is not required in all settings. Rather, support is needed for each proposition that underlies a proposed test interpretation for a specified use" (AERA et al., 2014, p. 14). The Standards do not offer justification for dropping the notion of a unitary concept. They simply call for the integration of the validity evidence deemed relevant to specific propositions engendered by intended score interpretation for specific uses into a coherent argument. This coherence criterion is also observed in Kane's (2006) validation arguments.

The Standards (AERA et al., 2014) acknowledge that "[t]he inclusion of test scores in educational accountability systems has become common in the United States and in other nations" (p. 205). The Standards, however, seek to restrict the responsibility of test publishers for accountability testing validity research and relegate educational accountability testing to Chapter 13: Uses of Tests for Program evaluation, Policy Studies, and Accountability.

The chapter suggests that test developers have a highly delimited role to play in accountability testing. Test developers are responsible for the development of the more scientific aspects of accountability (e.g., efforts that pertain to the development and production of growth scale and value-added models/accountability indices). The reasoning behind this orientation, I argue, is to limit the responsibility of test developers for engaging in the kind of socially engaged research that accountability testing demands or to have test developers/publishers be held accountable for the broad test outcomes. It is worth observing that given the authors of the Standards as well as the intended audience, the whole conversation is primarily among professionals in the field; teachers, school administrators, and program evaluators are not likely to be reading and/or commenting on the Standards.

The Standards (AERA et al., 2014) have a particular orientation to validity. Validity is score-based, technical, and utilitarian in terms of its approach to selecting and accumulating validity evidence. The sequenced propositions based on score interpretation and use and the lines of evidence, selected from five sources, to support those propositions are put together to form the argument for validity. The Standards' scope of validity research is largely measurement-directed, and the scope of responsibility is narrowly focused. The Standards hold to this orientation when discussing educational accountability testing. The orientation in this edition of the Standards seems to echo key features of Kane's (2006) validation approach.

Kane's Argument-Based Validity Approach

Kane (2006, 2013, 2017), similar to the Standards (AERA et al., 2014), emphasizes a score-based approach to validity and moves away from a unitary, construct validity approach. Kane explains that the uniform validity model does not lend itself easily to operational work. Kane pursues an argument-based validity (ABV) approach that specifies where to start, how to proceed, and when to end. Kane suggests first laying out the claims that are said to support intended score interpretation and use, which he calls the interpretive argument (IA) and then pursuing investigations to examine those claims. He calls this latter phase the validation argument (VA). Unlike the five, flexible sources of evidence in the Standards (AERA et al., 2014), Kane's (2006) ABV process is systematically delineated.

Kane (2006) presents a diagram to explicate how the IA is laid out for trait-based interpretations, as displayed in Figure 13.1. Kane starts with delineating the IA, which specifies the network of inferences and assumptions or a chain of claims underlying intended score interpretation. The IA, which pertains to the right side of Figure 13.1, starts with observed performances and progresses to trait interpretations. Test developers lay out IA claims regarding scoring, generalization, extrapolation, explanation, utilization, and so forth. Research (i.e. the VA) is then undertaken focusing on the specified claims. The VA amasses evidence to support or refute the intended inferences embedded in score interpretations and planned uses. Judgment of the quality of the IA and VA includes their coherence, completeness, clarity, and plausibility. Kane (2006, 2012) points out that this ABV process is to help organize the claims and systematize the research without engaging in validation research *forever*.

As Chapelle (2012) points out, ABV focuses on score inferences and analyses; however, it largely ignores test development processes, which include elaborations of traits, contexts, and methods. ABV pays indirect and retrospective attention, through score analysis, to the complex design and development processes undertaken before measurement specialists begin to analyze test score data. It is important to reaffirm the obvious statement that test development processes impact the quality of a testing program. Validity needs to document the quality of design and development operations in a testing program as well as documentation of test scores. Validity documentation needs to integrate both development and measurement arguments (Chalhoub-Deville & O'Sullivan, 2020). This is especially important for language testing professionals and ELP specialists whose scholarship is rooted in issues of construct, content, and standards.

Since his 2006 publication, Kane (2013) has increasingly become a proponent of documenting use and paying attention to outcomes and consequences as part of test documentation. Kane views "adverse impact and unintended systemic effects … as serious issues that need to be addressed in evaluating high-stakes

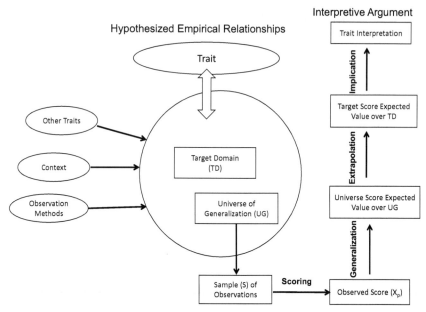

FIGURE 13.1 Kane (2006) measurement procedure and interpretive argument for trait interpretations. Reproduced with permission.

testing programs" (Kane, 2013, p. 59). Kane questions a definition of validity that engages with consequences only in relation to aspects of the construct (construct-relevance and representation), as observed with the Standards (AERA et al., 2014). Kane posits that scholarly engagement is needed to explicate the kinds of social consequences that we need to focus on, the criteria to adopt to evaluate consequences, and the framework to help delineate responsibility for evaluating consequence.

Kane makes his opinion clear as to whether test developers should consider test outcomes and consequences to be part of validity. He argues that test developers cannot relegate research responsibility for social aspects of test use, outcomes, and consequences to test users. Test developers need to engage in the social aspects of test score interpretation and use beyond the psychometric qualities of test scores (Kane, 2017). Kane urges engagement among policy makers, test providers, educational testing reserachers, relevant professional groups, and other key organizations to delineate the scope of consequences to be integrated into the IA argument and to allocate whose responsibility it is to undertake relevant investigations. This process is not straightforward. After all, "… perceptions about the seriousness of various kinds of consequences may be highly variable across stakeholders and across groups of stakeholders" (Kane, 2013 p. 48). In addition, different stakeholder groups have different financial resoures and experitise.

In short, Kane (2006, 2013, 2017) proposes a validation model that calls attention to score interpretation and use as well as to consequences. The model, nevertheless, remains anchored in individual test scores, which does not accommodate accountability testing realities.

Bachman and Palmer Assessment Use Argument

In language testing, the prevailing validity model is Bachman and Palmer's (2010) AUA. The model follows the validity tradition that focuses on the analysis and documentation of the quality of test score interpretation and use. AUA, however, represents a clear departure from the long-held language testing tradition in the United States to anchor validity in construct validity and to have the L2 construct be the point of departure for analysis. With AUA, Bachman and Palmer adopt a structured validation approach, similar to that advanced by Kane (2006). AUA, as shown in Figure 13.2, links inferences from intended/actual consequences, intended/actual decisions, intended/actual interpretations of test taker's language ability, and assessment records/scores to assessment performance and the embedded assessment tasks. A strong differentiating feature of AUA is its explicit attention to test development. Bachman and Palmer's AUA, unlike Kane's ABV, provides a guiding framework for test development, in addition to using evidence from the test development process to support the validity argument. AUA demarcates test development as a central phase in the evidence accumulation process to support the validity argument. Another key point of departure from Kane's validity arguments is AUA's grounding all lines of reasoning and justification in consequences. With AUA, validity is clearly focused on intended and actual consequences expected from a testing program. In comparison to Bachman and Palmer's strong affirmation of consequences as the cornerstone for the inferential links, Kane's IU/IUA accommodates consequences at the tail end of validity operations.

Bachman and Palmer's approach is illustrated in Figure 13.2 with two arrows calling attention to aspects of assessment development and interpretation and use. One arrow, pointing down, indicates that validation starts with assessment development. This assessment development sequence anchors the validity argument or justification in claims targeting intended consequences. AUA prompts developers to lay out consequences, claims, and hypotheses intended as part of a testing program implementation and to gear development operations to those contentions. The line of justification also targets inferences that need to be attended to in order to support intended decisions, interpretations, and aspects of performance description and scores. This process of evidence documentation then attends to claims that uphold performance and related task features. The other arrow in AUA, as shown in Figure 13.2, points upwards and directs attention to a sequence that starts with that test taker's performance, converted to

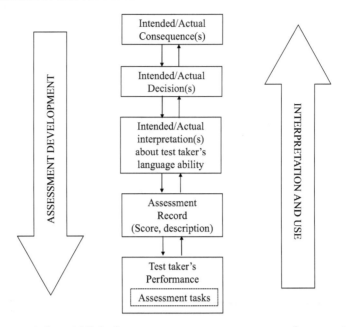

FIGURE 13.2 Inferential links from consequences to assessment performance. Reproduced by permission of Oxford University Press from *Language assessment in practice* by L. F. Bachman and A. S. Palmer © Oxford University Press 2010.

some record, score, and/or description. This arrow focuses efforts on justification for actual interpretation, use, and consequences.

It could be said that the validation embedded in the interpretation and use arrow, pointing upward, resembles Kane's IA/IUA sequence of inferences. A critical difference between the two, however, is the role consequences play in validity. While AUA's interpretation and use inferential links resolutely point to validation that targets actual consequences of a testing program and its outcomes, ABV includes consequence-related claims in the IU/IUA validity framework at the very end of the sequence of inferences. AUA represents a marked departure in terms of its representation of validity. AUA considers consequences to be unequivocally part of validity. Consequences are also considered at the very beginning of test design and development. Moreover, AUA upholds consequences as the anchor for the whole justification or validity enterprise.

AUA seems to target broad social consequence claims that generally speak to issues of beneficence, i.e., "the degree to which the consequences of using an assessment and of the decisions that are made promote good and are not detrimental to stakeholders" (Bachman & Palmer, 2010, p. 105). Bachman and Palmer call attention to consequences related to individual test takers and teachers, as well as education systems and society. The authors write that consequences have the "potential for affecting not only individuals, but the educational system as well" (Bachman & Palmer, 2010, pp. 209–210). In terms of roles, Bachman and Palmer consider the traditional allocation of responsibility, as commonly observed in the Standards (AERA et al., 2014), whereby test developers take responsibility for test development and construct-related consequences, and test users/decision makers assume responsibility for assessment uses in the real-world. The authors state that such a "neat division of labor" (Bachman & Palmer, 2010, p. 433) is not tenable with AUA where all activities and claims are anchored in intended consequences. Bachman and Palmer point out that the complex testing situations do not lend themselves to a formulaic way of allocating activities/investigations to developer and user groups. The authors acknowledge that a way forward involves "inter-action and negotiation" (Bachman & Palmer, 2010, p. 433) among relevant stake-holder groups.

In summary, AUA brings together a focus on test development and score interpretation and use as part of quality documentation. AUA, similar to Kane's (2006) ABV, embraces a systematic sequence of inferences targeted in the validation process. However, unlike Kane and the Standards (AERA et al., 2014), Bachman and Palmer anchor their approach in consequences, broadly defined, and urge test developers to pay closer attention to engagement and negotiation with key stakeholder groups. These distinctive features of AUA are groundbreaking and useful when thinking through validity issues for reform-driven, including L2, accountability testing systems.

Validation and Accountability

Traditionally, the focus of assessments, including language tests, is at the indi-vidual student level. The field has amassed statistical, operational, and valid-ation tools to deal with such scores. For example, in terms of validity, Kane's ABV fleshes out research to be undertaken to support validation of scores at the individual student level. Accountability tests move beyond a traditional focus at the individual level. Accountability testing systems intend to shift focus through rewards and punishments and drive teacher effectiveness and school performance. Student performance results are integral to the equation used to evaluate teachers. Value-added modeling, for example, estimates "the contribution of individual schools or teachers to student performance by means of complex statistical techniques that use multiple years of student outcome data, which typically are standardized test scores" (AERA et al., 2014, p. 225). This aggregated data is a centerpiece of educational reform policies. Aggregated scores are the unit of accountability; this is where validation needs to be anchored.

The Standards (AERA et al., 2014) call for a validity argument in areas such as accountability where aggregated scores are employed to make causal inferences about teacher effectiveness. This call for a validity argument to support accountability indices, albeit limited to technical aspects, is appropriate and overdue. The reality is that scholarship in this area is undertheorized and insufficiently investigated. The Standards state, "Developers and users of indices should be aware of ways in which the process of combining individual scores into an index may introduce technical problems that did not affect the original scores" (AERA et al., 2014, p. 210). Of note in this quote is the separation of technical qualities related to test score interpretation and the use of an individual test score from documentation related to aggregated scores. At a technical level, this is an accurate statement. We currently undertake validation of the individual student scores separately before we turn attention to aggregated scores. This separation, however, is not tenable in accountability testing where (e.g., as observed in value-added accountability indices) individual and aggregated scores are entangled. The focus of accountability testing is less, if at all, on individual test scores. The unit of accountability is the aggregate. In accountability testing, evidence based on individual scores is necessary but not sufficient. Validity in accountability testing has to undertake aggregate score inferences.

Validation in accountability testing necessitates that we revisit established validity models. In the context of accountability testing, validity models, even when focused only on technical documentation, cannot realistically focus on individual score interpretation and use and ignore engagement with validation of group- and system-level data. The goals in accountability testing are to build on student performance, hold teachers/schools accountable, and explicitly or implicitly embed socio-economic goals. Acree, Hoeve, and Weir's (2016) validation model illustrated in Figure 13.3 is an adaptation of Kane's (2006, 2013) ABV approach to validity to accommodate accountability testing that demands aggregate-level considerations. This figure conveys an understanding of the single and aggregate sore entanglement represented in accountability testing and the research needed at various inference levels. It is not sound to think of accountability indices as an added inference in the traditional sequence of single score inferences. Accountability-related validity documentation permeates all inferences. Another interesting feature of Figure 13.3 is how it moves the scope of validity beyond scoring, generalization, and extrapolation to engaging with decisions and consequences using aggregate level data.

The depiction of validation in Figure 13.3 is distinctive from that of the other models reviewed in this chapter. The depiction, for example, counters the restricted engagement with consequences observed in the Standards (AERA et al., 2014). The scope of validation is also singular as it explicitly addresses issues of aggregate scores, as realistically observed in accountability testing. Neither ABV nor AUA presents such an explicit depiction of the nature of validation as commonly observed with accountability, including ELP testing.

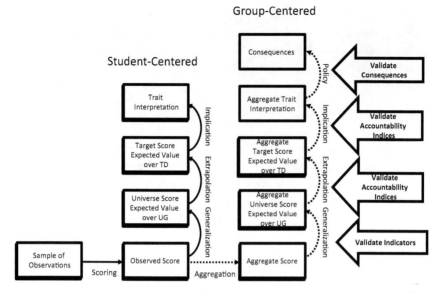

FIGURE 13.3 Validation for accountability testing by Acree et al. (2016). Reproduced with permission.

Consequences and Accountability Testing: A Shared Responsibility

As pointed out earlier, the role of consequences in key documents in the field such as the *Standards* (AERA et al., 2014) is highly restrictive. For example, Standard 13.8 states:

> Those who mandate the use of tests in policy, evaluation and account-ability contexts and those who use tests in such contexts should monitor the impact and should identify and minimize the negative consequences.
>
> *(AERA et al., 2014, p. 212)*

Policy makers and test users, as the quote indicates, are to be held responsible for consequences because they are better situated to address consequences that pertain to their own decisions and/or actions. Test developers seem to be exempt from this process. However, Kane (2013) argues, "… but a test devel-oper who provides a test to the user shares this responsibility. In particular, test developers who suggest that a test can be used in a particular way have an obligation to support the claims that they make" (p. 62). By responding to a call from an agency to develop a test, developers share in the responsibility for consequences, whether explicitly or implicitly stated. Test providers create tests, with *some* understanding of the consequences entailed by the testing program, but they are reluctant to engage in validaion to uphold these consequences. Reluctance to engage in socially embedded consequences may be understandable, given the messiness of policies and politics, the socio-educational complexity of the endeavor, and the limited experience the field has in terms of engaging policy makers.

Language testing and measurement researchers do not generally have ongoing working relations with policy makers. To the extent that the profession works with the policy making sector, roles are typically fixed. In this fixed-role allocation, policy makers mandate, or call for, a test-related product, and language testing professionals undertake independently test development and quality research within the scope mandated. In such traditional situations, test professionals assume responsibility for test quality documentation in terms of intended score interpretation and use; other interpretations and uses are said to be documented by pertinent stakeholder user groups. Additionally, policy makers and testing professionals embrace different notions of quality documentation. Quality assurance for testing professionals is commonly a validation of intended interpretation and use of test scores. It is principally a technical endeavor involving construct depiction, domain representation, score generalizability, DIF, and other psychometric properties. Policy makers, one can argue, consider the effectiveness of a testing program in terms of cost-benefit analysis/return on investment to yield desired outcomes. Policy makers approach testing as an investment option that allows them to achieve educational, economic, and social types of benefits. Testing represents a commodity that can help focus attention to areas of interest, improve teaching quality, produce decisions based on testing outcomes, affect social/equity change, and enhance economic competitiveness. These different roles and preoccupations come uneasily together in accountability testing.

With accountability testing, policy makers at various levels and test developers come together to shape testing systems. The federal government and various state agency professionals increasingly direct the development, interpretation, and use of accountability assessment systems. Test developers are financially compensated to undertake the development and related operations of a testing system that has an explicitly stated, expansive socio-educational reform agenda. Role conflation, as well as the expanded mandate for accountability test score interpretation and use, necessitates better collaboration between testing professionals and policy makers. In accountability testing, including ELP testing systems, consequence-related research, regardless of whether it is included in validity, is unavoidably a shared responsibility. Chalhoub-Deville (2016) builds on the work of Nichols and Williams (2009) to promote the concept of the zone of negotiated responsibility to make explicit and upfront the need for shared responsibility for consequence-related research. Chalhoub-Deville (2009a, 2009b, 2016) argues that fixed, a priori allocation of roles for quality assurance research is not tenable with accountability testing where roles are conflated, the stakes are far-reaching, and the stakeholder groups have different resources and expertise. For example, test developers either have resources or can develop needed resources. Alternatively, test developers can collaborate with other professionals to engage in the type of research accountability testing requires. Test user and policy maker groups are likely to have the financial resources and knowledge of outcomes and pitfalls that need to be accessed to undertake investigations needed.

Accountability testing calls for an uneasy but necessary partnership among stakeholder groups and requires negotiation of responsibilities for validity activities and/or claims embedded in these testing systems. Focused scholarship is needed to explore and develop workable negotiation frameworks that afford two-way and ongoing communication to clarify partnership roles, delineate responsibilities, allocate funds needed, target goals intended, and institute mitigation plans to handle unintended and negative consequences. These frameworks should be anticipatory in nature. In the next section, I present the argument that accountability policies and testing systems need to be refashioned at the design level to incorporate more thoughtful and systematic processes that can better target intended outcomes and consequences. I call for an anticipatory, forward-focused approach to designing policies and articulating validity research in accountability testing systems.

Accountability Testing and Anticipatory Research: Social Impact Analysis and Theories of Action

Throughout the recent era of accountability testing, the measurement and language testing fields have continued to play catch-up to accountability policies and testing mandates. Measurement and language testing professionals need to become more adept at anticipating the mandates of the next iteration of accountability testing. Professionals need to work with policy makers to design workable policies and negotiate the allocation of funds and responsibility for quality documentation. Researchers and test publishers need to push for scholarship to innovate and develop the research tools needed to meet accountability stipulations. For example, validity investigations of accountability testing systems have been reactive. Score-based research is typically undertaken after a policy has been implemented and the tests are operational. While this reactive approach is important, it should not be the only manner of conducting research. Investigations of intended and unintended outcomes should start at the policy-making stage where testing systems are key to policy implementation. This introduces us to the idea of considering consequences before they actually arise at the policy-making stages. What I am calling for differs from what is proposed by Bachman and Palmer (2010) where consequences are considered at the beginning of test development, after a policy has been finalized and rolled out.

Educational reform initiatives have typically sought accountability testing to realize far-reaching socio-educational goals; ultimately, they seek to improve the performance of students, teachers, and schools. It is reasonable to expect, given the stakes, that policies, deliverables, and processes be subjected to rigorous vetting and piloting before they are enacted. Chalhoub-Deville (2009a, 2009b) discusses social impact assessment (SIA), which addresses a proactive approach to policy research. SIA is "the process of assessing or estimating, in advance, the social consequences that are likely to follow from specific policy actions or project development …. SIA as a process and methodology has the potential to contribute greatly to the planning process" (Burdge & Vanclay, 1996, p. 59). Where testing is part of an accountability policy endeavor, SIA necessitates that accountability testing professionals work with policy makers upfront to inform policy design. An SIA approach necessitates that measurement and language testing professionals engage in the scholarship of accountability policy design to enhance the effectiveness of testing programs.

Policy theories, research procedures, and collaborative engagement systems are needed to investigate and address potential (intended/unintended, positive/negative) consequences at the policy planning stages. Simulation studies, ethnographic research, and focus groups, among others could be undertaken to study the variety of claims embedded in a testing system as envisioned in the planned policy. A confirmationist approach to validation evidence, as suggested by Kane (2006), is emphasized at this stage, akin to the improvement-oriented approach followed in test item piloting. Evidence obtained is used to revise and strengthen the effectiveness of the policy under development to better achieve desired goals (see Chalhoub-Deville, 2009b, 2016).

As part of this cooperative, coordinated, anticipatory-based approach, policy makers and related professionals should underscore in the request for proposals (RFP)[1] the need for test publishers to pay close attention to not only the intended technical qualities but also socio-educational goals and claims. The RFP should also request that mitigation plans be developed to minimize negative outcomes. Once the RFP is successful and test publishers engage in the design and development of the testing system, it behooves them to utilize frameworks that strengthen their attention to desired processes and outcomes as well as target research to minimize unintended negative results. Once a policy is rolled out, approaches that draw attention to anticipatory research and development (R&D) are needed. In the field of program evaluation, theory of change/theory of action (TOA) frameworks and logic models promote anticipatory research that also attends to actual desired objectives as well as unintended outcomes.

A few researchers have been publishing on the TOA approach in the context of measurement R&D (Bennett, 2010; Bennett, Kane, & Bridgeman, 2011; Sabatini, Bennett, & Deane, 2011). Bennett (2010) asserts that a TOA research "gives greater prominence to the effects of the assessment system on individuals and institutions as well as to the underlying mechanisms behind those effects" (p.71). Sabatini et al. point out that given that the testing instrument and related procedures are the intervention sought by accountability policies to drive particular outcomes, technical quality should address how the intervention is performing as well as "the impact (negative and positive) of instrument use on students, teachers, classroom practice, school functioning, and the larger education system as a whole" (2011, p. 14). A TOA framework stresses that attention be paid at the outset to deliverables such as accountability purposes and consequences. This translates into an R&D and validity system geared to address not only individual student scores but also aggregate results that target teachers, schools, and the larger social/educational contexts. Additionally, a TOA framework makes explicit the need to consider "[p]otential unintended effects and what will be done to mitigate them" (Bennett et al., 2011, p. 6). Frameworks such as TOA are relatively new in the measurement and language testing fields, but they are highly promising. The use of frameworks such as TOA invites systematic and anticipatory research that can help us move beyond traditional, individual-focused test scores and related technical quality documentation. Such frameworks can help us attend to actual desired socio-educational goals embedded in a policy (or a client's request) and address research into unintended outcomes.

In language testing, as part of the design phase for a testing project, Bachman and Palmer (2010) urge professionals to adopt an anticipatory R&D approach. Because of its attention to consequences, their AUA is anchored in such forward-outcome considerations. Bachman and Palmer ask professionals, for example, to articulate at the outset of a project issues such as: "Who are the intended test takers? How will they be affected? ... Who else will be affected? How will they be affected?" (p. 450). Bachman and Palmer also encourage test developers to attend to stakeholders and consequences. Such consequences are related to individuals (e.g., experiences of test preparations, feedback received, equitability, etc.), teachers, (e.g., washback and impact on instruction), and education systems and society (e.g., community values and legal requirements). Bachman and Palmer are explicit in terms of the need to address not only intended but also unintended consequences—one can reason that they mean negative unintended, consequences. To be able to identify unintended negative consequences is a considerable challenge.

Given the nascent nature of anticipatory R&D research such as SIA and TOA, much needs to be tackled. Below I present a few questions that delineate some of the issues that professionals in the field need to engage in to move the knowledge base in the field forward. Given how integral the EL population is to accountability decisions, all questions presented, including those that do not mention ELP are pertinent to EL professionals. Research questions to consider in the area of accountability testing and validation include:

- What models/frameworks and inherent processes are useful in identifying and isolating factors that yield desired socio-educational outcomes?
- To what extent do we need to link individual student-level inferences to those at the aggregate level? Do we need to do that for all inferences? For

EL students, this needs to be considered in conjunction with the associations that typically exist between ELP and content area educators.

- What EL- and ELP-specific variables need to be considered for each of the inferences?
- How can risks and unintended outcomes be identified and engaged in to remedy potential negative outcomes?
- What criteria should be adopted to identify adequate and appropriate documentation of actual outcomes? For example, how is success of a policy to be operationalized? What criteria should be used to determine success?
- To what extent can we identify causal links or relationships between testing activities and the desired outcomes?
- How do we structure interactions and negotiations among relevant stakeholder group to identify differentiated roles and allocate responsibility for consequence-related claims? What are the financial, personnel, and expertise resources required for the various research activities?

The present chapter is not a critique of accountability testing but rather a look at how changes observed in this area alter the landscape for validity theory, research, and operations. The listed questions draw attention to some salient issues in accountability testing that need to be considered in the re/formulation of validity to help guide our thinking and practices.

Concluding Remarks

Testing prior to NCLB held individual test takers accountable. With NCLB and other recent acts, accountability testing has become fundamentally about aggregate scores. The present chapter explores the extent to which validity models have addressed the changes that accountability testing has introduced. Throughout the chapter, I make the argument that the validity conceptualization that addresses accountability testing systems for the general student population applies to the EL population. Starting with NCLB, accountability regulations have held teachers, schools, and districts responsible under Title III for meeting rigorous targets for EL students. Funding and personnel consequences were in place to ensure compliance. With ESSA, we observe an added importance to the EL population where ELP is considered part of Title I. Of course, validation issues for EL students necessitate some inferences, which are specific to this student group (e.g., the use of ELP scores for appropriately exiting students). Nevertheless, the overall validity orientation and framework apply to professionals and structures that work with EL and non-EL populations.

The chapter demonstrates that validation increasingly involves explicit propositions or inferences that could be sequenced and investigated using various sources of evidence. Traditionally, validity arguments have been technical and geared toward the measurement community at large. Consequences are given a delimited scope within validity documentation, primarily with a focus on research that impacts construct/ability representation. The approach followed by Bachman and Palmer (2010) stands apart. Bachman and Palmer's AUA builds on Kane's (2006) ABV approach but is anchored in consequences. However, even with AUA, attention to the specifics of accountability testing is implicit if not silent. Given the scope of influence that accountability testing systems exert on the EL population, education at large, the test publishing industry, the measurement field, and the language testing community, validity models need to explicate and support accountability specific inferences as well as the connections between individual test scores and aggregate scores.

Policy-driven testing necessitates engagement with consequences. Additionally, the enmeshed roles commonly observed in accountability testing systems imply that traditional and fixed allocation of responsibility for consequences are no longer tenable. Engagement with consequence-related research is a shared responsibility among key stakeholder groups such as test developers, test users/decision makers, and policy makers. Interaction to allocate responsibility and negotiate funding requires that we pay attention to the varied resources available to different groups. Scholarly explorations are needed to develop validity models that connect with policies and set outcomes as the guiding principles for test development and documentation. SIA and TOA could be employed to assist R&D efforts move forward with explicit attention to not only technical documentation of individual score interpretation and use but also broad aspects of aggregate and socio-educational consequences. The measurement and the language testing fields and the public would benefit if our scholarship pays more attention to these matters.

Note

1 An RFP is where a policy or some other agency requests proposals, typically through a bidding process, from interested test developers/publishers who are interested in undertaking targeted testing projects.

References

Acree, J., Hoeve, K., & Weir, J. B. (2016). Approaching the validation of accountability systems. Unpublished paper and presentation. ERM 600: Validity and Validation, University of North Carolina at Greensboro.

American Educational Research Association, American Psychological Association, and National Council on Measurement in Education. (2014). *Standards for educational and psychological testing*. Washington, DC: Author.

Bachman, L. F., & Palmer, A. S. (2010). *Language assessment in practice*. Oxford, UK: Oxford University Press.

Bailey, A. L., & Wolf, M. K. (2020). The construct of English language proficiency in consideration of college and career readiness standards. In M. K. Wolf (Ed.), *Assessing English language proficiency in U.S. K–12 schools*. New York, NY: Routledge.

Bennett, R. E. (2010). Cognitively based assessment of, for, and as learning: A preliminary theory of action for summative and formative assessment. *Measurement: Interdisciplinary Research and Perspectives, 8*, 70–91.

Bennett, R. E., Kane, M. T., & Bridgeman, B. (2011). *Theory of action and validity argument in the context of through-course summative assessment*. Paper presented at invitational Research Symposium on Through Course Summative Assessment, Atlanta, GA. Retrieved from https://www.ets.org/Media/Research/pdf/TCSA_Symposium_Final_Paper_Bennett_Kane_Bridgeman.pdf

Brindley, G. (2001). Outcomes-based assessment in practice: Some examples of emerging insights. *Language Testing, 18*, 393–407.

Broadfoot, P. (1996). *Education, assessment, and society: A sociological analysis*. Buckingham and Philadelphia, PA: Open University Press.

Burdge, R. J., & Vanclay, F. (1996). Social impact assessment: A contribution to the state of the art series. *Impact Assessment, 14*, 59–86.

Chalhoub-Deville, M. (2009a). Standards-based assessment in the U.S.: Social and educational impact. In L. Taylor & C. J. Weir (Eds.), *Language testing matters: Investigating the wider social and educational impact of assessment*. Studies in Language Testing 31 (pp. 281–300). Cambridge: Cambridge University Press and Cambridge ESOL.

Chalhoub-Deville, M. (2009b). The intersection of test impact, validation, and educational reform policy. *Annual Review of Applied Linguistics, 29*, 118–131.

Chalhoub-Deville, M. (2016). Validity theory: Reform policies, accountability testing, and consequences. *Language Testing, 33*, 453–472.

Chalhoub-Deville, M. (2018, March). The next generation of policy-driven language testing systems: Accountability, consequences, and learning. Invited joint symposium: The International Language Testing Association and the American Association of Applied Linguistics (AAAL). AAAL Annual Meeting, Chicago, IL.

Chalhoub-Deville, M., & O'Sullivan, B. (2020). *Validity: Theoretical development and integrated arguments*. London: British Council Monographs, Equinox.

Chapelle, C. A. (2012). Validity argument for language assessment: *the framework is simple … Language Testing, 29*, 19–27.

Deville, C., & Chalhoub-Deville, M. (2006). Test score variability: Implications for reliability and validity. In M. Chalhoub-Deville, C. Chapelle, & P. Duff (Eds.), *Inference and generalizability in applied linguistics: Multiple research perspectives* (pp. 9–25). Amsterdam, The Netherlands: John Benjamins Publishing Company.

Deville, C., & Chalhoub-Deville, M. (2011). Accountability-assessment under No Child Left Behind: Agenda, practice, and future. *Language Testing, 28*, 307–321.

Every Student Succeeds Act. (2015). Public Law No. 114–354.

Gottlieb, M., & Chapman, M. (2019, March). Language proficiency assessment and social justice in the US K–12 educational context. A symposium conducted at the Language Testing Research Colloquium (LTRC) conference, Atlanta, GA.

Haertel, E., & Herman, J. (2005). *Historical perspective on validity arguments for accountability testing* (CSE Report 654). Los Angeles, CA: University of California, Los Angeles.

Hopmann, S. T. (2008). No child, no school, no state left behind: Schooling in the age of accountability. *Journal of Curriculum Studies, 40*, 417–456.

Jin, Y. (2018, March). Re-visioning a language testing system in China: Key drivers of change. In M. B. Chalhoub-Deville (chair), *The next generation of policy-driven language testing systems: Accountability, consequences, and learning.* An invited joint symposium of the International Language Testing Association (ILTA) and the American Association of Applied Linguistics (AAAL) presented at the AAAL conference, Chicago, IL.

Kane, M. (2006). Validation. In R. Brennan (Ed.), *Educational measurement* (4th ed., pp. 17–64). Westport, CT: American Council on Education and Praeger.

Kane, M. (2012). Validating score interpretations and uses. *Language Testing, 29*(1), 3–17.

Kane, M. (2013). Validating the interpretations and uses of test scores. *Journal of Educational Measurement, 50*, 1–73.

Kane, M. (2016). Explicating validity, assessment in education. *Principles, Policy & Practice, 23*, 198–211.

Kane, M. (2017). Loosening psychometric constraints on educational assessments. *Assessment in Education Principles Policy and Practice, 24*(3), 447–453.

Klinger, D. A., DeLuca, C., & Miller, T. (2008). The evolving culture of large-scale assessments in Canadian education. *Canadian Journal of Educational Administration and Policy, 76*, 1–34.

Mathis, W. J., & Trujillo, T. M. (2016). *Lessons from NCLB for the every student succeeds act.* Boulder, CO: National Education Policy Center. Retrieved from http://nepc.colorado.edu/publication/lessons-from-NCLB

Nichols, P. D., & Williams, N. (2009). Consequences of test score use as validity evidence: Roles and responsibilities. *Educational Measurement: Issues and Practice, 28*, 3–9.

No Child Left Behind. (2002). Act of 2001, Pub. L. No. 107–110, 115 Stat. 1425.

OECD. (2011). *How are schools held accountable?* Education at a Glance 2011: OECD Indicators. Paris: Author. Retrieved from https://doi.org/10.1787/eag-2011-32-en

Rupp, A. A., & Vock, M. (2007). National standards in Germany: Methodological challenges for developing and calibrating standards-based tests. In D. Waddington, P. Nentwig, & S. Schanze (Eds.), *Making it comparable: Standards in science education* (pp. 173–198). Muenster, Germany: Waxmann.

Sabatini, J. P., Bennett, R., & Deane, P. (2011). *Four years of cognitively based assessment of, for, and as learning (CBAL): Learning about through-course assessment (TCA).* Princeton, NJ: Educational Testing Service.

Sahlberg, P. (2011). *Global educational reform movement is here!* Retrieved from http://pasisahlberg.com/global-educational-reform-movement-is-here/

Sahlberg, P. (2016). The Finnish Paradox: Equitable public education within a competitive market economy. In F. Adamson, B. Astrand, & L. Darling-Hammond (Eds.), *Global educational reform: How privatization and public investment influence education outcomes* (pp. 110–130). New York, NY: Routledge.

Sato, E., & Thompson, K. D. (2020). Standards-based K–12 English language proficiency assessments in the United States: Current polices and practices. In M. K. Wolf (Ed.), *Assessing English language proficiency in U.S. K–12 schools.* New York, NY: Routledge.

UNESCO. (2017). *Accountability in education: Meeting our commitments.* A 2017–2018 global education monitoring report. Paris: Author. Retrieved from https://unesdoc.unesco.org/ark:/48223/pf0000259338

U.S. Department of Education. (2003). *Final non-regulatory guidance on the Title III state formula grant program—Standards, assessments and accountability.* Retrieved from www2.ed.gov/programs/nfdp/NRG1.2.25.03.doc

U.S. Department of Education. (2009). *Race to the top*. Retrieved from www2.ed.gov/pro grams/racetothetop/index.html

U.S. Department of Education. (2016). *Non-regulatory guidance: English learners and Title III of the Elementary and Secondary Education Act (ESEA), as amended by the Every Student Succeeds Act (ESSA)*. Retrieved from www2.ed.gov/policy/elsec/leg/essa/essatitleiii guidenglishlearners92016.pdf

Wixson, K. K., Dutro, E., & Athan, R. G. (2003). The challenge of developing content standards. *Review of Research in Education, 27*, 69–107.

SUBJECT INDEX

Title III (Language Instruction for Limited English Proficient and Immigrant Students) 21, 22, 23, 25, 38, 247, 260
TOEFL iBT 112
TOEFL Junior Comprehensive 210, 215, 216
tutorial 117, 122, 126

Universal Design 188, 194, 199
Universal Design for Learning 86
universal tools 59, 64–6, 70, 190, 191; *see also* accessibility
usability 112, 128, 198

validation 9–11, 76–9, 84, 85–8, 166, 245, 248, 251, 253–4, 259; *see also* validity
validity 9, 75, 78, 95, 99, 107, 112, 164, 183, 186, 191–4, 207, 208, 222, 239, 245, 247–53, 254, 260; concurrent validity 81; consequential validity 82, 83, 86; construct validity 251; validity framework 9, 78, 86, 252

validity evidence 9–10, 75, 79–83, 113–4, 135
verbal protocol analysis 114, 128
vertical scaling 10, 135, 140, 141, 151–5

WIDA 8, 27, 29, 30, 43, 55, 57, 76, 77, 80, 111, 227, 229
word error rate (WER) 210, 217
writing 25, 29, 43, 57, 58, 61, 64, 70, 82, 104–5, 118, 119, 124–5, 127, 136, 137, 144, 150, 151, 211, 214–5, 219, 228, 235
written language 41, 70, 136, 137–8, 143, 151, 152, 154

young English learners (ELs) 28–9, 63, 86–7, 208–9, 222; *see also* young learners
young learners 11, 61, 66, 67, 69–71, 76, 84, 86, 196, 209

zone of negotiated responsibility 256